Dilthey and the Narrative of History

Dilthey and the Narrative of History

Jacob Owensby

CORNELL UNIVERSITY PRESS
Ithaca and London

First published 1994 by Cornell University Press.

Printed in the United States of America

Library of Congress Cataloging-in-Publication Data

Owensby, Jacob, b. 1957
    Dilthey and the narrative of history / Jacob Owensby.
        p.   cm.
    Includes bibliographical references and index.
    ISBN 0–8014–3011–9
    1. History—Philosophy.   2. Dilthey, Wilhelm, 1833–1911—
    Contributions in philosophy of history.   I. Title.
    D16.8.09   1994
    901—dc20   94-15982

To Joy

Contents

Preface

Wilhelm Dilthey (1833–1911) proposed but never produced a Critique of Historical Reason. In its place he left a wide array of writings without clearly defining their systematic unity. I contend that life, narrative, and historical understanding are the three themes that, taken together, define the problem-set of his critique, and in this book I use these themes to draw his scattered reflections into a single, systematic foundation for historical understanding.

For Dilthey, all knowledge is rooted in life itself as it is given in lived experience. Life is not, however, reducible to subjectivity. Rather, life is an I-world relation prior to the subject-object distinction. Consciousness is always integrated within and conditioned by sociohistorical structures. Consequently, the task of critical philosophy is to show how historical understanding is made possible by both the structures of human consciousness and the structural social and political systems within which we are immersed.

Because Dilthey's approach to historiography was largely narrative, his critical treatment of life must show that narrative structure is grounded in life itself. This means, first of all, that he must show that life unfolds like a story. To do so, he devises a theory of time that serves as the foundation on which he builds a narrative concept of the diachronic coherence of life. In addition, a narrative account of others is a matter of discerning how their lives unfold in relation to various sociohistorical settings or contexts. To justify the interpretive process of locating actions and expressions within a specific set of contexts, he articulates the category of the historical setting or context and demonstrates how some actions are proper to a certain context and how contexts may be said to be appropriate to the understanding of an action or expression.

The final theme of a Critique of Historical Reason is historical understanding itself. Our involvement in historical contexts at once forms the basis for and presents the greatest difficulty to historical understanding.

That is, because interpreters are immersed in a historical context different from that in which the actions and texts they seek to understand are situated, it would appear that we could never be assured of confronting anything other than a construct of our own sociohistorical horizon. Dilthey argues for a revised notion of objectivity, contending that historical understanding draws on the same imaginative capacities that enable poets to transcend the limits of their own sociohistorical conditions.

I thank the National Endowment for the Humanities for a Summer Stipend, which supported research for this project. The release time and research grants provided by Jacksonville University were very helpful.

My interest in Dilthey began when I was a graduate student at Emory University, and I owe a great deal to the guidance and continued support of Rudolf Makkreel. A German Academic Exchange Service (DAAD) fellowship made my dissertation work on Dilthey's early writings possible, and I am grateful for the direction provided by Frithjof Rodi of the Ruhr University-Bochum during the term of this fellowship.

I am grateful to the following: the *Journal of the History of Philosophy* for permission to republish portions of my article "Dilthey's Conception of the Life-Nexus" (25 [October 1987]: 557–572); the *Journal of Aesthetics and Art Criticism* for permission to use parts of my article "Dilthey and the Historicity of Poetic Expression" (46, no. 4 [Summer 1988]: 501–507); Vandenhoeck & Ruprecht for permission to translate passages from Dilthey's *Gesammelte Schriften;* and Princeton University Press for permission to use passages from volumes 1 and 5 of Wilhelm Dilthey, *Selected Works.* Copyright © 1989 by Princeton University Press. Reprinted by permission of Princeton University Press.

The comments and criticisms of my colleagues have been invaluable in the development of this project. In particular I thank Thomas Flynn, Tom Nenon, Ray Clines, and Mark Ledbetter for their comments on drafts of the manuscript. Sharon Scholl's and Andrea Weisberger's comments on portions of the work were very helpful. I am especially grateful to my students Paul Welty, Doug Atkinson, and Jennifer Benson for their questions, insights, and persistent skepticism.

Above all I am indebted to my wife, Joy, without whose patience and support this project could not have been completed.

JACOB OWENSBY

Jacksonville, Florida

Abbreviations

Aufbau	Dilthey, *Der Aufbau der geschichtlichen Welt in den Geisteswissenschaften*
BT/SZ	Heidegger, *Being and Time / Sein und Zeit*
CR	Kant, *Critique of Pure Reason*
"Descriptive Psychology"	Dilthey, "Ideas concerning a Descriptive and Analytic Psychology"
ED	Dilthey, *Das Erlebnis und die Dichtung*
"Fragments"	Dilthey, "Fragments for a Poetics"
GS	Dilthey, *Gesammelte Schriften*
Introduction	Dilthey, *Introduction to the Human Sciences*
"Poetics"	Dilthey, "The Imagination of the Poet: Elements for a Poetics"
Spurs	Derrida, *Spurs: Nietzsche's Styles*
SW	Dilthey, *Selected Works*
TM	Gadamer, *Truth and Method*
"Understanding Other Persons"	Dilthey, "Understanding Other Persons and Their Expressions of Life"
WD	Derrida, *Writing and Difference*

Dilthey and the Narrative of History

Introduction

Wilhelm Dilthey's name is most often linked with the title of a nonexistent book: Critique of Historical Reason. Although he never published a work under this title, most if not all of his mature philosophical and historical writings were devoted to such a critique or were used at least in part for developing concepts crucial to it. In this book I attempt to forge from his unsystematic corpus a unitary foundation for historical understanding from a Diltheyan perspective. This volume is not, then, the reconstruction of an unfinished text from notes and drafts or a text-by-text exposition of Dilthey's corpus in order to trace the evolution of his thought. Rather, I have here identified the problems at issue in a Diltheyan Critique of Historical Reason, and while remaining sensitive to the developments and shifts in his thought, I have drawn from his work as a whole to provide the solutions. The central problems of the critique are characterized by three broad themes: life, narrative, and historical understanding.

The first of these problems is to determine the very nature of the critical project itself. Dilthey maintained that all knowledge is empirical, and thus he sought to provide the conditions for experience in order to show how historical understanding is possible. In this respect, Dilthey is clearly an heir of Kantian critical philosophy. But whereas Kant sought to show that experience is grounded in pure, autonomous reason, Dilthey contends that experience, hence historical understanding, is rooted in life as it is lived. Life is a life-nexus, an I-world relation prior to the subject-object distinction. Human consciousness is always already immersed not only in a network of one-to-one relationships but also within more encompassing historically developed and continually developing social structures. Accordingly, the critical project is to ground historical understanding in both the volitional, emotional, and cognitive structures of humans as practical agents and the structural social and political systems that function as objective meaning frameworks for human action.

In Chapter 1, I show that his approach to this task evolved in two phases. Before 1900, Dilthey maintained that the conditions of knowledge were given immediately in lived experience itself and needed only to be articulated by a descriptive psychology. With the new century, Dilthey's confidence in description waned as he came to see that many of the conditions of experience transcend the present lived experience, for example, our own past experiences and the sociohistorical systems in which we participate. The conditions of experience could be found only indirectly through the interpretation of expressions, because these expressions pull together and articulate the conditions of experience which transcend the present. Accordingly, hermeneutics assumes the foundational role from psychology.

Nevertheless, the conditions for historical understanding reside in the structures of the life-nexus itself, and it remains the transcendental task to articulate these structures. Thus, after settling the issue of transcendental methodology, the transcendental task proper still remains. That is, we must trace the categories used in historical understanding to structures in the life-nexus. Chapter 2 is devoted to a further clarification of Dilthey's concept of life as a practical life-nexus of lived relations between I and world. I argue that the subject-object relation is for Dilthey a derivative, one-sidedly intellectual interpretation of life, and consequently life-philosophy must not be construed as a philosophy of the subject in the Kantian tradition. On the contrary, subjectivity is redefined by Dilthey as a function of the life-nexus. Dilthey insisted in all his writings that knowledge always arises in the service of life. In his pretwentieth-century writings, Dilthey portrayed life as the practical, adaptive interaction of human agents and their environments. In Dilthey's final writings, this organic model of life is placed within the broader context of the communicative relations between agents and the social systems that make communication possible.

The second problem is derived from the fact that Dilthey took a largely narrative approach to historiography. Because the transcendental project is to articulate the structures of the life-nexus which ground our historiographical categories, narrative structure must be grounded in life itself. This involves two tasks. First, it must be shown that life unfolds like a story. In Chapter 3, I explain how Dilthey's theory of time serves as the foundation on which he builds a narrative concept of the diachronic coherence of life. I show that the coherence of life is a reflective achievement that assumes a narrative structure, one not imposed on life externally but elicited from life itself. Second, a narrative account of others is for Dilthey a matter of discerning the ways in which their actions and expressions unfold as either a part of or at odds with a myriad of sociohistorical settings or contexts such as the economy, religious institutions, language, artistic schools or movements, political structures, familial relations, and professional associations. The task of a historical critique is then to justify the interpretive process of locating actions and expressions within a specific set of contexts. Accordingly, in Chapter 4, I concentrate on the category of the historical setting or context and demonstrate how some actions are proper to a certain context and how contexts may be said to be appropriate to the understanding of an action or expression.

In the fifth chapter I turn to the third problem of a Critique of Historical Reason, namely, historical understanding. Our involvement in historical contexts forms the basis for but also presents the greatest difficulty to historical understanding. That is, because interpreters are immersed in a historical context different from that in which the actions and texts they seek to understand are situated, it would appear that we could never be assured of confronting anything other than a construct of our own sociohistorical horizon. I will use Dilthey's discussions of the poet's imagination and of worldviews to argue that historical understanding uncovers the temporal structure of life as it unfolds in history. The object of historical understanding is not a fixed essence but the unfolding meaning of human life—concrete humans in concrete sociohistorical contexts. Historical understanding is not the mirroring of an object that stands at a distance from us but a critical confrontation with a social and historical context other than our own. Historical understanding, then, is philosophical. It is a confrontation with other ways of living which not only demonstrates the impoverishment or enrichment of our own ways of living but which also provides a sense of life's inexhaustible multidimensionality.

Some questions may have arisen by this point about my characterization of Dilthey's theory of understanding as narrative. After all, Dilthey himself did not systematically employ the term "narrative," and his death precedes the rise of contemporary narrative theory of history by more than half a century. To address these questions, I turn next to a brief discussion of his relationship to this more recent work.

Dilthey's Hermeneutics and Narrative History

Arthur Danto's *Analytical Philosophy of History* broke significant ground with a chapter devoted to the analysis of narrative sentences.[1] Danto

---

1. Arthur C. Danto, *Analytical Philosophy of History* (Cambridge: Cambridge University Press, 1965).

showed that the past is not a fixed object but an object constituted by the reflective position of the historian. He argues that if the past were a fixed object, then a perfect history could be written by a sort of ideal chronicler, that is, an observer with a God's-eye view on human happenings who is capable of recording in proper sequence each event as it occurs.[2] But the document that such an observer could produce would be nothing but a chronologically correct series of eyewitness descriptions, that is, descriptions of what is present. It would not contain narrative sentences, since these kinds of sentences describe an event in terms of events that occur some time afterward. To use Danto's example, at the time of Denis Diderot's birth, it would have been impossible to say that the author of *Rameau's Nephew* was born in 1717 because the earlier event (Diderot's birth) is described in terms of a later event (the writing of the text), one completely unknown to an eye witness. Although Dilthey devoted no energies to the analysis of narrative sentences, his doctrine of *Besserverstehen*, that is, that interpreters can understand authors better than the authors understood themselves, also entails the acknowledgment that the past studied by historians is a reflective achievement. Events are understood in their significance when interpreted as antecedents or as anticipating later events.

Danto's analysis of narrative sentences reveals the peculiar temporal structure of narrative. But because the analysis is done at the level of the sentence, it can only suggest, not fully articulate, the ways in which individual events are parts of the larger temporal whole of an individual's life and that individual's developing sociohistorical context. In *Philosophy and the Historical Understanding*, W. B. Gallie in effect extends Danto's work by discussing the larger framework of events, namely, the story.[3] According to Gallie, a story is defined by its followability. That is, the actions and experiences of individuals and groups in various settings are not simply arranged in a chronological order but are described such that the changes in setting or the reactions of the agents to their setting produce problems or reveal previously hidden problems that call for some further response. The reader expects from the concatenation of

2. Whereas Danto seems to suggest that the meaning of events is always open to transformation by successive events, Raymond Aron argues that events as such are always the historian's reconstruction. See Aron, *Introduction to the Philosophy of History: An Essay on the Limits of Historical Objectivity*, trans. George J. Irwin (Boston: Beacon Press, 1961), p. 118.

3. W. B. Gallie, *Philosophy and the Historical Understanding*, 2d ed. (New York: Schocken Books, 1968).

actions and settings certain outcomes, such that a sense of movement toward a conclusion occurs. This is, of course, not to say that the conclusion could be deduced or systematically predicted, only that the various episodes of the story should culminate in some way that, in retrospect, seems plausible or acceptable. Naturally, any number of stories exist whose conclusions are farfetched, and we often deem them as poor or amateurish. But the existence of such stories only underscores Gallie's point. A story directs us toward an ending that is called for in the movement of the episodes themselves, and it is only by virtue of this that we can be disappointed by an ending. Although Dilthey never speaks explicitly in terms of a story's ending, he makes it quite clear that life has a teleological dimension. Our actions are incorporated into the larger movement toward purposes that we set for ourselves or assume as members of some group or institution. Understanding for Dilthey thus involves following these actions through to their conclusion.

Dilthey's account of the role of judgment in this process is fuller than Gallie's, however. Gallie's phenomenological account of the story certainly suggests that the reader's capacity to follow is the necessary condition for the occurrence of a story. But Dilthey recognizes that the historian not only reads but also constructs the story to be told. Before reading a story in the direction it was lived, the historian must work backward from the story's conclusion to see individual events in their narrative significance. Dilthey insists that, in this construction of historical narratives, judgment serves to explicate structures embedded in life itself, and this insistence sets him at odds with some contemporary theorists. According to Louis O. Mink, for example, narrative structure is a "cognitive instrument."[4] We use narrative structure to organize the sea of past events with which we are confronted. But these events themselves are not already a part of a narrative simply waiting to be read or discovered. The narrative structure of the historian's account is the contribution of the historian's judgment, which is thus much closer to the productive, literary imagination than to scientific judgment. It is precisely this point that Hayden White expands with his view of historiography as emplotment, namely, that historians utilize already established plot structures to

4. Louis O. Mink, "Narrative Form as a Cognitive Instrument," in *The Writing of History: Literary Form and Historical Understanding,* ed. Robert H. Canary and Henry Kozicki (Madison: University of Wisconsin Press, 1978), pp. 129–149; see also Mink's "History and Fiction as Modes of Comprehension," *New Literary History* 1 (1970): 541–558.

present their material. They do not elicit plots from the historical data itself.[5]

Whereas Mink and White suggest a radical discontinuity between life as lived and its historical representation, Paul Ricoeur argues for an indirect connection between the temporality of human action and historiography.[6] According to Ricoeur, the temporal structure of action is not itself narrative. Narrative is a conceptual schema that redescribes the temporal world of action. But this is not to say that narrative imposes externally an order on complete chaos. The narrative instrument of plot certainly integrates heterogeneous elements such as "agents, goals, means, interactions, circumstances, unexpected results," and plot is not a structure of action.[7] Nevertheless, the temporal structures of action "call for narration."[8] Carving out a coherent life story from the discordant elements of life is an essential component of action. Thus, although our narratives do not re-present or explicate a structure embedded in action, they do arise in the service of action. Ricoeur's connection between the lives we lead and the narratives we construct about them would still be too weak for Dilthey. Dilthey would readily acknowledge that our lives assume narrative shape only on reflection and that these narratives are constructed to serve life. But he contends that reflection explicates the implicit structures of life as lived, and on this point, Dilthey's position resembles David Carr's. Carr seeks to show that literary and historical narratives are themselves rooted in the temporal structures of our everyday experience and action.[9] This is not to say that Carr reduces narrative structure to the structures of individual experience. On the contrary, he uses the concept of narrative to move from the individual to the social dimensions of experience, arguing that the constitution of a community is bound up with the production of a common narrative. Similarly, Dilthey bases narrative not only on the temporal structures of individual experience but also on the dynamic structures of the sociohistorical systems or contexts

5. Hayden White, *Metahistory: The Historical Imagination in Nineteenth-Century Europe* (Baltimore: Johns Hopkins University Press, 1973); in addition see his "The Historical Text as Literary Artifact," in *The Writing of History*, ed. Canary and Kozicki, pp. 41–62, and "The Value of Narrativity in the Representation of Reality," in *On Narrative*, ed. W. J. T. Mitchell (Chicago: University of Chicago Press, 1981), pp. 1–23, especially p. 23.

6. Paul Ricoeur, *Time and Narrative*, vol. 1, trans. Kathleen McLaughlin and David Pellauer (Chicago: University of Chicago Press, 1984).

7. Ibid., p. 65.

8. Ibid., p. 59.

9. David Carr, *Time, Narrative, and History* (Bloomington: Indiana University Press, 1986).

within which individuals are situated. Unlike Carr, however, Dilthey does not view these contexts as themselves narrative productions but as conditions for the possibility of narratives. Sociohistorical contexts are, for Dilthey, objective systems to which our actions and expressions always already belong and by virtue of which they are meaningful.

Dilthey's practice of situating the actions and the expressions of individual agents in their proper contemporary context or contexts may seem to diminish the continued relevance of his hermeneutic approach, as much contemporary work has undermined the concepts of the intentional subject and the privileged context. The work of Jacques Derrida in particular appears to pose serious problems for the Diltheyan approach, for he makes these points against Husserl and Heidegger—figures who have been rightly seen as closely related to Dilthey's position in various ways.[10] Excellent work has been done in the attempt to reconcile hermeneutics with or defend it against poststructuralism. Calvin O. Schrag and John D. Caputo, for example, have produced important studies that demonstrate ways in which hermeneutics can put the work of deconstruction to its own uses.[11]

In *Communicative Praxis and the Space of Subjectivity*, Schrag takes the deconstruction of the subject not as a signal of its ultimate demise but as the occasion for formulating a decentered conception of subjectivity as a function of communicative praxis. Schrag's rehabilitation of the subject transforms the insights of Merleau-Ponty and Ricoeur and involves the claim that communicative praxis is characterized by a "texture" which is constitutive not only for spoken communication and action but for textuality as well. He is thus able to analyze the structures of speech, action, and text as internally related forms of life without reducing them to the structures of a text. The subject is then situated "within the folds of communicative praxis" as an event or achievement.[12] The constitution of the

---

10. One of the earliest and most extensive comparisons of Dilthey, Husserl, and Heidegger is Georg Misch, *Lebensphilosophie und Phänomenologie* (Stuttgart: B. G. Teubner, 1967). A more recent series of excellent comparative essays appears in *Dilthey and Phenomenology*, ed. Rudolf A. Makkreel and John Scanlon (Washington, D.C.: Center for Advanced Research in Phenomenology and University Press of America, 1987). For further comparisons of Dilthey, Husserl, and Heidegger, see also the essays in *Dilthey und die Philosophie der Gegenwart*, ed. Ernst Wolfgang Orth (Freiburg / Munich: Verlag Karl Alber, 1985).

11. Calvin O. Schrag, *Communicative Praxis and the Space of Subjectivity* (Bloomington: Indiana University Press, 1986); John D. Caputo, *Radical Hermeneutics: Repetition, Deconstruction, and the Hermeneutic Project* (Bloomington: Indiana University Press, 1987).

12. Schrag, *Communicative Praxis*, p. 146.

subject involves "a comprehension of its historical posture at the intersection of past and future in the life of discourse and social practices."[13]

Caputo argues in *Radical Hermeneutics* for the primacy of the flux. He seeks in the marriage of hermeneutics and deconstruction a way to philosophize which remains true to factical, dynamic human existence. His claim is that all conceptual systems, whether theoretical or practical, are attempts to structure the flow of human existence, to make it manageable. Although these conceptual systems arise from the flux, they ossify and obscure the volatile foundation on which they are built. It is the task of "radical hermeneutics" to keep us conscious of the flux and thus to expose the temporary and provisional nature of all conceptual schemes. Radical hermeneutics has its origins in Martin Heidegger's hermeneutics of facticity, a project worked out in lecture courses in the 1920s and first published in *Being and Time*. Caputo reads this project as a "hermeneutics that writes from below," and he uses Derrida to develop it further into a postmetaphysical hermeneutics that "exposes us to the ruptures and the gaps, let us say, the textuality and difference, which inhabits everything we think."[14]

Schrag and Caputo clearly diverge in the degree to which they incorporate deconstruction into their hermeneutic projects. Schrag uses it as motivation to revise basic hermeneutic concepts. Caputo's hermeneutics adopts a deconstructive, liberating edge. Nevertheless, these studies demonstrate ways in which hermeneutics is not simply displaced or superseded by poststructuralism. I contend that the relevance of Dilthey's hermeneutics remains undiminished even admitting the validity of certain poststructuralist claims, namely, the deconstruction of subjectivity and of the notion of an appropriate context, and I shall at various junctures set Derrida's work in motion with Dilthey in order to make this point.

As I indicated at the outset, I draw on the full range of Dilthey's work to make my case. Because his thought underwent considerable development, in each chapter I do not merely state a completed version of Dilthey's position but trace the evolution of his approach to the problem at hand as well. It is widely accepted that in his pre-twentieth-century writings, Dilthey argued for a foundational role for psychology, whereas he gave hermeneutics this role after 1900. Controversy arises, however, in

13. Ibid., p. 147.
14. Caputo, *Radical Hermeneutics*, p. 6.

determining the relation between the writings before and after the turn of the century. Some commentators draw a rigid line between the early and late writings and view later developments as a renunciation of the earlier; others apparently recognize no significant differences, as they juxtapose materials from each period indiscriminately.[15] By providing a brief overview of Dilthey's major works, I point up both the continuities and the shifts to be discussed at greater length in the following chapters.

An Overview of Dilthey's Works

Dilthey was born in 1833, the son of a clergyman in Biebrich on the Rhine. His university studies began in 1852 at the University of Heidelberg, where he took up theology. In 1853 Dilthey transferred to the University of Berlin, but not before learning from his first mentor, Kuno Fischer, the importance of a study of the history of philosophy. While at Berlin, Dilthey's theological interests first became integrated in and then were eclipsed by historical and philosophical projects, and he was influenced by the historicists August Böckh, Leopold von Ranke, Theodor Mommsen, and Jakob Grimm.[16] In 1860 Dilthey wrote a prize-winning essay on Friedrich Schleiermacher's hermeneutics, on the basis of which he was invited to complete an edition of Schleiermacher's correspondence and to write Schleiermacher's biography.[17] Dilthey's break with theology became complete in 1861, when he transferred from the

15. The tendency to divide Dilthey's work into two rigidly distinct periods, that is, an early psychological and a late hermeneutical phase, was greatest in commentaries written before World War II. See, for example, Dietrich W. Bischoff, *Wilhelm Diltheys geschichtliche Lebensphilosophie* (Leipzig: B. G. Teubner, 1935), and Carl Theodor Glock, *Wilhelm Diltheys Grundlegung einer wissenschaftlichen Lebensphilosophie* (Berlin: Junker und Dünnhaupt, 1939). Nevertheless, some more contemporary commentators also view Dilthey's development in this same way. See Robert C. Scharff, "Non-Analytical, Unspeculative Philosophy of History: The Legacy of Wilhelm Dilthey," *Cultural Hermeneutics* 3 (March 1976): 295–331. H. P. Rickman takes an almost diametrically opposed position on Dilthey's development, arguing for a continuity in his thought which allows for the juxtaposition of early and late writings. I discuss Rickman's commentaries below.

16. Elzbieta Paczkowska-Lagowska demonstrates the enduring influence of the historical school on Dilthey's thought in "The Humanities in Search of Philosophy: Dilthey and the Historical School," *Reports on Philosophy* 6 (1982): 3–16.

17. Dilthey published the first of a promised two volumes in 1870 but failed to complete the project. His work on the massive project is contained in his *Gesammelte Schriften* (to be abbreviated as *GS*), 20 vols. (Stuttgart: B. G. Teubner; Göttingen: Vandenhoeck & Ruprecht, 1914–90), vol. 13 and vol. 14. Unless otherwise noted, translations of Dilthey's *GS* are my own.

theological to the philosophical faculty. Under Friedrich Trendelenburg's direction, Dilthey completed his dissertation ("De principiis ethices Schleiermacheri") and his *Habilitationsschrift* ("Versuch einer Analyse des moralischen Bewusstseins")[18] in 1864.

As early as 1865, Dilthey began sketching out the distinctions between the studies of human, historical reality and the natural sciences (*GS*, 18:1–16), but his first major publication in this vein appeared in 1875 with the essay "Über das Studium der Geschichte der Wissenschaften vom Menschen, der Gesellschaft und dem Staat" (On the Study of the History of Man, Society, and the State) (*GS*, 5:31–73).[19] Naming these sciences moral-political, Dilthey began the task of bringing the history of the development of what he would later call the human sciences (*Geisteswissenschaften*) up to the refined level of the history of the natural sciences. Rather than actually tracing this historical development, his brief essay concentrates on some of the philosophical implications and underpinnings of such a historical study.

This essay served as a springboard for the *Einleitung in die Geisteswissenschaften* (*Introduction to the Human Sciences*), the first volume of which appeared in 1883.[20] In the dedication to his friend and close philosophical associate Graf Paul Yorck von Wartenburg, Dilthey wrote that this work had arisen from a plan, revealed to Yorck during one of their first conversations, for a critique of historical reason (*GS*, 1:ix). Precisely when Dilthey began work on the *Introduction* is difficult to determine. There is no specific mention of it before 1880 in the Dilthey-Yorck correspondence. The first written evidence of Dilthey's work on the *Introduction* is a letter dated May 12, 1880, from the Duncker and Humblot publishers. The letter remarks on the lengthy period Dilthey has spent editing the first proofs of the *Introduction*, thus indicating that Dilthey's work on it extends back into the 1870s. Hans-Ulrich Lessing dates the beginning of the planning of the *Introduction* at 1877, which coincides with the first contact between Yorck and Dilthey, apparently partly on the

18. *GS*, 6:1–55.

19. Preliminary notes toward this essay and two drafts toward its expansion are contained in *GS*, 18:17–37, 57–111.

20. This first volume of the *Introduction to the Human Sciences* (to be abbreviated as *Introduction*) is contained in *GS*, vol. 1. It is translated, together with the projected second volume, in *Selected Works* (to be abbreviated as *SW*), 6 vols., ed. Rudolf A. Makkreel and Frithjof Rodi, trans. Michael Neville, Jeffrey Burnouw, Franz Schreiner, and Rudolf A. Makkreel (Princeton: Princeton University Press, 1985–), vol. 1. Only *SW*, vol. 1 and *SW*, vol. 5 have been published as of 1993.

evidence of Dilthey's dedication to Yorck. At first glance the absence of written exchange between the two men during the writing of the *Intro-duction* seems strange because Dilthey regularly and eagerly shared his thoughts with Yorck. But both men lived in Breslau until Dilthey's departure for Berlin in 1882, and most of their exchanges were probably face-to-face conversations. Thus, sometime between 1877 and 1880 Dilthey began a project with which he was to be more or less occupied until 1896.[21]

As stated in the preface to the first of two proposed volumes of the *In-troduction*, the overall plan of the work entailed a historical investigation into the development of the human sciences and their philosophical-epistemological bases in order to prepare the way for a systematic, critical grounding for historical reason (*SW*, 1:47; *GS*, 1:xv). Much impressed by the work of those of the historical school, Dilthey wanted to provide an epistemological basis for their work grounded in experience but avoiding the reductionistic narrowness of positivism. At the same time, he sought to include human purposes and values in historical analysis without postulating speculative claims that have no ground in experience.

As with Kant, Dilthey's conception of a critical foundation involves defining the limits and conditions of knowledge. Unlike Kant, however, he is not satisfied with a deduction of the transcendental, purely intellectual grounds for the unity of experience. Dilthey begins with lived experience given as an already connected whole and describes the way in which intellectual, emotional, and volitional processes are interwoven. The critical ground of the human sciences can be provided only by a *Selbstbesinnung,* or self-reflection on the connections immanent in psychic life. The conditions for understanding history are not merely intellectual but volitional and evaluative as well. Knowledge is a function of psychic life, and only descriptive psychology can provide the analysis of the given connections between intellectual, volitional, and evaluative processes adequate to the task of grounding the human sciences.

The *Introduction* was to contain five books, the first two appearing in volume one and the final three in volume two. Book 1 begins with an overview of the individual human sciences and their character as a system, then evaluates their epistemological footing. The second book

21. Hans-Ulrich Lessing, *Die Idee einer Kritik der historischen Vernunft: Wilhelm Diltheys erkenntnistheoretisch-logisch-methodologische Grundlegung der Geisteswissenschaften* (Munich: Verlag Karl Alber, 1984), pp. 105–106.

provides a historical study of the development of the human sciences through the period of their metaphysical grounding. The second volume of the *Introduction* was to contain a further historical study of the development of the human sciences and epistemology to the present (book 3), and Dilthey's own epistemological foundation for the human sciences was to compose the fourth and fifth books (*GS*, 1:xix). Volume 2 of the *Introduction* was not published during Dilthey's lifetime.

Nevertheless, Dilthey did write two drafts of the second volume of the *Introduction*, separate essays meant for inclusion in the second volume, and works not meant for inclusion in the second volume but which explore and develop concepts central to Dilthey's descriptive psychology. Already in 1880 Dilthey had written a draft of the second volume containing what is now known as the "Breslauer Ausarbeitung" ("Breslau Draft") (*GS*, 19:58–295; *SW*, 1:243–455). Whereas the published first volume of the *Introduction* had projected a fourth and fifth book devoted to methodology, epistemology, and logic, the later plan adds a sixth book. Book 4 is called "Grundlegung der Erkenntnis" ("Foundation of Knowledge") and begins with a primitive, indeterminate level of consciousness, prior to a subject-object split, in which the acts and objects of consciousness are taken as facts of consciousness. This indeterminate level of consciousness is articulated first in an analysis of outer, then inner, perception. Book 5 is devoted to the logic of the human sciences, analyzing the rules, forms, and categories of thought. Finally, book 6 contains methodological studies.

In 1893, Dilthey drew up another, less detailed draft of the second volume known as the "Berliner Entwurf" ("Berlin Draft") (*GS*, 19:296–332; *SW*, 1:459–492). An outline of book 3 suggests that it would still be a historical analysis and an assessment of the current epistemological problems of the human sciences as projected in the *Introduction*. Book 4 is composed of a study of psychic life in descriptive and comparative psychology. The "Grundlegung der Erkenntnis" is shifted from its original position in book 4 to book 5 and begins with an analysis of thought as a function of life. The sections of book 5 are mostly titles without text. The titles nonetheless suggest that the analysis was to proceed with a discussion of the relation between perception and reality whose center addresses the reality of the self and the external world. The final section, equally incomplete, seems to deal with the logical problems worked out in the fifth book of the earlier draft. In book 6, the limits of knowledge and the power that knowledge bestows on humans are discussed.

There are also three important essays not incorporated into the drafts discussed above but probably meant for inclusion in the second volume of the *Introduction*. The essay "Beiträge zur Lösung der Frage vom Ursprung unseres Glaubens an die Realität der Aussenwelt und seinem Recht" (Contributions to the solution of the problem of the origin and validity of our belief in the reality of the external world) (1890) criticizes the theoretical proofs for the reality of the external world (*GS*, 5:90–138). Dilthey argues that our most fundamental relation to the world is volitional, not intellectual, and the ground for our belief in external reality is our experience of its resistance to our will. In "Erfahren und Denken" (Experience and thought) (1892) Dilthey rejects the Kantian position that the structure of experience is imposed externally by a purely formal reason. Structure is not imposed on but immanent in lived experience, which is given as an already connected whole (*GS*, 5:74–89). The third essay, "Leben und Erkennen" (Life and knowledge), was written between 1892 and 1893, and its title would suggest that it could be included in the first section of book 5 of the "Berliner Entwurf." In this essay Dilthey discusses perception and thought as a function of the purposive nexus of life and derives the categories of life from the structures immanent in lived experience (*GS*, 19:333–388).

During the 1880s and 1890s Dilthey was also involved in historical and philosophical analyses of pedagogy, ethics, and aesthetics. Continuing work begun in 1874, he developed his lectures on pedagogy between 1884 and 1894 and in 1888 published "Über die Möglichkeit einer allgemeingültigen pädagogischen Wissenschaft" (On the possibility of a universally valid pedagogical science) (*GS*, 9). Especially in his lectures, Dilthey discusses the role of volition in the purposiveness of psychic life and places purposiveness at the core of his conception of human development. In those on ethics, which were also developed around 1890 from earlier work, Dilthey discusses the connection between different levels of instinct and feeling, from primitive reflexes to reflective responses, and volition in our responses to our environment (*GS*, 10).

Although Dilthey explored and developed concepts central to his descriptive psychology in both these projects, he did so to a greater extent in the aesthetic writings. "Dichterische Einbildungskraft und Wahnsinn" (Poetic imagination and insanity) was published in 1886 (*GS*, 6:90–102) and "Die Einbildungskraft des Dichters: Bausteine für eine Poetik" ("The Imagination of the Poet: Elements for a Poetics") the following year (*GS*, 6:103–241; *SW*, 5:29–173). Not only did Dilthey develop a conception of the imagination which stresses its capacity to bring to focus rather than create connections in lived experience, he also formulated the conception of the acquired psychic nexus which would figure so prominently in his notion of the development of the individual.

In 1894 Dilthey wrote his "Ideen über eine beschreibende und zergliedernde Psychologie" ("Ideas concerning a Descriptive and Analytic Psychology").[22] Though not necessarily intended for inclusion in the drafts of the second volume of the *Introduction*, "Descriptive Psychology" was clearly meant to address the task of the required descriptive, psychological base of the human sciences. Rejecting explanatory psychology, Dilthey provided descriptions of the structure and the development of the full range of psychic life as lived. Dilthey's final work related to the epistemology of the *Introduction* was an essay called "Beiträge zum Studium der Individualität" (Contributions to the study of individuality) (1896), which was part of a more ambitious work, "Über vergleichende Psychologie" (On comparative psychology) (1895), withdrawn from the publisher (*GS*, 5:241–316). After 1896 Dilthey abruptly halted work on the second volume of the *Introduction* and never returned to it. Thus, the period during which Dilthey was occupied with completing the systematic portion of the second volume of the *Introduction* begins around 1877 and ends in 1896.

From 1896 to 1905 Dilthey turned to historical studies of Leibniz and his age, Frederick the Great and the German Enlightenment, and the eighteenth century and the historical world (*GS*, vol. 3). He also completed a study of the development of the thought of the young Hegel (*GS*, vol. 4), which was to be very influential on his view of the sociohistorical determinants of meaning. In roughly the middle of this period of historical reflection, Dilthey published "Die Entstehung der Hermeneutik" (The rise of hermeneutics) (1900), in which he sketches the methodological approach that was to characterize his work from this point forward (*GS*, 5:317–331). Understanding others as well as ourselves begins with the interpretation of expressions, particularly written expressions, rather than with psychological descriptions.

From 1905 to the end of his life in 1911, Dilthey returned to the task of a Critique of Historical Reason. Dilthey published the *Aufbau* in 1910,

22. This essay appears in *GS*, 5:139–240, and as "Ideas concerning a Descriptive and Analytic Psychology" in Dilthey's *Descriptive Psychology and Historical Understanding,* trans. Richard M. Zaner and K. L. Heiges (The Hague: Martinus Nijhoff, 1977), pp. 23–120. I shall refer to this essay as "Descriptive Psychology."

claiming that he was resuming the task he had begun in the *Introduction* (*GS*, 7:117). The *Aufbau* is not, however, the second volume of the *Introduction* but a separate work that takes up the same problem anew and sharpens the hermeneutical perspective issued in with "The Rise of Hermeneutics." In other words, Dilthey's earlier work had assumed that the conditions of lived experience were present, albeit indeterminately, in lived experience itself and thus yielded up to neutral description. In his later work Dilthey turns more explicitly to the role played by our objective sociohistorical contexts in the constitution of meaning and of lived experience itself. Although the influences of such systems are never adequately presented in our immediate lived experience, they are embedded in the expressions to which our lived experiences give rise. Thus we can come to understand our experience more fully through expressions than we ever could through immediate observation and description. Nevertheless, while refraining from indiscriminately mixing the views of the *Aufbau* and the *Introduction*, I shall show that elements of Dilthey's earlier descriptions of the structures of the relation between the practical agent and its environment remain operative in his hermeneutical writings as crucial components for providing the basis for a narrative conception of historical understanding.

Approaches to Dilthey

Commentators on Dilthey's work have used a variety of strategies and principles for organizing his scattered and sometimes conflicting writings into a single, coherent philosophical position. To more clearly define my own use of the problems of narrative history as such an organizing principle, I outline here some of the other approaches to Dilthey's critical theory of history and differentiate them from the present study. One such strategy is to focus primarily on Dilthey's late writings. Howard Nelson Tuttle equates the problem of the possibility of historical knowledge with that of objective and universal validity.[23] He is in part led to this view by his own methodological device of accepting later formulations as Dilthey's final position wherever shifts or contradictions between the *Introduction* and *Aufbau* occur. Tuttle's view of the critique is derived for the most part, then, from the *Aufbau*. Similarly, after dividing Dilthey's de-

---

23. Howard Nelson Tuttle, *Wilhelm Dilthey's Philosophy of Historical Understanding: A Critical Analysis* (Leiden: E. J. Brill, 1969).

velopment into three periods corresponding roughly to the *Introduction* (1883), the "Descriptive Psychology" (1894), and the *Aufbau* (1910), Theodore Plantinga concentrates on the post-1900 phase of Dilthey's work.[24] Plantinga maintains that in these works, Dilthey drops his preoccupation with psychology and picks up the more fruitful approach of interpreting the meanings of acts as expressions of *Erlebnis* (lived experience). In contrast to both Tuttle and Plantinga, I try to show the continued relevance of Dilthey's psychological descriptions to his reflections on the methodological problems of understanding. This approach allows me to discuss the epistemological and methodological problems of objectivity and universality in connection with Dilthey's analyses of the reality of the self and the external world which place these problems in proper perspective as functions of life.

Rudolf Makkreel uses a Kantian perspective derived from the third *Critique* to argue for the continuity of Dilthey's thought as a whole.[25] Makkreel maintains that Dilthey's aesthetic writings are not only central to his thought as a whole but that the theory of the imagination developed there also has crucial implications for how we should conceive of the Critique of Historical Reason. According to Makkreel, the critique can be viewed as an aesthetic of history, that is, as an examination of the aesthetic conditions of historical experience as disclosed through the workings of the imagination. Dilthey's theory of the imagination leads Makkreel to argue that historical reason is replaced by a model of historical understanding similar to Kant's reflective judgment. In Makkreel's view Dilthey in effect rejected the traditional synthetic conception of the imagination associated with ordinary determinant judgment. Synthesis is required only if there is no original connectedness of lived experience. For Dilthey, the imagination begins with an already connected whole and does not need to make further connections; rather, it articulates or brings to a sharper focus parts that typify the whole. Historical judgment, then, does not synthetically construct a historical system by externally imposing an order on experience. Instead, historical understanding assesses the meaning of history by situating parts within a given whole.

Makkreel's use of Kant's conception of reflective judgment demonstrates the continuity of Dilthey's thought while allowing him to be sensi-

---

24. Theodore Plantinga, *Historical Understanding in the Thought of Wilhelm Dilthey* (Toronto: University of Toronto Press, 1980).

25. Rudolf A. Makkreel, *Dilthey, Philosopher of the Human Studies* (Princeton: Princeton University Press, 1975).

tive to Dilthey's development, conceptual shifts, and reformulations. I take a somewhat different approach to achieve a similar effect. Whereas Makkreel places at the organizational center of his interpretation Dilthey's conception of the imagination, I emphasize Dilthey's insistence on the facticity of human existence.[26] Makkreel's approach leads to an aesthetic of history investigating the imaginative and reflective conditions of historical judgment, whereas my approach yields a hermeneutic ontology of the lived relations that make narrative historical understanding possible.

Hans Ineichen takes what he calls a historical-genetic approach to Dilthey's epistemology and methodology of the human sciences.[27] His book is divided into three parts corresponding to his organization of Dilthey's work into three periods. In the first section, Ineichen deals with the works up to 1880, in which Dilthey develops the idea of a historical critique. The second section is limited to the period from 1880 to 1900 and analyzes the critique as formulated in the first and second volumes of *Einleitung in die Geisteswissenschaften*. In the final section, Ineichen examines the writings from 1900 to Dilthey's death in 1911, in which Dilthey shifts from his predominately psychological concerns to the methodological problems, found mostly in the *Aufbau*, involved in understanding the historical world.

Ineichen characterizes his interpretation as having two aspects: positive-receptive and critical-negative. The positive-receptive moment assesses Dilthey's arguments on their own terms and appropriates useful concepts. Perhaps more indicative of Ineichen's position is the critical-negative moment. Arguing for this approach, Ineichen justifies criticism of Dilthey from the position of transcendental philosophy because Dilthey's project was a critique of historical reason that maintains the Kantian structure of a transcendental aesthetic and analytic. This critical-

---

26. On this point my position diverges somewhat from that of Manfred Riedel and Herbert Schnädelbach. Although I agree with their view that Dilthey's *Aufbau* resumes the project he began in the *Introduction,* I find too strong their claim that Dilthey's psychological writings were an interruption in this otherwise continuous development. I will show that Dilthey's psychological writings provide a portrait of factical human existence integral to Dilthey's hermeneutics. See Riedel's introduction to Wilhelm Dilthey's *Der Aufbau der geschichtlichen Welt in den Geisteswissenschaften* (Frankfurt am Main: Suhrkamp Verlag, 1970), pp. 33–63, and Schnädelbach's *Geschichtsphilosophie nach Hegel: Die Probleme des Historismus* (Munich: Verlag Karl Alber, 1974), pp. 120–121.

27. Hans Ineichen, *Erkenntnistheorie und geschichtlich-gesellschaftliche Welt: Diltheys Logik der Geisteswissenschaften* (Frankfurt am Main: Vittorio Klostermann, 1975).

negative approach leads Ineichen to criticize Dilthey's theories of psychic structure and categories as an anthropomorphic sketch lacking a priori character. Although his epistemological anthropomorphism is too one-sided, Dilthey does, according to Ineichen, develop important concepts for the logic of the human sciences, such as *Erlebnis,* expression, and understanding. To be epistemologically adequate, however, the anthropomorphic one-sidedness of these concepts must be corrected by a transcendental approach.

Ineichen's interpretation fails to take Dilthey on his own terms, however. His claim that Dilthey's critique maintains the structure of a transcendental aesthetic and transcendental analytic is true only in a very limited way. Like Kant, Dilthey maintains that the form of outer sense is space and that the form of inner sense is time. Further, Dilthey arrives at categories that structure experience. But he deliberately rejected a transcendental deduction of a priori principles of experience for the sake of a broadened empirical approach that describes the structures immanent in lived experience. Thus, to criticize Dilthey from the standpoint of Kant's vision of transcendental philosophy is to approach his thought from a perspective that Dilthey intended to supersede. Rather than eliciting the internal unity of Dilthey's thought from the uniqueness of his position, Ineichen externally imposes a Kantian unity on Dilthey's critique.

Michael Ermarth recognizes the development of Dilthey's thought but rejects the common tendency to separate his work into periods whose overall approaches differ.[28] The changes in emphasis and reformulations of important problems and concepts in Dilthey's thought do not represent major reorientations that break with what came before. They are parts of a continuous but perhaps uneven development that is characterized by *Aufhebungen* (syntheses of apparently contradictory positions) rather than breaks. True to this conception of Dilthey's development, Ermarth organizes his book according to major themes, problems, and concepts and demonstrates their development and changing importance in Dilthey's work as a whole.

Ermarth derives the principle of the continuity of Dilthey's thought by situating him within his own turbulent historical context. Dilthey's project can be understood as an attempt to synthesize the two major, opposing philosophical influences of his time—idealism and positivism. That is, Dilthey wished to study human *Geist* (mind or spirit) without indulg-

28. Michael Ermarth, *Wilhelm Dilthey: The Critique of Historical Reason* (Chicago: University of Chicago Press, 1978).

ing in a speculation that loses contact with experienced reality, and he wanted to ground his knowledge in an empirical approach not so barrenly limited as to exclude the evaluative and volitional aspects of human existence. Ermarth calls this position *Idealrealismus*, or ideal-realism, and maintains that it is Dilthey's enduring orientation that provides the continuity in the shifts in Dilthey's thought. In contrast to Ermarth's position, I locate the enduring themes of Dilthey's thought in the elements required to ground a narrative conception of historical understanding. Ermarth's "ideal-realism" is quite accurate as a general characterization of Dilthey's life-philosophy, but it remains too vague to be used to locate the systematic links between Dilthey's diverse writings.

H. P. Rickman has written extensively about Dilthey, his most notable work being perhaps *Wilhelm Dilthey: Pioneer of the Human Studies*.[29] In each chapter he deals with a different concept or problem in Dilthey's thought, only one of which is devoted to Dilthey's critique. Maintaining a continuity in Dilthey's thought, Rickman draws no distinction between the *Introduction* and *Aufbau* positions and juxtaposes quotations from different times in Dilthey's life without reference to disparities in overall context. In *Dilthey Today*, Rickman departs from his earlier role as sympathetic expositor of Dilthey's work and both argues for Dilthey's current relevance and critically assesses his shortcomings.[30] He does not, however, set as his major task a sustained confrontation with current theoretical work from a Diltheyan perspective. Rickman draws no detailed connections or contrasts between Dilthey and poststructuralism but tries instead to show the relevance of Dilthey's hermeneutics to the practices of, among others, historians, psychoanalysts, and politicians. In his central criticism, Rickman focuses on Dilthey's fusion of epistemology and philosophy of life, a fusion that results in subordinating reason to sociohistorical life. Here, Rickman takes a Kantian position and faults Dilthey for sacrificing the autonomy of reason. By infusing the veins of the knowing subject with real blood, Dilthey loses, according to Rickman, the objective claim to validity offered by transcendental philosophy. I shall show that Dilthey does not so much relinquish any claim to objectivity as he reformulates objectivity in a way suitable to the historical character of human understanding.

29. H. P. Rickman, *Wilhelm Dilthey: Pioneer of the Human Studies* (Berkeley: University of California Press, 1979).
30. H. P. Rickman, *Dilthey Today: A Critical Appraisal of the Contemporary Relevance of His Work* (New York: Greenwood Press, 1988).

Hans-Ulrich Lessing's book *Die Idee einer Kritik der historischen Vernunft* has a twofold purpose, represented in its division into two parts. In part 1, Lessing traces the development of Dilthey's conception of a critique in his writings from 1852 to 1876. This development culminates in the *Introduction,* and part 2 of Lessing's work is devoted to reconstructing the genesis and systematic connection of the *Gesamtkonzept,* or total concept, of the *Introduction.* To this end, Lessing analyzes the texts from the period between 1877 and 1896. As Dilthey abruptly stopped his work on the *Introduction* in 1896, Lessing includes only the texts up to this date in those which conform to the idea of the critique as developed before and during the writing of the *Introduction* itself. Thus, Lessing's work is a reconstruction of the proposed second volume of the *Introduction* which does not attempt to integrate these early writings with the later.

In this book, I attempt to produce a systematic response to what I believe are the problems that constitute a critique of historical reason, namely, revision of the transcendental project, location of the structures of narrative historiography in life itself, and delineation of the process of historical understanding. In the next chapter I turn specifically to the first of these problems, discussing the way in which Dilthey transforms the transcendental project from the Kantian deduction of a priori categories to the articulation of structures embedded in lived experience itself.

Chapter One

Revising the Transcendental Project

Dilthey is perhaps most widely known for distinguishing between the human sciences and the natural sciences methodologically, that is, for claiming that the natural sciences seek to explain and the human sciences seek to understand. Yet, this claim is only partially true, and it can obscure the real thrust of Dilthey's work. Delineation of the human and the natural sciences was crucial to his project, but Dilthey's primary concern was to provide a critical foundation for the human sciences. Methodological considerations were for him always an outgrowth of more fundamental epistemological considerations. His work is thus not primarily methodological but transcendental. Genuine science is empirical; so finding the foundation of the human sciences involves discerning the conditions of experience. In this respect Dilthey continues the Kantian tradition. But he rejected Kant's deductive approach and pioneered his own transcendental method. Accordingly, this chapter is devoted to an analysis of Dilthey's revised transcendental method.

As I will show, his view of how we can arrive at the conditions of experience evolved with time. From at least 1880 to 1895, the grounding science of the human sciences is construed as a descriptive psychology. The conditions of experience are immediately but indeterminately given, and the task of this descriptive psychology is to explicate these conditions through neutral descriptions. That is, the conditions are implicit in experience itself and need only be made explicit. But from 1900 to the end of his life in 1911, Dilthey gradually came to see that because description is limited to observations of present lived experience, it cannot adequately grasp the conditions of experience which transcend our present experience. Dilthey thus turns to the interpretation of expressions of lived experience, arguing that in expressions we are able to see how our past lived experiences and our sociohistorical world condition our experience. Hermeneutics thus seems to displace descriptive psychology at the foundation of the human sciences, and we are left to ponder the relevance, if any, of the results of the earlier descriptions for the hermeneutic phase of Dilthey's thought. I shall show that description continues to play an important albeit revised role in the hermeneutical writings and that the earlier descriptions of lived experience can be viewed as a framework within which to situate Dilthey's later discussions of interpretation theory. As a first step, I turn to a general characterization of the Diltheyan view of a philosophical ground.

A Philosophical Foundation without Metaphysics

Often cited as an indication of Dilthey's conception of a philosophical ground is a passage from the preface to *Introduction to the Human Sciences:* "Apart from a few beginnings, such as those of Herder and Wilhelm von Humboldt, which were not scientifically developed, previous epistemology—Kant's as well as that of the empiricists—has explained experience and cognition in terms of facts that are merely representational. No real blood flows in the veins of the knowing subject constructed by Locke, Hume, and Kant, but rather the diluted extract of reason as a mere activity of thought" (*SW*, 1:50; *GS*, 1:xviii). Traditional epistemology is hampered by a one-sidedly intellectual model of the knower. Our cognitive operations are always internally related to volitions, emotions, and instincts and arise in the service of our practical existence. In the *Introduction* and the writings that were to follow for almost a decade and a half, Dilthey sought to remedy this one-sidedness with the aid of descriptive psychology. In his last writings, the role of descriptive psychology becomes difficult to discern, and hermeneutics comes to the fore as the foundational discipline. Nevertheless, Dilthey's attempt to provide a foundation for the human sciences continued throughout his life to do justice to the knower as a practical agent, thus his remarks prefacing this early work accurately characterize his life's project as a whole.

What is often not appreciated, however, is the extent to which Dilthey's work transforms the very notion of a philosophical ground.[1] This transformation is particularly important given the antifoundationalist tenor of much of contemporary philosophy. For example, Richard Rorty has ar-

---

1. A notable exception is Makkreel, who credits Dilthey with recognizing that the hermeneutic circle involves a non-foundationalist conception of the philosophical starting point. See his *Dilthey, Philosopher of the Human Studies,* p. 302.

gued forcefully from the perspective of Anglo-American philosophy that grounding is a bankrupt project. It can be traced back to a conception of mind as a "glassy essence" devoted to mirroring adequately an extramental world. The task of epistemology, the modern science of grounding, is to find an Archimedean point that guarantees the correspondence of representations to being; this foundational position then allows philosophy to validate and invalidate other sectors of culture, especially science and religion.[2] The goal of epistemology, as Rorty sees it, is the attainment of a single set of rules for governing systems of discourse. With the destruction of the metaphor of mind as mirror comes the dissolution of the theory of knowledge as accurate representation and the demise of epistemology understood as the search for a single foundation.

Arguing just as persuasively, if perhaps more obliquely, Jacques Derrida questions the continuing relevance of philosophy as the activity of grounding from the space left after his own deconstruction of structuralism and phenomenology. Grounding returns again and again to the self-presence of mind or consciousness. Indeed, the history of metaphysics, as Heidegger had also argued, is construed as the history of the dominance of presence over thinking. That is, philosophy again and again, even Hegel's attempt to reconceive Being as dynamic, assumes some fixed point of reference to stabilize its considerations. Derrida has shown that any ostensibly simple presence bears within it the trace of *différance*, a differing and deferring prior to any presence at all. There is, then, no simple presence on which to ground the play of thought.[3]

As successful as these arguments are in undermining foundationalism, they do not compromise the Diltheyan project. Indeed, they are not inconsistent with Dilthey's own assessment of metaphysics. Although it cannot be argued that Dilthey explicitly construed epistemology as fatally bound to the mirror metaphor or thematized metaphysics as the fixation of thought on presence, it is quite clear that Dilthey viewed his own philosophical project as philosophy after the demise of metaphysics, as an attempt to philosophize in a postmetaphysical way. The concepts of metaphysics are fixed and dead and have become detached from the fac-

2. Richard Rorty, *Philosophy and the Mirror of Nature* (Princeton: Princeton University Press, 1979), especially chapters 1, 3, and 8.

3. There are many examples of Jacques Derrida's attack on the metaphysics of presence. His extended criticism of Husserl in *Speech and Phenomena*, trans. David B. Allison (Evanston: Northwestern University Press, 1973) is particularly relevant considering Dilthey's descriptive approach.

tical existence from which they arose. Metaphysical thinking obscures life precisely because it fixes its object.[4] Dilthey does not seek merely to replace the metaphysical concepts of the past with more adequate concepts. He undermines the metaphysical manner of concept formation and tries to employ a way of thinking that does not transform its object into something rigid and changeless. For Dilthey, the activity of grounding is neither the description of a ground as absolute presence nor the discovery of fundamental propositions that accurately mirror their object. Dilthey's reference to life as a "ground" is not the foundationalist's project of building an epistemic house on a firm, self-identical foundation.

Dilthey repeatedly stresses that life is *unergründlich,* or unfathomable. Life cannot be intellectually penetrated. We cannot get to the bottom of it. For example, in the essay "Leben und Erkennen" ("Life and Knowledge") (1892–93) he writes: "Life remains unfathomable for thought. . . . Thought cannot go behind life, because it is an expression of life" (*GS,* 19:347). Life is not simply the first proposition in a demonstrative system. Rational discourse is in a sense based on life, but not in the manner in which one proposition is justified by another or corresponds to a referent. Rational discourse certainly involves reference to standards of justification, but life is not such a standard. Life is not *er*-gründlich. It cannot be made into a ground in the traditional metaphysical sense of rational justification. Life-philosophy claims that praxis and discourse are made meaningful by finite, historically developed common contexts within which they occur. But there is no monolithic context within which everything will ultimately reside, and these contexts are not, as Rorty describes epistemological systems, purely intellectual constructs that control commensuration. They are rather the practical contexts of values, ideas, and purposes within which we live our lives. Dilthey maintains that there is a practical purpose to discourse, namely, the fulfillment of life.

Metaphysical thinking is shaped by two closely related presuppositions. First, the knower is conceived of as purely intellectual. But because our immersion in the world is largely a practical affair involving evalua-

---

4. Dilthey explicitly addresses the problem of metaphysics at length in three places: book 2 of the *Introduction* (*GS,* 1:123–408; *SW,* 1:173–240), "Das Wesen der Philosophie" (*GS,* 5:339–416), and the *Weltanschauungslehre* (*GS,* vol. 8). There are also a number of excellent discussions of Dilthey's departure from metaphysics. Among these, see especially Manfred Riedel, "Dilthey und das Problem der Metaphysik," *Philosophisches Jahrbuch* 76 (1968–69): 332–348.

tive and conative relations, this one-sidedly intellectual model of the knower divorces it from worldly attachments and results in the second presupposition, namely, that of an inner-outer dualism. The knower is an "inner" realm whose access to itself is immediate but whose access to extra-mental, "outer" reality is mediated by representations. As a result of the mind's representational access to reality, knowledge can be a matter of correspondence only. Dilthey undermines inner-outer dualism and its correlate, the correspondence theory of truth, by reformulating the knower as an agent who is volitional, instinctual, and emotional as well as intellectual. In the *Introduction* he writes: "From the perspective of mere representation, the external world always remains only a phenomenon. On the other hand, for the whole human being who wills, feels, and represents, external reality is given simultaneously and with as much certitude as his own self. That which is independent of us, whatever its spatial characteristics, is thus given as part of life, not as a mere representation" (*SW,* 1:51; *GS,* 1:xix). The knower is engaged in the world from the first, making thought a function of this engagement with the world rather than an autonomous reflection of this world's essential structures.

Dilthey summarizes his early approach to the ground of the human sciences in the so-called Althoff Letter: "All science, all philosophy, is experiential. All experience derives its coherence and its corresponding validity from the context of human consciousness. The quarrel between idealism and realism can be resolved by psychological analysis, which can demonstrate that the real world given in experience is not a phenomenon in my representation; it is rather given to me as something distinct from myself, because I am a being that does not merely represent, but also wills and feels" (*SW,* 1:493–494; *GS,* 19:389). All science begins with experience, and the grounding activity of philosophy is devoted to analyzing the consciousness that conditions this experience. Kant arrived at these conditions deductively, whereas Dilthey insists that they can be explicated descriptively. Dilthey continues: "The main difference between Kant and myself [lies in my view that] the intellect also transforms its own conditions of consciousness through its engagement with things. Kant's a priori is fixed and dead; but the real conditions of consciousness and its presuppositions, as I grasp them, constitute a living historical process" (*SW,* 1:500; *GS,* 19:44). That is, Dilthey replaces Kant's ahistorical transcendental conditions with historically developed presuppositions. Whereas Kant reserves an a priori status for the forms of intuition and the categories, Dilthey insists that the presuppositions which shape our experience of the world are themselves formed, tested, and rejected in our practical engagement with this world.

As I indicated in the Introduction, there was an important turn in Dilthey's thought around 1900 marked by the essay "Die Entstehung der Hermeneutik" (The rise of hermeneutics) and culminating in the *Aufbau* (1910). Throughout the 1880s and 1890s Dilthey applied a descriptive method to the structures of consciousness, but in his late works he seems to cast doubt on the possibility of neutral description and maintains that lived experience can be understood only mediately through an interpretive approach to the expressions to which it gives rise. Thus, Dilthey appears to replace the immediate, descriptive approach to lived experience with a mediate, interpretive approach. But the case is not quite so simple. As I show in the final section of this chapter, descriptions of lived experience still have an important role to play in Dilthey's late work. Further, his earlier writings are ambiguous with respect to the notion of life which provides the conditions for experience. The psychological approach construes experience as always under the conditions of consciousness. But Dilthey's writings on life as consciousness are interwoven with writings that explicitly formulate life in terms of a life-nexus, an I-world relation prior to subjectivity. The discussions of the life-nexus integrate the subjectivistic analysis of consciousness with the analysis of categories of life. The categories may be read as an interpretive explication, a laying out, of our situatedness, our ways of belonging to, larger life-contexts. From this perspective, lived experience can be viewed as conditioned not only by consciousness but also by more encompassing sociohistorical contexts. Dilthey in his later work increasingly construes lived experience along this second line and in so doing provides a more thoroughly *socio*historical account of the knower. To make this case, we must turn first to the descriptive approach of the *Introduction*.

Distinguishing the Human Sciences from the Natural Sciences

Dilthey's discussion of the human sciences in book 1 of the *Introduction to the Human Sciences* is devoted to demonstrating that the human and the natural sciences are different systems of science and require different epistemological analyses. There, it would appear that the distinction between these systems of sciences is based on two different realms of experience rather than on a single life-nexus. According to Dilthey, science in general is a system of propositions whose elements give rise to constant, determinate concepts that are valid throughout a conceptual system. These propositional parts are formed into a whole whose aim is to communicate either propositional representations of reality or general propositions that may serve as practical rules for directing and understanding human activity (*SW*, 1:56–57; *GS*, 1:4–5). This distinction should not lead one to conclude, however, that the human and the natural sciences can be differentiated according to the Kantian distinction between theoretical and practical reason. Dilthey does not limit the distinction between these sciences to the inclusion or exclusion of factual or evaluative propositions. Rather, the human sciences combine theoretical and practical reason.[5]

Dilthey begins with a pretheoretical portrait of the general conditions and limits of consciousness from whence the distinction between the systems of science arises. Human self-consciousness entails volitional efficacy, a feeling of responsibility for one's actions, and the capacity to order things into a conceptual system. In Dilthey's words, "Even before he is concerned to investigate the origin of the human spirit, man finds within his self-consciousness a sovereignty of the will, a responsibility for actions, a capacity for subjecting everything to thought and for resisting, from within the stronghold of his personal freedom, any and every encroachment. This distinguishes him from the rest of nature" (*SW*, 1:58; *GS*, 1:6). Values and purposes are facts of our consciousness and thus are effective in our psychic life. Accordingly, we are commonly aware of (prior to any epistemological reflection) a purposive realm of history in contraposition to the mechanical necessity of nature. "And since only that exists for him which is a fact of his consciousness, every value and every purpose in life lies in this independent world of mind within him— the goal of his every action is to produce spiritual facts. Thus from the realm of nature he distinguishes a realm of history" (*SW*, 1:58; *GS*, 1:6). Dilthey intends to develop this pretheoretical representation critically through analyses of the methods and presuppositions of the natural and the human sciences and suggests that further analysis will lead to two different regions of experience underlying the two types of science, that is, outer and inner experience for the natural and the human sciences, respectively.

5. Lessing makes much the same point. See *Die Idee einer Kritik der historischen Vernunft*, pp. 202–203.

The terms "inner experience" and "outer experience" are, however, unfortunate, for they connote an inner-outer dualism of a subjective flow of representations over against the objective data of the senses. It was precisely such a dualism that Dilthey spent much of his intellectual energies to overcome. Dilthey did narrow outer experience to the facts of the five senses and the synthetic judgments about such facts. Further, inner experience is not reducible to and cannot be derived from the objects of sense perception; nevertheless, it always has reference to them (*SW*, 1:269; *GS*, 19:80–81). As I shall show in more detail in the following section of this chapter and in Chapter 2, inner experience is actually more inclusive than is outer experience.[6] The human sciences are concerned with sensible objects insofar as they are related to human purposes and values. That is, they employ an empirical method (*Empirie*) which can include the sensible objects studied by the natural sciences but which, unlike the empiricism (*Empirismus*) of the natural sciences, is not limited to the objects of the five senses. The *Empirie* of the human sciences takes its evidence from the whole spectrum of lived experience.

The distinction between the human and the natural sciences is, then, based on the incommensurability of the analysis of *Gesamterlebnis* (total lived experience) as found in the human sciences with the analysis of sense experience in the natural sciences (*SW*, 1:61; *GS*, 1:9). For Dilthey, the precise distinction between inner and outer experience cannot be derived from a merely static analysis but requires a genetic analysis of the process by which inner and outer are differentiated. As I will demonstrate at length in the next chapter, the inner-outer distinction is for Dilthey a derivative one. It arises from a life-nexus whose primordial structures are prior to such distinctions as subject-object, inner-outer.

One may nevertheless wonder why Dilthey began his *Introduction* with a distinction that so easily belies his intention to provide a common ground for both systems of science. The answer lies in the purpose of this first of six books in the overall plan of the *Introduction*.[7] At this point in the *Introduction*, Dilthey is largely concerned with distinguishing the human sciences from the natural sciences in contrast to thinkers such as Auguste Comte, who would grant the former no autonomy from the

6. Makkreel and Rodi also discuss this point. See *SW*, 1:37.

7. For a discussion of the development of the second volume of the *Introduction to the Human Sciences*, see my introduction to this book, Rodi and Helmut Johach's introduction and notes to *GS*, vol. 19, and Makkreel and Rodi's introduction to *SW*, vol. 1.

latter.[8] In the first book is an overview of the human sciences as an autonomous system, with the systematic underpinning of the human sciences to be given in later books (which were published only posthumously). Dilthey notes that in his discussions of inner and outer experience, he is making only preliminary distinctions (*SW*, 1:60–61; *GS*, vols. 1, 8–9). As Rudolf Makkreel and Frithjof Rodi have pointed out, book 2 (section 4) of the *Introduction*, which was included in the edition published in 1883, already speaks of grounding the human and the natural sciences, thus these two regions of experience, in *the* life-nexus.[9]

One of the basic problems of the Critique of Historical Reason is to determine the relationship between the psychic facts of inner experience and the regularities of material processes found in outer experience. Dilthey clearly rejects the metaphysical approach to the problem, which associates these two kinds of facts with two kinds of substance. As exemplified by Descartes, the metaphysical problem became one of how an immaterial substance can affect an extended, material substance and vice versa. For Dilthey, Descartes's interactionism and Nicolas Malbranche's occasionalism are equally implausible; indeed, the mind-body problem "was a constant embarrassment which eventually led to the dissolution of the metaphysical standpoint in general" (*SW*, 1:60; *GS*, 1:8). But positing two hermetically sealed realms of experience would also be a mistake. The subject matter of the human sciences is not merely the isolated mental life of human beings. It is psychophysical life-units, embodied practical agents immersed within a sociohistorical as well as a natural environment.

This same object can be studied by the natural sciences and, in particular, by biology. For example, as Dilthey notes, "I can start from the world of physical nature, as I see it before me, and perceive psychic facts ordered within space and time; I then see changes within spiritual life subject to external interference—natural or experimental—consisting of physical changes impinging on the nervous system" (*SW*, 1:67; *GS*, 1:15). In other words, there is no absolute distinction between human and natural scientific facts. Inner states and physical processes alike may be facts for both types of science. But natural scientists restrict their analysis to

8. H. A. Hodges provides an excellent discussion of Dilthey's distinction from Comte and Mill. See *The Philosophy of Wilhelm Dilthey* (London: Routledge and Kegan Paul, 1952), pp. 162–165.

9. Makkreel and Rodi, *SW*, 1:22.

causal explanation. Dilthey's model of explanation resembles covering law theory—that is, to explain is to determine a causal relation between events and to show that this causal relation is an instance of a law or a regularity. Human scientists, by contrast, strive to construct a narrative within which the meaning of life emerges. For Dilthey, explanations and causal analyses can be used in the construction of historical narratives, but narrative accounts can be neither reduced to nor displaced by explanation.[10] Dilthey anticipates Gallie's point that explanations "are essentially aids to the basic capacity or attitude of following [a story], and only in relation to this capacity can they be correctly assessed and construed."[11] Explanations eliminate contingency because they allow us to deduce the occurrence of an event from the occurrence of its antecedents and the appropriate historical law or regularity.[12] Stories, on the other hand, trace sequences of events in a way which preserves contingency. Following a story does not mean that we can deduce one event from another. Stories present individuals or groups in various settings containing conditions that call for a response. The changes resulting from these responses present problems or reveal hidden tensions that call for further responses, and so on, such that we as readers anticipate not only outcomes of each individual action but also an outcome that will provide a coherence for the entire sequence of actions. It is this coherence-granting final outcome that constitutes the conclusion of a story. Explanations are used to facilitate our ability to follow the story. In Dilthey's words, "We can combine knowledge of how nature shapes human beings with insight into how it provides us with material for action" (*SW*, 1:70; *GS*, 1:18).

The transcendental task, as Dilthey construes it, is to show that the categories used to construct a historical narrative are inherent in the life-nexus. As I have indicated, Dilthey replaces Kant's deduction of the conditions underlying experience with a description of structures imma-

---

10. Although Dilthey refers in this context only to the use of natural scientific explanations, the same point can also be said to hold for explanations given by human scientists, e.g., economic or demographic analyses.

11. Gallie, *Philosophy and the Historical Understanding*, p. 105.

12. This brief sketch is drawn largely from Carl Hempel's model, because it seems most consistent with Dilthey's view of explanation. As Gallie indicates, however, this model has itself undergone serious criticism. For example, in *Laws and Explanations in History* (London: Oxford University Press, 1957), William Dray argues that causal analysis in history need not make use of historical laws.

nent in lived experience itself. He outlines this transcendental approach to life in the so-called principle of phenomenality.

The Principle of Phenomenality

It is perhaps best to begin by disposing of a common but I think mistaken characterization of Dilthey's view of consciousness. He is charged by commentators such as Ineichen and Hans-Georg Gadamer with a barely latent Cartesianism.[13] Their claims seem justified on the basis of such passages as the following: "In nature there appear only signs for properties unknown to us of a reality that is independent of us. In contrast, mental life is given in inner experience as it is in itself. Thus, something real is there for us in its full reality in self-reflection" (*GS*, 19:272). This theme is found throughout Dilthey's writings, namely, that inner experience gives direct access to reality in itself, whereas sense perception presents only *signs* of an independent, extra-mental reality. And it is difficult to deny that this passage invites comparisons with Descartes's distinction between the mind's immediate givenness and our mediated acquaintance with things beyond the mind.

This Cartesian interpretation initially seems reinforced by Dilthey's first principle of philosophy, the principle of phenomenality. Dilthey begins his discussion of the principle of phenomenality by recounting an example of the everyday interpretation of life with which it stands in contrast: "When I examine my earliest memories, I find that objects, much like those that surround me today, have always been there for me. My life stands within this relation to an external world that is independent of me. The farmer who guides his plow through the earth changes matter by means of matter. The inventor of the steam engine overcomes real spatial distance . . . by means of an apparatus that can move at greater speed" (*SW*, 1:245; *GS*, 19:58). From this largely prescientific perspective, our lives unfold in the context of a sociohistorical and a physical world independent of us. The fundamental science of the human sciences entails a more primordial view of life and its surrounding world, and begins by reconstruing the objects, persons, and institutions that sur-

---

13. See Ineichen, *Erkenntnistheorie*, p. 106; Hans-Georg Gadamer, *Truth and Method*, translation ed. Garrett Barden and John Cumming (New York: Continuum Publishing, 1975), pp. 192–214. Translated from *Wahrheit und Methode*, 2d ed. (Tübingen: J. C. B. Mohr, 1965). I will abbreviate *Truth and Method* as *TM*.

round us as "facts of consciousness" (*SW*, 1:245; *GS*, 19:58). Acts and contents are equally facts of consciousness: "Whatever is there for us, because and insofar as it is there for us, stands under the condition of being given in consciousness" (*GS*, 19:60; cf. *GS*, 5:90). Other people, things, so-called internal states, and, indeed, even the axioms and concepts of science are to be viewed first as facts of consciousness and as given under the conditions of consciousness. Dilthey's orientation thus takes on something of a Kantian tenor.

But this reduction to the region of facts of consciousness is not a reduction to representational consciousness; to so insist would be to commit "the error of regarding consciousness as a space into which perceptions or representations come and go" (*SW*, 1:246; *GS*, 19:59). From this perspective, facts of consciousness would simply be mental images or representations that should be distinguished from extra-mental objects. In contrast, Dilthey contends that "consciousness" refers only to "the various modes and ways in which some psychic content exists for me" (*SW*, 1:246; *GS*, 19:59). Accordingly, to construe the objects of our everyday experience as facts of consciousness is merely to view them as they are given to me perceptually, intellectually, emotionally, and volitionally. Some facts of consciousness, such as physical objects and other persons, may thus be said to exist independently of me. But this independence must be explicated in terms of how they are related to my consciousness rather than positing an in-itself apart from all consciousness.

The principle of phenomenality is meant to initiate an approach to life as lived which is prior to the traditional, theoretical distinction between immanence and transcendence. For Dilthey: "These facts exist precisely because I experience them. They constitute the realm of reality above all because my whole life is made up of them" (*SW*, 1:250; *GS*, 19:63). Facts of consciousness constitute the primordial, indubitable sense of reality because they constitute my practical existence, what Dilthey calls an implicit reality. What is there for me is a pre-reflective component of my lived existence (*SW*, 1:248; *GS*, 19:61). Dilthey distinguishes inner and outer as ways in which facts of consciousness are given.

Our awareness of facts of consciousness is prior to reflective questions of scientific objectivity, and at this level of analysis Dilthey denies that the world is given only mediately (*SW*, 1:257–258; *GS*, 19:70). Insofar as it is given pre-reflectively, the external world is real as lived: "The external world is given to me with as much immediacy as any mood or exertion of will" (*SW*, 1:258; *GS*, 19:70). I and world are given components in lived experience before questions of the objectivity of representations are raised. Though Dilthey's use of the language of consciousness obscures the point, the world is not given first as a system of representations, and it is not indubitable qua a collection of mental contents. Rather, to live is to be situated in a world prior to the split between theory and practice. The theoretical world of the natural sciences arises as an abstraction from this lived, practical context, and it is given mediately as a representational construct.

The traditional question asks how we can speak of a thing as at once in my consciousness and an object of the external world which is other than, independent of, me (*SW*, 1:249–250; *GS*, 19:62). But it does not arise at this level of analysis because it presupposes the very transcendence-immanence distinction that the principle of phenomenality undercuts. It is, so to speak, a misguided question. Yet it is prompted by an important problem. Namely, objectivity must be reformulated in a way that is consistent with using practical, lived existence as a starting point. The principle of phenomenality asserts only the implicit reality of the facts of consciousness—that is, they are components of my real, lived existence. But because the modes in which these facts of consciousness are given differ, the kinds of reality we should ascribe to them will emerge as we make explicit how they are given. Dilthey's strategy is to show that whereas psychic acts exist simply because they are lived, things of the external world are ascribed an objective reality because of the way in which their sensory presentation changes with our own changing position (*SW*, 1:250–251; *GS*, 19:63). The explicit reality of external things can be called into question, but not their implicit reality as facts of consciousness.

It is tempting to view the principle of phenomenality as a forerunner of Edmund Husserl's epochē. But this temptation should be resisted, for it obscures important differences between these two philosophers.[14] Admittedly, both Dilthey and Husserl seek to describe the structures of lived experience without employing the presuppositions of naturalistic sciences. Each brackets, then, the inner-outer dualism of the naive, natural standpoint. But Husserl's phenomenological reduction entails putting the question of the Being of the natural world on hold. Transcendence is redefined as transcendence-in-immanence, and the field of conscious-

---

14. The differences between Dilthey and Husserl will become even clearer in the final section of this chapter, where I discuss the essays in which Dilthey explicitly comes to terms with Husserl.

ness is construed as transcendental subjectivity—a new sphere of individual Being. Phenomenological analysis is then devoted to the essence of consciousness transcendentally conceived.[15] Dilthey's principle of phenomenality does not lead us back to transcendental subjectivity as a new realm of Being. It opens up empirical consciousness, with its historically developed presuppositions, as the condition of our encounters with the natural and social world. Further, the field of consciousness is a practical field where our actions are always intertwined with those of others. Although Dilthey's psychological terminology obscures this central point, the field of consciousness is mine, but it is also common. Reflection on my own consciousness is not divorced from social praxis: "The task of philosophy is today human self-reflection and the reflection of society upon itself" (*SW*, 1:461; *GS*, 19:304). Even though Dilthey expends great effort explicating the structures of our experience of Others,[16] he never brackets their existence. Thus his analysis of the presentation of the Other is not driven by the Cartesian doubt that motivates Husserl's *Fifth Meditation*. From the first, we are sociohistorical beings for Dilthey.

Description of the Psychological Nexus

The method for clarifying lived experience is derived from the second principle of philosophy, which itself emerges as a result of considering how to solve the problem of the objectivity of external things. According to this principle, the nexus that contains the facts of consciousness "is psychological, i.e., it is contained in the totality of psychic life," and the manner in which these facts are connected can be discovered only in an "analysis of psychic life as a whole" (*SW*, 1:75; *GS*, 19:75). Because our starting point is the region of facts of consciousness, both psychic content and psychic acts are part of this same psychic nexus. Thus the solution to the problem of the otherness of psychic content cannot be explained by going beyond this nexus, that is, by providing either a natural scientific

15. Edmund Husserl, of course, reworked the reduction any number of times, so there are many formulations of it. Some of the more familiar are found in *Ideas: General Introduction to Pure Phenomenology*, trans. W. R. Boyce Gibson (New York: Collier Books, 1962), sections 27–34.

16. See Dilthey's discussion of our belief in the reality of other persons in "Beiträge zur Lösung der Frage vom Ursprung unseres Glaubens an die Realität der Aussenwelt und seinem Recht" of 1890 (*GS*, 5:110–114).

or a metaphysical explanation. Only an empirical or, in other words, descriptive and analytic science may ultimately provide the ground for the human sciences (*GS*, 19:77). Everything there for me—psychological processes, other persons, physical objects, even the propositions, axioms, and evidence of the sciences—are facts within the overarching nexus of psychic life, the interconnections and modes of givenness of which must be examined. Dilthey calls this analysis *Selbstbesinnung*, or self-reflection, and explicitly distinguishes it from epistemology. Whereas epistemology focuses narrowly on the intellectual conditions of knowledge, "self-reflection finds equally the groundwork for action and for thought in the nexus of the facts of consciousness" (*GS*, 19:79).

Dilthey begins by rejecting what he perceives as Kant's overly rigid distinction between form and content, thought and intuition. For Kant, the form of experience is imposed by the a priori forms of space and time and the transcendental categories of the understanding, and the formless content of experience comes from without.[17] In "Erfahren und Denken" (1892), Dilthey argues that if the content of experience provides the diversity and variety with which we are confronted daily, it is a contradiction to hold that content is devoid of form. Diversity already presupposes differences, and, according to the Kantian formula, differences presuppose the formal relation of content by the mind: "A sense manifold can neither be separated from the connecting consciousness nor only represented, much less exist. It would be a *contradictio in adjectio*. For multiplicity presupposes distinctions. But every distinction is a relation between contents" (*GS*, 5:77–78). Dilthey contends that it would be impossible to relate individual parts of the sense manifold consistently so long as there is no formal distinction between them which provides a criterion for their relation. That is, if there is no means in the given content of experience on which to justify the relations imposed on it by the mind, there can either be no relating, or the relating is merely arbitrary and cannot be properly called knowledge (*GS*, 5:78).

The forms, principles, and categories of thought must be immanent in life itself if knowledge is to be possible at all. As Dilthey writes, the

17. Kant's dualisms of form-content and thought-intuition have met with much criticism. For an excellent discussion of the merits of the latter Kantian distinction, see Daniel C. Kolb, "Thought and Intuition in Kant's Critical System," *Journal of the History of Philosophy* 24 (April 1986): 223–241. The complexities of the distinction, particularly the difficulties in determining the meaning of "concept" and "intuition," are outlined by Henry E. Allison in *Kant's Transcendental Idealism* (New Haven: Yale University Press, 1983), pp. 66–68.

structures in lived experience are given as an indeterminate system of relatedness.

> Life itself, vitality, behind which I cannot go, contains connections that all experience and thought explicate. And here lies the decisive point for the very possibility of knowledge. Only because life and experience contain the entire nexus that appears in the forms, principles, and categories of thought, only because it can be analytically shown in life and experience, is there knowledge of reality. Even the mere analysis of logical forms and principles is impossible if the flow of representations is really completely different from the thought process. (*GS*, 5:83)

We cannot go behind the structure of life to ground knowledge because knowledge itself occurs within the context of life. Thus, as the basis of valid judgment, Dilthey proposes a reciprocal relation of immediate and mediated experience. Reality is given to us, unmediated by thought, in the vitality of lived facts. Only through the mediation of thought are the relations immediately yet indeterminately present in lived experience made determinate (*GS*, 5:85). Lived experience is already a unity of inter-relations, and this is to be the epistemological starting point. Thought mediates the facts of consciousness only after they are present in their relatedness, for this relatedness is itself already a fact of consciousness. There is no such thing as an unrelated fact of consciousness. Thought does not synthesize all the relations between impressions but articulates relations already given in lived experience, an articulation that does not distort lived experience.[18]

The tone of "Erfahren und Denken" might leave the impression that the structures of consciousness are purely given and that descriptive analysis simply records but does not constitute them. But in the essay "Leben und Erkennen"—written at roughly the same time (1892–93)—Dilthey seems to acknowledge that the description of the relations of lived experience is in some way a reflective achievement. But this does not transform description into production or suggest that description always distorts its object. Dilthey couches the discussion in terms of the problem of the given. He begins by insisting that we must assume a given

18. This leads Makkreel to argue that Dilthey's conception of historical judgment is patterned after reflective judgment as described in Kant's *Critique of Judgment*. See Makkreel, *Dilthey, Philosopher of the Human Studies*, pp. 160–202.

that cannot be reduced to the psychic processes which operate upon it, writing: "There must be something in us which these processes already find, that they presuppose, but that is *toto coelo* different from them. In the color blue, in the feeling of pain, in the C note there is a core that cannot arise from relations" (*GS*, 19:334). But this does not mean that the given occurs in experience or perception devoid of its relations to the rest of the nexus. It "is only separated, only given in my analysis. Such a direct given never constitutes a psychic process. It never comes to inner perception independently. It is separated only in analytic thought" (*GS*, 19:334). The given is not an intuitively given simple. Dilthey argues here for a logical distinction between the psychological processes with which we order experience and that which is ordered by these processes. We should not and could not isolate the given and then reconstruct consciousness from it. The given is not so much a starting point as it is a well-founded assumption: "We may and must assume such a given" (*GS*, 19:333). Experience is organized by virtue of the agent's selection of a focal point in which the myriad of lived relations intersect, in much the same way that we make sense of a painting or musical composition. These focal points at once produce and are produced by the context of which they are a part. But the selection of a focal point is not purely arbitrary. Some focal points will simply fail to produce a coherent unity. Such experiences lead us to believe that there is a given that we have improperly contextualized. Again, we are not capable of a pure intuition of such a given which could guide its proper contextualization. It leads us only to seek out a more successful focal point.

Because we begin with a nexus that is always already indeterminately ordered, Dilthey concludes that perception itself is already intellectual (*GS*, 19:335). That is, perception is more than a purely passive reception of data, a sort of blank stare: "Perception (*perceptio*) in the original sense of taking and preserving (*wahrnehmen*) is a finding, a coming upon, an immediate consciousness in which what is found is not only noted, but noted by virtue of an interest in apprehending the fact" (*SW*, 1:269; *GS*, 19:80). Because facts of consciousness are always already related, "apprehending the fact" should be read as seeing things as contextualized *as if* by the work of an intellect. Intellectual reflection on perception thus amplifies the connections already given (albeit indeterminately) there. This is no less the case for outer than for inner perception. But only inner perception need concern us in this context because Dilthey defines inner experience in a way that can incorporate outer experience, and inner experience is "the correlative of the concept of 'fact of consciousness' " (*SW*, 1:269; *GS*, 19:81). Dilthey claims that perception becomes experience or knowledge through intellectual analysis, and he claims that intellectual analysis is judgment. In Dilthey's words: "Experience (*empeiria, experientia*) is knowledge on the basis of perception. Perception as such is not yet experience; rather, the latter consists of judgments and involves an extension of the knowledge of facts" (*SW*, 1:270; *GS*, 19:81). Dilthey then insists that "the concept is first formed in the judgment" (*SW*, 1:419; *GS*, vol. 20).[19] That is to say, thought acts to articulate the indeterminate unity found in perception; it seeks to discover a concept that adequately expresses this unity rather than beginning with a concept in order to forge a unity from isolated units.[20] Dilthey's view of judgment is thus patterned after the Kantian view of reflective judgment as distinct from determinant judgment. As Kant writes in the *Critique of Judgment*, "Judgment in general is the faculty of thinking the particular as contained under the universal. If the universal (the rule, the principle, the law) be given, the judgment which subsumes the particular under it . . . is *determinant*. But if only the particular be given for which the universal has to be found, the judgment is *reflective*."[21] Further, Dilthey's grounding of judgment in the intellectuality of perception parallels Kant's claim that a system of empirical, reflective judgments "must be considered in accordance with such a unity as they would have if an understanding (although not our understanding) had furnished them to our cognitive faculties."[22]

The distinction between the form and content of knowledge must be recast to be compatible with this view of thought and perception. Because what is given in perception is already indeterminately ordered, form must be reconceived both as a given relation between contents and as the intellectual operations such as ordering, connecting, and separating used by the interpreter to articulate these indeterminate relations. Dilthey illustrates what he means by form and content using varying shades of color: "The difference in intensity of two colors is proper to the

19. Dilthey's discussion of judgment in *SW*, vol. 1 is a translation of a portion of his "Basel Logic," in *GS*, vol. 20.

20. In this respect, Makkreel's argument that Dilthey's conception of judgment follows Kant's notion of reflective judgment is borne out.

21. Immanuel Kant, *Critique of Judgment*, trans. J. H. Bernard (New York: Hafner, 1951), p. 15.

22. Ibid., p. 16.

consciousness that makes these distinctions, and it is there only for this consciousness. The intensity of the one and of the other color is proper to the content, but it attains to knowledge only in the system of gradations of intensity which each has gained in his experiences" (*GS*, 19:340). This is not to say that consciousness constituted the relation between the two colors. Rather, the implicit perceptual relations between these two colors is made explicit knowledge only by the reflective judgment of the observer. Dilthey insists further that whatever is ordered by these processes is the content: "In distinction from the form of consciousness I call the material of knowledge that which is connected, separated, related, ordered" (*GS*, 19:340). He refuses to limit the matter of knowledge rigidly to atomic elements and defines it in relation to the intellectual operations of the investigator, thus allowing for the study of different levels of society—from the individual to increasingly encompassing systems such as the state—without turning the sociohistorical world into a constructionist system. Social systems need not be viewed as an aggregate of epistemological or metaphysical atoms reducible ultimately to sense data or individuals but as systems of real connections that form the content of knowledge by virtue of being articulated by the human scientist.

Dilthey's characterization of the nexus of facts of consciousness as *psychological* does not, however, do justice to his view of the sociohistorical nature of knowing. The psychological analysis of lived experience locates the conditions of this experience one-sidedly in the cognitive-volitional-emotional activity of a subject. Even though Dilthey redefines consciousness in a way that undercuts the subject-object distinction, his insistence that the psychological perspective is most inclusive appears either to preclude finding social conditions of experience or to make them somehow secondary to psychological conditions. But as we have seen, Dilthey maintains that the conditions of consciousness which shape our experience are themselves the product of a sociohistorical development. In contrast to this psychological approach, Dilthey's discussion of the categories of life develops the principle of phenomenality from the perspective of a life-nexus rather than the psychic nexus and suggests that we should construe experience as a function of our actively integrating ourselves within a nexus of factical conditions. Here, experience is still certainly conditioned by psychological operations, but it is also conditioned by the structures of life more broadly construed as practical contexts.

The Life-Nexus and the Life-Categories

In the essay "Leben und Erkennen," Dilthey claims that the categories appropriate to the human sciences are immanent in the life-nexus, which he characterizes thus: "Life is structure. Structure is a life-nexus" (*GS*, 19:355). By structure, here, Dilthey does not mean something static, such as a geometrical shape. On the contrary, he uses structure to designate dynamic, internal relations on analogy with the organic relations between the parts of the body. The basic structure that characterizes life is not limited to psychic structure. Rather, life is characterized by the dynamic, internal relation between an inner psychic life and an object to which it reacts; according to Dilthey, life "exists where a structure exists that moves from stimulus to response" (*GS*, 19:344). To speak either of an object or of psychological processes in isolation is an abstraction. A sensory object can be called a stimulus as such only if it is considered in relation to an inner life that it excites. Correlatively, a psychological process is a response only if it is a reaction to something that stirs us or matters to us. Because sensory objects and psychological processes are primordially stimulus and response, they are from the first connected to each other in a practical relation. I turn to a detailed analysis of the conception of the life-nexus in the next chapter. In the next chapter I show how the turn to the life-nexus broadens the conditions of experience to include not only psychological processes but objective structures as well.

Insisting in "Leben und Erkennen" that the life-nexus must be approached descriptively, Dilthey provides an analysis of the role of volitional processes that are involved in our experience of the world which amplifies the descriptions of consciousness we have seen thus far. But Dilthey also insists that the things we confront in the world can also form life-nexuses: "A tree stands before me. This is a life-nexus in which parts become attached to a whole" (*GS*, 19:356). Centered in the tree is an internal relation between its roots, leaves, branches, and fruit. Further, it is "by virtue of [this structure that] it lives and stands in vital relation to its milieu" (*GS*, 19:356). This is not to say that we see the structure of the tree simply the way it is in itself. We confront the tree or anything from the perspective of our own practical interests. Without a relation to our will, "it would be a mere picture, a shadow, a decoration for us" (*GS*, 19:356). There is an objective structure with which we must come to terms, but the way in which we are able to construe this structure is limited by our own practical interests and our cognitive and perceptual operations. "We glimpse in it the countenance of a life-whole. . . . But as a rule a point of interest dominates in this whole, from which we construe it" (*GS*, 19:356). This relationship between psychic life and the life-structures of things in the world is the life-nexus that provides the condition for the possibility of experience, and Dilthey maintains that this structural relation is given in experience itself.

The analysis of the life-nexus takes the form of a doctrine of categories, and a closer look at Dilthey's conception of a category will help clarify how experience is grounded in the life-nexus. This life-nexus is not produced by but rather "is expressed in a number of real categories" (*GS*, 19:360). According to Dilthey, categories have been understood since Kant as the intellectual conditions of experience, as concepts that "express or produce a connection" (*GS*, 19:360). Such categories (e.g., identity, difference, etc.) are purely formal and impose their order externally on representational facts (*GS*, 19:361). In contrast to these categories, Dilthey introduces real categories or categories of life, maintaining that "they are the nexus of life" (*GS*, 19:361). They are the structures of life itself and emerge in a reflexive awareness (*Innewerden*) of life itself. For Dilthey, reflexive awareness is not so much a Cartesian intellectual seeing as a precognitive having, a possessing of life as mine, which can be made cognitively more articulate through analysis. It is an indeterminate sense of life belonging to "me" prior to the differentiation of the "I" of either substance-accident metaphysics or Kantian transcendental philosophy.[23] Life-categories are not purely intellectual functions that synthesize representational contents but the structures of my practical involvement in a factical context. They do not represent an alternative set of categories which are to be applied in the same manner as formal categories. They represent a completely different approach to knowing.

In his "Berlin Lectures on Logic and Epistemology," Dilthey attempts to show that the formal, purely intellectual principle of identity is derived from the dynamic structures of the life-nexus. In his view, "The principle of identity is the expression of a reality that is experienced within ourselves, according to which we remain constant despite changes of time and of acts of thought" (*SW*, 1:409; *GS*, vol. 20). This is not to say that the principle of identity is the result of the intellectual intuition of a self-identical ego. Rather, the logical formula $a = a$ originates from our indeterminate awareness of the unity of our own lives throughout changing

---

23. For a more extended discussion of reflexive awareness, see Chap. 2.

circumstances. As we shall see more fully in Chapter 3, the unity of our lives is like a narrative that we must continually revise. Accordingly, it is an achievement, not a static given. In keeping with his view of the life-nexus as an I-world relation, Dilthey contends that the constancy of life is "also a basic property of the external world" and thus that the principle of identity arises from the life-nexus as a whole, not merely our inner lives (*SW*, 1:409; *GS*, vol. 20). As we saw above, the things of the pretheoretical, lived world form coherent structures, and Dilthey maintains that these structures, like that of our own inner lives, are dynamic. The principle of identity expresses the constancy of the life-nexus in a way that obscures its dynamism, but the life-categories explicate its structures without fixing them.

George Misch, a student and son-in-law of Dilthey's, recognized quite early important connections between Dilthey's categories of life and Heidegger's existentialia.[24] On the face of things, Heidegger's sharp distinction between categories and existentialia would seem to distance the *Daseinsanalyse* from Dilthey's categories of life.[25] For Heidegger, categories are tied to substance-accident metaphysics and analyze the properties of entities understood as present-at-hand. Existentialia, conversely, open up *Dasein*'s existence-structure, its dynamic ways of being: "*The 'essence' of Dasein lies in its existence.* Accordingly those characteristics which can be exhibited in this entity are not 'properties' present-at-hand of some entity which 'looks' so and so and is itself present-at-hand; they are in each case possible ways for it to be, and no more than that" (*BT, 67; SZ, 42*). Because *Dasein* is Being-in-the-world, its way of being always involve reference to the world. But this conception is very similar to Dilthey's own attempt with the life-categories to determine the structure by which life unfolds. Heidegger's lectures before *Being and Time* was published underscore this similarity. In the lecture course *Phänomenologische Interpretationen zu Aristoteles: Einleitung in die phänomenologische Forschung* (Phenomenological interpretations of Aristotle: introduction to phenomenological research) given in the winter semester of 1921–22, Heidegger himself uses a variation of the Diltheyan term—*Grundkategorien des Lebens,* or fundamental categories of life—to refer to the living

24. Misch, *Lebensphilosophie und Phänomenologie*, pp. 53–56.
25. Martin Heidegger, *Being and Time*, trans. John Macquarrie and Edward Robinson (New York: Harper and Row, 1962), pp. 70–71/44–45; translation of *Sein und Zeit* (Tübingen: Max Niemeyer Verlag, 1979) (to be abbreviated as *BT/SZ*).

structures of factical existence.[26] There, Heidegger follows Dilthey's rejection of the purely formal conception of categories, stating, "One does well to keep the concept 'form' at a distance from the concept 'category.' "[27] The fundamental categories of life are not purely logical "*Gitterwerke* [grids], rather they are in a more primordial way *alive in life itself* [*im Leben selbst am Leben*]."[28] For Heidegger and Dilthey alike, the life-categories are not life's static properties but the ways in which we sort out the meaning of our lives as we live them.

Heidegger does, however, perceive himself as making a clear advance on Dilthey's work. Heidegger understands the *Daseinsanalyse* as a part of the larger project of disclosing the meaning of Being. Indeed, he specifically criticizes Dilthey for his failure to ask the ontological question of the Being of life (*BT*, 72; *SZ*, 46). In his seminar of summer 1925, *Prolegomena zur Geschichte des Zeitbegriffs*,[29] Heidegger praises Dilthey's rejection of the purely theoretical approach of neo-Kantianism and empirical psychology in favor of viewing the fundamental structure of life as the object of history, his grounding of psychology in an understanding of factical, historical man, and his attempt to philosophize radically on the basis of the *Sache selbst* (the thing itself, experience as given). But, Heidegger insists that this radical tendency remained covered over by the inadequate means of anthropological psychology and Dilthey's own uncertainty about his philosophical intentions.[30] In a lecture series titled *Wilhelm Diltheys Forschungsarbeit und der gegenwärtige Kampf um eine historische Weltanschauung*, (Wilhelm Dilthey's work and the contemporary debate on a historical worldview) given April 16–21, 1925, in Kassel, Heidegger suggests that Dilthey was at once aware of the radical nature

26. Carl Friedrich Gethmann traces the development of the existentialia from an earlier conception of fundamental categories of life in "Philosophie als Vollzug und als Begriff: Heideggers Identitätsphilosophie des Lebens in der Vorlesung vom Wintersemester 1921/ 22 und ihr Verhältnis zu *Sein und Zeit*," *Dilthey-Jahrbuch* 4 (1986–87): 35–37, 50.

27. Martin Heidegger, *Gesamtausgabe*, vol. 61, ed. Walter Bröcker and Käte Bröcker-Oltmanns (Frankfurt am Main: Vittorio Klostermann, 1985), pp. 86–87.

28. Ibid., p. 88.

29. Ibid., vol. 20, ed. Petra Jaeger (Frankfurt am Main: Vittorio Klostermann, 1979); translated by Theodore Kisiel as *History of the Concept of Time: Prolegomena* (Bloomington: Indiana University Press, 1985).

30. Frithjof Rodi makes this point in "Die Bedeutung Diltheys für die Konzeption von *Sein und Zeit*," *Dilthey-Jahrbuch* 4 (1986–87): 162–163. Rodi uses Heidegger's early lectures to discuss the degree to which Heidegger's departure from Husserl and neo-Kantianism was influenced by Dilthey.

of the question of the essence of history but also limited by his own approach. Heidegger maintained that Dilthey had not come to ask the question about histor*icity* as such; hence in this way his thought is limited. He had penetrated to historical reality but had not analyzed the Being of historical beings.

This criticism suggests that Heidegger takes Dilthey's analysis of life's meaning-constituting structures to be limited to ontical connections such as a career, particular family involvements, or volunteer work, but not to what Heidegger came to call the existentialia. But Dilthey's analysis of the life-nexus is clearly not an attempt to situate particular persons in their concrete historical circumstances. A stimulus-response relationship is a structure of any factical life-relation whatsoever, not a particular, concrete relation. It is true that Dilthey's theory of categories is not part of a larger ontological project. But it could be argued that Dilthey did not merely fail to ask the ontological question or somehow overlooked it. Rather, Dilthey *refused* to ask about the Being of life, and this may be viewed as an advantage of the Diltheyan approach. Dilthey's analysis is designed to help us clarify the structures of human interaction in socio-historical contexts different from our own. To see the analysis of the structures of the life-nexus as a route to the disclosure of Being is for Dilthey an abstraction from life itself and a distraction from a more pressing matter, namely, a focus on the widely varying, historically developed forms of human interaction in order to discern the effect on us of our own practices.[31]

As we have seen, in "Leben und Erkennen" Dilthey held that description was the only means adequate to the task of delineating the conditions of experience. Experience and knowledge are grounded in the life-nexus, which as a structure immanent in experience itself can be made explicit through observation of experience. This was to remain Dilthey's approach for the remainder of the 1890s, but his methodological approach to experience changed with the dawn of the new century.

Hermeneutics and the Status of Psychology

In 1910 Dilthey published *Der Aufbau der geschichtlichen Welt in den Geisteswissenschaften* (The formation of the historical world in the human sciences), in which he claims to resume the task of a critique of historical

---

31. For a detailed discussion of this point, see Chapter 5.

reason begun in the *Introduction*. The *Aufbau*, however, grounds the human sciences on "the relation between lived experience, expression, and understanding" (*GS*, 7:131)—that is, Dilthey now maintains that experience can be adequately grasped only through the interpretation of human expressions and particularly of written expressions. Not only is psychology dislodged from its previous place at the foundation of the human sciences, but the status of the descriptive approach to lived experience so central to the *Introduction* appears uncertain. A closer look at the development of the *Aufbau* position will show, however, that description itself leads to a more mature conception of lived experience which transforms but does not eliminate the usefulness of the results obtained through the earlier psychological descriptions.

The *Aufbau* developed in part from, and Dilthey's conception of "lived experience" gradually matured in, three lectures delivered to the Prussian Academy between 1905 and 1909. The first of these—"Der psychische Strukturzusammenhang," or "Psychic Structure"—very clearly was written under the influence of Husserl's *Logical Investigations,* as Dilthey refers to the "excellent investigations of Husserl" as support for his own descriptive psychology (*GS*, 7:10). Nevertheless, Dilthey does not follow Husserl's methodological lead of purifying lived experience by suspending all talk of transcendence. To the contrary, Dilthey's descriptions of lived experience move "completely within the presuppositions of empirical consciousness. The reality of external objects and other persons is presupposed in this consciousness" (*GS*, 7:12). Makkreel summarizes Dilthey's position nicely: "The reality of external objects remains presupposed, but is not affirmed. As a consequence, the world is neither naturalistically posited, nor phenomenologically bracketed. Both *Erlebnis* and outer experience refer then to the world, the former qua concern of the *Geisteswissenschaften,* the latter qua object of the *Naturwissenschaften.*"[32] As we have already seen, in the 1880s Dilthey insisted that some facts of consciousness are independent of me. But without the tool of intentionality, Dilthey was unable to express adequately the way in which consciousness may be said to refer beyond itself. He could only distinguish different modes of givenness. Husserl's *Logical Investigations* gave him this tool and reinforced his devotion to the descriptive approach.

In the lecture "Der Strukturzusammenhang des Wissens" (The structural nexus of knowledge), which he also presented in 1905, Dilthey

---

32. Makkreel, *Dilthey, Philosopher of the Human Studies,* p. 283.

employs a static conception of structure rather than the fluid structure of interaction discussed in the previous section. He argues that feelings, volitions, and representations form conscious, stable structures in lived experience and that structurally similar lived experiences become related. He uses the structural relations between lived experiences to account for the objective reference of *Erlebnis*. He asserts, "The world is only the totality or the order of what has been objectively apprehended" (*GS*, 7:25). This may sound at first as if Dilthey merely incorporates the world into *Erlebnis*. But such is not the case. The world exists always for us *through* lived experience and specifically through the mode of lived experience called objective apprehension (*gegenständliches Auffassen*). Dilthey makes a clear distinction between the lived experience and the object to which the lived experience has reference, and this object partially transcends lived experience.

The object is at once immanent in and transcends *Erlebnis*. Dilthey uses the example of spending a sleepless night worrying about completing his work at his advanced age. His manuscript becomes an object for him: "What I notice and the content by which I discern the object is contained in lived experience itself. . . . To this extent the object is immanent in lived experience. On the other hand, the lived experience is sorted out from the object. The object partially transcends the lived experience" (*GS*, 7:28). Thus, when I speak of my lived experience of an object, I may focus on the lived experience itself or the object to which the lived experience refers. The former is simply there for me. There can be no doubt about it. But this certainty regarding the lived experience has nothing to do with whether there is actually an object (*GS*, 7:26). The lived experience contains worries, sense perceptions as well as the awareness that these worries and perceptions refer to an object. These perceptions and their reference to an object are indubitably there for me. The object, on the other hand, is not. But, according to Dilthey, "This partial transcendence is grounded in lived experience itself" (*GS*, 7:28). That is, structural elements within the present lived experience can be isolated. These structural elements are related to such elements in previous lived experiences, which ground the objectivity of the present lived experience.

This objectivity does not, then, return to a naive sense of transcendence. On the contrary, Dilthey is concerned to show that the transcendence of the object is inextricably bound up with the way in which our past lived experiences both transcend and affect the present: "The remembered lived experience is transcendent for the consciousness that lives in the present lived experience. It is something that lies beyond. It is not posited as completely transcendent of consciousness but as transcendent of the present moment of this consciousness which is fulfilled by lived experience" (*GS*, 7:29). Consciousness has a temporal structure, and this temporal structure is the condition for the presentation of transcendent objects.[33] Dilthey does not, however, wish to construct the object from a multiplicity of lived experiences. He is only describing the way in which we are always related to objects through lived experience. This analysis of lived experience has two important consequences.

First, because lived experience is now understood as the relation to a world that transcends it, Dilthey can approach lived experience both as the subject's perspective on the world and as a function of the objectivities to which it is related. This conception transforms the place of lived experience in the human sciences. It is no longer a starting point, but it remains a condition of knowledge. Lived experience is incorporated in the world rather than, as he had previously thought, inclusive of the world. Lived experience is our perspective on and relation to the world from within the world. Because lived experience is our vantage point, we cannot speak of the world as it is in itself. Nevertheless, lived experience is a system of relations to the world, so understanding lived experience is a matter of understanding how it is related to a world that partially transcends it.

Second, because the given structures of present lived experience are constituted by past experiences, the value of descriptions of what is given in lived experience is unclear. This point becomes especially evident in the third lecture—"Die Abgrenzung der Geisteswissenschaften" (The delimitation of the human sciences)—delivered to the Prussian Academy in 1909 (*GS* 7:70–75) and in his revision of the "Poetics" of 1907–8 (*SW* 5:223–231; *GS* 6:313–320). As we have already seen, Dilthey's earlier position was that judgment is capable of eliciting the structures of lived experience given in introspection without distorting them. But if, as the later formulations suggest, our past lived experiences shape the present lived experience, then the adequacy of description is suspect. In his revision of the "Poetics," Dilthey questions the accuracy of introspection: "Observation itself is conditioned by the questions that I pose" (*SW*, 5:228; *GS*, 6:317–318). Direct observation of lived experience is not adequate to understand it because of the very nature of lived experience

---

33. I discuss the temporal structure of consciousness in detail in Chapter 3.

itself. Lived experience refers beyond itself to a nexus of structurally related experiences that ground it but are not themselves present. Dilthey concludes: "Only a different method can lead us further. It must proceed through an intermediary" (*SW*, 5:229; *GS*, 6:318). By intermediary, Dilthey means expression. Description focuses on only the present lived experience. But the present lived experience is always formed by its relation to the past. This relation of lived experiences to one another is not accessible to description. The fullness of lived experience, however, including its relation to the past and its reference to the world, is articulated in expressions. An unfolding relation between the subject and its world emerges in expressions (*SW*, 5:229; *GS*, 6:318).

Yet it is important to note that even though he now insists that lived experience can be adequately approached only through the mediation of expression, Dilthey nevertheless remains firm in the conviction that lived experience can come to understanding undistorted. Certain kinds of expressions simply articulate relations already implicit in lived experience. Dilthey's analysis of the relation between lived experience, expression, and understanding will be discussed in detail in Chapter 5. In the present context, it is important only to determine what role the psychological description of lived experience has left to play and in this way to discern the relation between Dilthey's early and late views.

The case seems initially to be quite clear. Dilthey omits psychology from the list of the disciplines of the human sciences in "Die Abgenzung der Geisteswissenschaften" (The delimitation of the human sciences) and thus appears to reject psychology altogether (*GS*, 7:70). But this cannot and should not be taken as conclusive. He also omits pedagogy, ethics, and linguistics from this list, which indicates that it is not meant to be an exhaustive enumeration of the genuine human sciences. Besides, even if it is not considered a human science, psychology could still have a vital relation to the human sciences. Dilthey suggests precisely this in the first draft of the essay: "And if psychology is related to [the human sciences]— grounding them on the one hand and making use of their data on the other—then this should at first just be taken as a fact, and whether it belongs to these sciences should remain an open question" (*GS*, 7:304). In the second draft he states more explicitly what kind of role descriptive psychology might play. Instead of grounding the human sciences, descriptive psychology "completes the group of the human sciences and gives them systematic unity" (*GS*, 7:313). That is to say, the human sciences are differentiated from the natural sciences because they are based on the relation between lived experience, expression, and understanding. Expressions mediate lived experience and understanding, but they do not make explicit the structural connection between them, a task that belongs to descriptive psychology. It must make explicit how "in lived experience and understanding themselves a nexus, a structure, that connects them is given in lived experiences themselves" (*GS*, 7:312). So, psychology still provides the crucial service of explicating the structures involved in producing a temporal nexus of lived experiences and how these structures are related to understanding. Because lived experience is now viewed as a nexus of lived relations to the world, the work of descriptive psychology could be understood as the clarifying of the structures of the life-nexus. Accordingly, those earlier writings which seek to elicit the structures of the life-nexus continue to have relevance to Dilthey's later, hermeneutical approach to the human sciences. They make explicit the overall structural framework within which and by virtue of which lived experience, expression, and understanding are connected.

In summary, we have seen that Dilthey's transcendental approach is motivated from the beginning by the desire to provide a knower with real blood in her or his veins. The knower is essentially sociohistorical, and this facticity is something which conditions knowledge, not something which must be stripped away to arrive at an ahistorical a priori. Human life itself is then the foundation of all knowing, and the transcendental task becomes an explication of those life-structures which make knowledge possible. Dilthey's earlier writings are somewhat ambiguous about the nature of life. In some formulations of the philosophical ground, he makes use of psychological interpretations of consciousness and seems to suggest that life is to be understood subjectively. Other formulations feature the life-nexus, a sort of I-world relation not unlike Heidegger's Being-in-the-world, and suggest a philosophical starting point that moves away from the philosophy of the subject. Descriptions of life as a life-nexus continue to play an important part in Dilthey's later, hermeneutical writings, and I contend that Dilthey's theory of historical understanding is rooted in his view of life as a life-nexus. Accordingly, in the next chapter I turn to a detailed discussion of the life-nexus itself.

Chapter Two

The Life-Nexus:
From Organic Milieu to Sociohistorical Context

In the preceding chapter we saw that Dilthey revised the transcendental project, placing life as it is lived at the foundation of all knowing and of historical understanding in particular. The transcendental task is to trace all concepts employed in historical understanding to their origins in the life-nexus and to explicate these concepts fully. As we shall see in succeeding chapters, historical understanding is a matter of understanding other persons and how their historical contexts make their lives meaningful. Accordingly, the concepts of the historical subject and the sociohistorical context must themselves be shown to be rooted in the life-nexus, and their meaning must be made explicit in order to justify their use by human scientists. In this chapter I show that these concepts are indeed embedded in the life-nexus and undertake their full analysis in the following two chapters.

The life-nexus is a practical I-world relation in which subject and surrounding world always presuppose or refer to each other. Dilthey's conception of the life-nexus developed in roughly two phases. From at least 1880 until 1894, Dilthey took a psychological approach to life and used organic metaphors to elicit the dynamic structure of our inner volitional, instinctual lives to its correlative world. In the twentieth century he placed greater emphasis on the objective cultural conditions for understanding, only rarely making use of organic metaphors. What emerges from this conceptual development is a transcendental foundation prior to the subject-object distinction and from which our categories of historical subject and historical context can be gradually articulated.

The Organic Interpretation of Life

In the "Descriptive Psychology" (1894), Dilthey maintains that life is characterized by a subjective-immanent purposiveness. Life is fundamentally a life-nexus defined in part by an adaptive reciprocity between an inner life of feelings and volitions and an environment of means, ends, and obstacles. Purposiveness, here, describes the relation, as given in lived experience, between the driving agency of feelings and instincts and the intellectual and volitional life of individuals within their milieu. The representational, emotional, instinctual, and volitional components of psychic life cooperate to promote an increasing articulation of the relation of individuals to their environment for the sake of the enhancement of life.[1] This purposiveness is subjective insofar as it describes the structure of lived experience and immanent because it refers to nothing beyond lived experience to ground it.

The formulation of this basic structure of life found in the "Descriptive Psychology" is representative of Dilthey's view through 1894 of life. In his analysis of life he concentrated on describing the way in which subjective psychological processes order and react to the external world, whereas in his twentieth-century hermeneutical writings he emphasized objective meaning relationships grounded in the shared sociocultural matrix of objective spirit. Even though this earlier approach can be characterized as psychological, it is important to realize that it is not psychological in a narrow sense that views the subject in isolation. Dilthey always stressed the reciprocity between the psychophysical individual and the environment.

Through 1894 Dilthey repeatedly used organic metaphors to convey his psychological view of life.[2] For example, in his "Grundlinien eines Systems der Pädagogik" of 1884, Dilthey describes the reciprocal structure of life. Emphasizing that reciprocity is a lived relation, Dilthey maintains that life can be understood only with reference to the nexus that surrounds and conditions the living individual: "The organism endowed with sensation and deliberate motion is determined in its preservation and improvement by its relations to the milieu in which it lives" (*GS*, 9:185).

This encompassing nexus provides both the limitations and possibili-

---

1. Cf. Rudolf A. Makkreel, "The Feeling of Life: Some Kantian Sources of Life-Philosophy," *Dilthey-Jahrbuch* 3 (1985): 102.

2. Frithjof Rodi first pointed out Dilthey's use of the concept of structure and the organic metaphors in a seminar at the Ruhr Universität-Bochum in 1984. Rodi further discusses Dilthey's use of the concept of structure and the origin of this concept in "Dilthey's Concept of 'Structure' within the Context of Nineteenth-Century Science and Philosophy," in *Dilthey and Phenomenology*, ed. Makkreel and Scanlon, pp. 107–121.

ties of the individual's preservation and satisfaction. Stimuli from the environment are analyzed by the representational component, that is, perceptual and intellectual processes, of psychic life and assessed with regard to their negative or positive influence on the individual. "Stimuli . . . are grasped in sensation, perception, and thought, then the relation of these stimuli . . . to self-preservation and the improvement of individual existence is assessed and felt according to its values in pleasure and displeasure" (*GS*, 9:185). In response to the emotional state, volitional acts arise "which adapt our private, inner life to the life-conditions or the life-conditions to our private, inner life" (*GS*, 9:185). That is, these acts aim either to order the environment in a manner more conducive to the needs of the individual or to reconcile and to adjust the individual's feelings and impulses to an unyielding situation.

Examples of Dilthey's emphasis on the stimulus-response in the analysis of life can also be found in "Dichterische Einbildungskraft und Wahnsinn" (Poetic imagination and insanity) (1886): "The play of stimuli evokes sensations, perceptions, and representations from the external world; then the value of these changes for individual existence is experienced in the manifold of feelings; and then the impulses and acts of will excited by the feelings react externally" (*GS*, 6:95). The external world is presented in representational processes that are emotionally evaluated for their significance for life. These feelings are then transformed into a volitional response to the state of affairs in the external world. The following year (1887), Dilthey uses the same model in his "Imagination of the Poet: Elements for a Poetics": "Thus there is a constant interaction between the self and the milieu of external reality in which the self is placed, and our life consists of this interaction" (*SW*, 5:72; *GS*, 6:143). To live is to be in constant, adaptive interaction with the surroundings. Stimuli are always evaluated with an eye to the preservation and fulfillment of the individual and the actions required to attain such fulfillment. The interaction between organism and environment is predominantly an evaluative and purposive relation, not a logical or dialectical relation whose structure is fundamentally rational. The logical connections made by the intellect do not exhaustively characterize the relation of the organism and the environment. Rather, thought serves a mediating role in this overarching relationship by providing representations of the external world for emotional evaluation and volitional response. The structure of the life-nexus is fundamentally characterized by an adaptive response to stimuli.

Because Dilthey repeatedly characterized life in the organic terms of adaptation and reciprocity, it is important to emphasize that Dilthey's conception of life is not primarily biological. Biology draws its evidence only from the five senses and explains perceptual phenomena with the use of hypotheses. The inner life of feelings and volitions is not a domain open to biological study as such. Correlations between the psychological and physiological can and certainly should be explored, but the biologist's method does not provide direct access to psychic states. Dilthey's descriptive psychology, however, draws from the entire breadth of lived experience, in which feelings and impulses are immediate facts of consciousness. As given in *Erlebnis,* life is the psychic structure of the reciprocity of the living being's inner responses to its environment as lived, and it need only be described.[3]

These organic metaphors allowed Dilthey to highlight two principles of life central to his concern with the psychological processes of the individual and the relation of these processes to the world. First, the reciprocity of the organism and its milieu served to illustrate that the structure of life is one in which the things of the external world are always being enlivened through their relation to feelings and the inner life of feeling is externalized in volitional responses to the world. Life is this interaction of inner and outer and can never be reduced to one or the other. Second, Dilthey used the purposiveness inherent in the organism to portray the internal unity of the representational, volitional, and emotional components of psychic life. Perception, thought, impulse, and feeling are parts of the larger whole of life which are unified in the organism's purposive assessment and response to stimuli. Thought and perception mediate the internalization of our external situation and the externalization of our internal responses. With Dilthey's shift to hermeneutics in the twentieth century, descriptions of the unity of psychic life give way in priority to analyses of the way in which cultural products stand in relation to tradition or objective spirit. This is not to say that psychological descriptions are to be abandoned altogether but that life is to be viewed as more encompassing than the psychological and thus is no longer adequately characterized by metaphors drawn primarily from the inner life of the individual. Even in the *Introduction* (1883) Dilthey had recognized the

---

3. Michael Ermarth maintains that "Dilthey stipulated emphatically that his use of the term 'life' was restricted solely to the human world." See Ermarth, *Dilthey: The Critique of Historical Reason,* pp. 114–115. Although this is clearly the case in the *Aufbau,* Dilthey repeatedly speaks of the same structure of life at all levels of life during the 1884–94 period.

inadequacy of organic metaphors for discussing sociohistorical systems. Thus, when he began in the *Aufbau* to focus on these systems as sociohistorical life, it was only natural that he would discard the organic metaphors used in the psychological writings.

The shift in Dilthey's conception of life is made explicit if we focus on his use of the theory of life-categories in the essay "Leben und Erkennen". "Leben und Erkennen" provides us with a formulation of the life-categories which differs from the discussions in the "Plan der Fortsetzung zum Aufbau der geschichtlichen Welt in den Geisteswissenschaften" (Plan for continuing the formation of the historical world in the human sciences) (1910), where Dilthey applies temporality to the life-categories of meaning, purpose, and value to enable him to view the course of the individual's life as a coherent whole.[4] To this late approach to the categories we can contrast the early by means of their respective formulations of the category of meaning. In the "Plan der Fortsetzung zum Aufbau," the category of meaning is the expression of the connection of individual moments of the past into a mnemonic whole. That is, the past is given as a remembered whole that forms a context within which individual events can be situated (*GS*, 7:201, 233). This formulation represents an objective approach to life in which the events of life are to be understood in their relation to other events and the cultural milieu of which they are a part. In "Leben und Erkennen" Dilthey does not view meaning as an objective part-whole relation; rather he proceeds more psychologically by defining meaning in terms of the subjective processes of feeling and willing whose fulfillment is the goal of life. The life-categories are used in this earlier work to describe the psychological processes involved in the individual's ordering of and reaction to the environment—that is, these categories function to detail the way in which stimuli evoke an emotional response that is then transformed into a volitional reaction. The life-categories as presented by Dilthey in "Leben und Erkennen" thus articulate a psychological view of life, whereas the later formulations reflect a move away from this psychological view.

As I indicated in the preceding chapter, Dilthey distinguishes the categories of life from the purely formal categories of Aristotle and Kant. According to Dilthey, the categories of life do not originate from the formal clarity of pure reason but from the structure of life itself (*GS*,

---

4. In Chapter 3, I discuss these categories at greater length and show their role in the formation of a life narrative.

19:361). The life-categories of acting (*Wirken*) and suffering (*Leiden*) arise in us from the awareness at once of our own spontaneity and the hindrance of this by external resistance. As Dilthey states, "The psychophysical life-unit itself lives in the consciousness of its free vitality; but also that which resists it, which therefore lies beyond its reality, is grasped by the life-unit itself as a volitional vitality since it determines the strength of the will" (*GS*, 19:369). The reciprocity of individual and world entails a volitional tension between the intentions of the individual and the obstinacy of the world.

In "Leben und Erkennen" the categories of purpose, value, and meaning are grouped with the categories of essence and sense (*Sinn*) because together they articulate "what makes life worth living" (*GS*, 19:375). They further explicate the correlativity of the life-nexus by describing our evaluative ordering of the world in relation to our concerns and purposes: "The center of the structure of life itself . . . expresses itself in [these] categories" (*GS*, 19:375).

Essence and meaning point to the system of concerns or inner life whose fulfillment is equivalent to the fulfillment of life. These categories bring to focus "the distinction between that which is indispensable and decisive [for life] and the unessential and indifferent" (*GS*, 19:376). Value is the relation of this system of concerns and feelings to the things presented in the sense manifold: "The manifold of stimuli in this its relation is evaluated by us; we call this, its relation to us, value" (*GS*, 19:375). The response to the sense manifold, insofar as it "springs from the instinctiveness and center of life and continually seeks to bring about adaptation" (*GS*, 19:375), that is, as an attempt to organize the practical field in a way conducive to the fulfillment of life, is described by purposiveness, or means-ends.

Each thing in our milieu is related to us as life-enhancing, life-thwarting, or indifferent to the fulfillment of life by virtue of its relation to feeling. In other words, individuals are always involved in value relations. But their orientation in the world is characterized by more than a series of discrete, more or less life-enhancing relations to particular things, and the historical world is more than an aggregate of internally unrelated things. Things are located in larger nexuses of values and purposes. As Dilthey states: "Thus the psychophysical life-unit comes to terms within itself with a gradation of interests from the middle point to the periphery of interest on all sides. Not only is there a gradation of these different values, but also a connection, a system" (*GS*, 19:376). At this level of the analysis of the life-nexus, Dilthey only hints at a more determinate and encompassing understanding of the world aspect of the I-world correlation. In the *Aufbau* Dilthey turned his attention to the historical world as a whole and its less encompassing sociohistorical systems. There he discussed the ways in which the individual is situated in a historical world that is a whole differentiated into systems of influences (*Wirkungszusammenhänge*). This view of the fundamentally social dimension of life marks an important point of difference between Diltheyan and Nietzschean life-philosophies, and given Nietzsche's influence on poststructuralist thought, it also foreshadows the point of contact between Diltheyan hermeneutics and poststructuralist critical theory.

For Dilthey and Nietzsche alike, life is not a property that belongs to a static substance but is itself a concept designed to displace the metaphysical category of substance. Life is an interaction, a tension between impulse and resistance. According to Nietzsche, life is will to power: "The essential thing in the life process is precisely the tremendous shaping, form-creating force working from within which *utilizes* and *exploits* 'external circumstances.'"[5] This vital interaction is construed in terms of self-assertion, dominance, and exploitation. Nietzsche's philosophy of life leads then to a kind of normative individualism where compromise and integration are conceived as succumbing to the herd instinct. Morality, our herd instinct, is life-denying. Dilthey's social view of life emerges from his initial organic view of life as the process not only of appropriation but of integration as well. The assimilation of standards governing social discourse, integration into larger social contexts, is for Dilthey a life-expanding act, not a sublimation of the will to power.

Although Dilthey and Nietzsche each insist that knowledge is a function of life, their respective views of life give this basic formula quite different interpretations. Nietzsche is wont to express this formula in stylistic flourishes such as "Truth is error," expressions that could not be found in Dilthey for reasons more substantial than Dilthey's own comparatively wooden style. "Truth" for Nietzsche is a belief that serves life's self-assertion. He writes, "The *valuation* 'I believe that this and that is so' as [sic] the *essence* of '*truth*'. In valuations are expressed conditions of preservation and growth. . . . Trust in reason and its categories, in dialectic, therefore the valuation of logic, proves only their usefulness for life."[6] Knowing for Nietzsche is then a kind of falsification justified by its en-

5. Friedrich Nietzsche, *The Will to Power*, trans. Walter Kaufmann and R. J. Hollingdale (New York: Vintage Books, 1967), p. 344.
6. Ibid., pp. 275–276.

hancement of our feeling of life, of power. His reference to "preservation" and "growth" does not mean merely survival but enhancement of the will to power as well, and such enhancement may mean the opposite of survival. Dilthey, too, would reject any "objective truth" devoid of any relevance to life, and he would perhaps agree that the natural sciences systematically distort or falsify life for the sake of control. Nevertheless, knowledge of human existence does not have to entail falsification. Certainly, a perfect, static representation of the "essence of man" is not attainable. But "truth" is also not derived from life's self-assertion. For Dilthey, truth involves a reflective attitude that includes the possibility of reconciliation with and resignation to what cannot be overcome just as much as self-affirmation in the face of limits. So, whereas Nietzsche asserts that history is an acceptable pursuit only insofar as it serves to further the life of the present,[7] Dilthey, as will be discussed in detail in the coming chapters, construes life as a narrative accounting of ourselves.

Dilthey and Nietzsche at least appear to part ways most drastically on their views of the relation of life to consciousness. Dilthey's organic conception of life is an attempt to reformulate "consciousness" as a philosophical term, whereas Nietzsche seems to reject the possibility of using consciousness as a starting point at all. For Nietzsche, consciousness is an "erroneous starting point, as if there existed 'facts of consciousness.' "[8] Consciousness is an epiphenomenon of deeper, "biological" life processes. It is not a simple given. But Nietzsche's conception of consciousness is precisely the one-sidedly intellectual view of the knower rejected by Dilthey, for whom consciousness is not the purely intellectual "seeing" of the cogito. Life is no theoretical, self-evident given. Consciousness is the instinctual, emotional, *and* intellectual doing that can be clarified through reflection and interpretation. Nietzsche's attacks on the concept of the ego as a simple, epistemological starting point and on consciousness as a self-given fundament have, of course, been sharpened and transformed by poststructuralists, particularly Derrida, in the process of undermining philosophies of consciousness such as Husserlian phenomenology. As we have seen, Diltheyan hermeneutics is grounded in a concept of life motivated by similar concerns, so Dilthey's hermeneutics is compatible with poststructuralism to some extent. This is made especially clear when we consider the differences between Husserl's and Dilthey's conceptions of life and Derrida's criticism of that of Husserl.

7. Friedrich Nietzsche, *Untimely Meditations,* trans. R. J. Hollingdale (Cambridge: Cambridge University Press, 1983), p. 59.
8. Nietzsche, *Will to Power,* p. 263.

Dilthey's emphasis on *Erlebnis* and his advocacy of a descriptive psychology have led a number of commentators, indeed Dilthey himself, to see important connections between Diltheyan life-philosophy and Husserlian phenomenology. Dilthey viewed the *Logical Investigations* as a vindication of his own project of providing a descriptive foundation for the human sciences. But he came to realize that the issues dividing him from Husserl were perhaps more significant than any agreement based on their shared terminological emphasis on lived experience and description. As we saw in the previous chapter, Dilthey viewed life as always factical, which differs significantly from the Husserlian conception of transcendental life.

Husserl himself apparently thought his own position quite compatible with Dilthey's. As he wrote in a letter to Dilthey, "So the phenomenological theory of religion requires, or rather, *is* for the most part, exactly what *you* demand again and again: a return to the *inner life*, to the 'life forms' which first come to be genuinely understood in the reliving [*Nacherleben*] of our inner motivations."[9] But what Husserl and Dilthey mean by "life" and "life-forms" is radically different, as Husserl's explanation of the phenomenological analysis of nature and religion in the same letter demonstrates: "The task of a phenomenological theory of nature is to submit the consciousness that is constitutive of nature to an eidetic investigation with regard to all of its structures and correlations, to the extent that all the principles under which being (in the sense of nature) is a priori, are finally clarified, and all the problems which, in this sphere, concern the correlations between being and consciousness can be resolved. In *exactly the same manner*, the task of a theory of religion (phenomenology of religion), with reference to possible religion as such, would be to examine the consciousness that is constitutive of religion in a suitable manner."[10] But this consciousness is "in no way limited by anthropological-historical

---

9. "The Dilthey-Husserl Correspondence," ed. Walter Biemel, trans. Jeffner Allen, in *Husserl: Shorter Works*, ed. Peter McCormick and Frederick Elliston (Notre Dame: University of Notre Dame Press, 1981), p. 206. This correspondence was initiated by Dilthey in response to Husserl's portrayal of him as a historicist in the now famous *Logos* article "Philosophy as a Rigorous Science" ("Philosophie als strenge Wissenschaft" [*Husserl*, trans. Quentin Lauer, pp. 166–197]). This charge will be discussed in Chapter 5 below. The correspondence consists of three letters: Dilthey's first letter was dated June 29, 1911; Husserl's response was dated July 5–6, 1911; and Dilthey's final letter was dated July 10 of the same year. Husserl promised to publish a clarification of his position indicating that he did not view Dilthey's approach as historicist. But Dilthey died shortly after this exchange, and no clarification was ever published.

10. "Dilthey-Husserl Correspondence," p. 206.

facticities."[11] Inner life is not for Husserl the empirical inner life of a concrete, sociohistorical human. It is transcendental consciousness purified of empirical entanglements in the world such as language, particular religions, or particular sciences. But, Dilthey does not posit a stratum of consciousness or inner life which precedes concrete, empirical attachments to the world. Whereas life-forms seem to suggest to Husserl the a priori forms of transcendental consciousness, they mean for Dilthey historically developed facticities. Inner life itself is always in interaction with a factical milieu.

Dilthey's divergence from Husserl on this point is especially important for the viability of Diltheyan hermeneutics in a poststructuralist climate, given the favorable reception of Derrida's criticisms in *Speech and Phenomena* of Husserl's insistence on the transparency and the purely transcendental character of consciousness. It should be noted that I am not here endorsing Derrida's reading of Husserl but merely demonstrating to those who do agree with Derrida on this point that these criticisms of Husserl do not apply to Dilthey. I leave it to Husserlians to argue for an alternative interpretation.

Derrida analyzes Husserl's claim in the *Logical Investigations* that there is no need for signs in the pure field of consciousness. Husserl distinguishes expressions into the sensible sign, which provides only an indicative function, and the mental act, which gives the sensible sign a meaning. He argues that because expressions continue to be expressions even in solitary life, their essential function cannot be indication. This follows from the fact that signs function to indicate something not immediately present, and the intentional acts of consciousness are given immediately. Signs are required only for communication with others, for our minds cannot be present to others' minds. The meaning-giving acts of consciousness are not, then, motivated by and do not depend on the sensible dimension of the word. In an internal monologue the word can be merely imagined, and its "non-existence neither disturbs nor interests us, since it leaves the word's expressive function unaffected."[12] The meaning-giving capacity of consciousness is left independent of any empirical sign or system of signs, thus of any empirical language, which means that the essential function of expressions is not indication but

---

11. Ibid., p. 205.

12. Edmund Husserl, *Logical Investigations*, 2 vols., trans. J. N. Findlay (N.J.: Humanities Press; London: Routledge and Kegan Paul, 1970), 1:279; translated from *Logische Untersuchungen*, 2 vols., 2d ed. (Halle: Max Niemeyer, 1913).

the achievement of the immediate presence of the meaning (i.e., the meaning-giving act).

Derrida's strategy is to turn Husserl's own view of monologue against him. Husserl claims that monologue is the internal representation of a dialogue with ourselves, although no real dialogue occurs because no indication occurs. In dialogue the sign is used to indicate, but in monologue it is not. Only real, empirical signs indicate. Imagined ones do not. But Derrida shows that Husserl's distinction between real and imagined signs is untenable, because real no less than imagined signs depend on re-presentation or repetition. Imagined signs depend, even according to Husserl, on the re-presentational capacity of the imagination. But real signs themselves are what they are only by virtue of re-presentation in a myriad of different contexts. Real signs also presuppose representation. In Derrida's words, "It can function as a sign, and in general as language, only if a formal identity enables it to be issued again and to be recognized. This identity is necessarily ideal. It thus necessarily implies representation: as *Vorstellung*, the locus of ideality in general, as *Vergegenwärtigung*, the possibility of reproductive repetition in general, and as *Repräsentation*, insofar as each signifying event is a substitute (for the signified as well as the ideal form of the signifier)."[13] Derrida thus argues that consciousness is always mediated by a preexisting system of signs. What is present to consciousness is not simply given, but given through a detour. Accordingly, phenomenological descriptions cannot be foundational in the way Husserl maintains.

But Diltheyan descriptions of consciousness do not assume a stratum of consciousness prior to empirical life-forms such as language or any other cultural system. Life is a dynamic interaction that produces oppositions such as subject-object, inner-outer. Inner life is given as a correlate of the world to which it is always already internally related. Consequently, Dilthey's use of life as a fundament for hermeneutics does not subject him to the criticisms leveled at Husserl by Derrida. This point is made especially clear by Dilthey's account of the genesis of our concepts of self and world.

The Constitution of the Self

The continuous reciprocity of self and world is not given initially as the intellectually clear distinction between a thinking subject and its repre-

---

13. Derrida, *Speech and Phenomena*, p. 50.

sentational objects but gradually emerges in stages of an awareness that Dilthey calls *Innewerden*. "*Innewerden*" is a term that defies easy and clear translation not only because it is one of those German words with no ready English equivalent but also because Dilthey himself uses the term in a number of different contexts.

In rendering *Innewerden* as reflexive awareness, I follow the convention adopted by Makkreel and Rodi, the editors of the *Selected Works* translation of Dilthey's writings.[14] They decided on this rather interpretive translation of the term in order to convey its self-given quality. That is to say, whereas reflection is a mode of consciousness in which the subject purposely takes some distance on an object so as to attain a certain perspective on it, in reflexive awareness that which is conscious is not separate from that which comes to consciousness. The German language does not distinguish between the reflective and the reflexive, and Dilthey himself did not draw this contrast. The English language, however, provides this distinction which helps underscore the self-givenness of *Innewerden*, and it is for this reason that Makkreel and Rodi translate *Innewerden* as reflexive awareness. But it is important to stress that reflexive awareness is not a Cartesian intellectual intuition or a Husserlian *Wesenschau* (intuition of an essence). It does not present consciousness to itself as indubitable scientific evidence. Reflexive awareness is a precognitive appropriation of life which more closely resembles Heidegger's *Jemeinigkeit* (mineness) than an intellectual seeing (*BT*, 68; *SZ*, 42–43). Dilthey is thus not resorting here to the transparency and pure self-givenness of consciousness characteristic of Husserl.

In the "Breslau Draft" (circa 1880), Dilthey emphasizes the reflexive character of *Innewerden* by distinguishing it from *Vorstellung*: "It is a consciousness that does not place a content over against the subject of consciousness (it does not re-present it); rather, a content is present in it without any differentiation" (*SW*, 1:253–254; *GS*, 19:66). Prior to any separation of subject and object, *Innewerden* is an awareness in which the acts and contents of consciousness are viewed in correlative togetherness. That is, reflexive awareness refers to the self-givenness of consciousness. In reflexive awareness something is *für-mich-da*, or there for me, as lived. Reflexive awareness is not a *vor-sich-stellen* (placing-before-oneself) in which a subject is confronted by an object. Subject and object are not separated in *Innewerden*. Representation, on the other hand, presupposes

14. See Makkreel and Rodi's discussion in *SW*, 1:26 and *SW*, 5:16.

the distinction of subject from object. *Vorstellen* (to represent) is a *vor-sich-stellen*, a conceptual operation in which scientific objects are posited whose existence is independent of my experiencing them (*SW*, 1:254; *GS*, 19:66–67).

Further, *Innewerden* is an awareness that is also an appropriation. That of which I am reflexively aware always has a sense of mineness. Reflexive awareness possesses its content prior to any contemplation or reflection on it. This content has an inextinguishable sense of mineness, even if not an intellectual clarity, for it is my life.[15] According to Ineichen, *Innewerden* is a reformed or broadened version of the Kantian "I think" which may accompany every representation.[16] Dilthey had, according to this view, merely criticized the narrowness of the Kantian investigation, thus broadening the "I think" to an "I think-feel-will" in order to incorporate the full range of psychic life. Although there are important similarities between the transcendental unity of apperception and *Innewerden*, Ineichen's formula blurs fundamental differences that, as we shall see, arise from Dilthey's rejection of the mere phenomenality of inner states.

Kant uses the transcendental unity of apperception to provide for the synthetic unity of consciousness. That it is possible for the representation "I think" to accompany all representations both unites the multiplicity of representations in a single consciousness and provides the identity of consciousness through the manifold of representations: "Only in so far, therefore, as I can unite a manifold of given representations in *one consciousness*, is it possible for me to represent to myself the *identity of the consciousness in* [*i.e., throughout*] *these representations.*"[17] The similarity to Dilthey's conception of *Innewerden* is clear. Both the "I think" and *Innewerden* must be able to accompany a moment of consciousness and are grounded in the unity of consciousness.

Closely related to this point is that both *Innewerden* and the transcendental unity of apperception are appropriative. As Kant states, "The manifold representations, which are given in an intuition, would not

---

15. Michael Ermarth situates *Innewerden*, or what he calls "primitive awareness of experience," within a seven-tiered hierarchy of awareness (*Dilthey: The Critique of Historical Reason*, pp. 130–131). According to Ermarth, *Innewerden* is a more determinate, although still "pre-predicative," awareness than is *Erleben*. I, however, claim that *Innewerden* is a more primordial awareness than *Erleben*.

16. Ineichen, *Erkenntnistheorie*, pp. 105–106.

17. Immanuel Kant, *Critique of Pure Reason* (to be abbreviated as *CR*), trans. Norman Kemp Smith (New York: St. Martin's, 1961), B133.

be one and all *my* representations, if they did not belong to one self-consciousness" (*CR*, B132–133). Insofar as the manifold of representations are within the unitary consciousness provided for by the "I think," they are *mine*. That is, they are for a subject, but not a personal subject: "Only in so far as I can grasp the manifold of the representations in one consciousness, do I call them one and all *mine*" (*CR*, B134).

Kant makes it quite clear that the "I think" is not a substantive subject. His rejection of rational psychology eliminates the possibility of an intellectual intuition of the "I." All intuition is sensible. The "I think" is a purely logical, mental representation without sensible content: "It is only the formal condition, namely, the logical unity of every thought, in which I abstract from all objects" (*CR*, A398). Any intuition of the "I" must be empirical, or put otherwise, conditioned by the form of inner sense, that is, time. "This original and transcendental condition is no other than *transcendental apperception*. Consciousness of self according to the determinations of our state in inner perception is merely empirical, and always changing. No fixed and abiding self can present itself in this flux of inner appearances. Such consciousness is usually named *inner sense*, or *empirical apperception*" (*CR*, A106–107). But an empirical apperception is not sufficient to provide the transcendental, unconditioned unity of consciousness. Empirical apperception presents only the appearance of the "I," not as it is in itself or as a transcendental condition for experience.

What Ineichen overlooks in this context is the significance of Dilthey's rejection of Kant's assertion that inner sense presents a merely phenomenal manifold. Inner states are perceived as they are in themselves. There is nothing beyond psychic life to which to refer as its ground and therefore no need to refer to a transcendental unity to ground the *real* flow of life. Dilthey's "I think-feel-will" does not express an empty, logical necessity but the reflexively appropriated structural components of psychic life. Further, even the appropriative character of the two concepts must be viewed differently. Whereas Kant's "I think" provides a logical link merely between all representations, *Innewerden* entails the personal possession of one's own life as actually lived. *Innewerden* is *not* a transcendental principle.

Innewerden is not the logical representation of an "I think" that provides the formal unity of consciousness. Rather, it is a reflexive awareness of the correlative togetherness of the acts and content of consciousness without either referring to a logical, transcendental "I" or presupposing a subject opposed to an object.

In the "Breslau Draft" we can distinguish three stages of the reflexive awareness of the life-nexus. In the most primordial reflexive awareness there is no separation between that which is aware and that of which it is aware, according to Dilthey: "We can immediately infer that whoever becomes reflexively aware possesses this state, or that whoever is in a state is reflexively aware of it. Reflexive awareness is the primary fact of being-for-oneself [*Für-sich-sein*]" (*SW*, 1:339; *GS*, 19:161). All acts and contents are self-given as correlative facts of consciousness. At this primitive level of awareness there is "no distinction between subject and object" (*SW*, 1:339; *GS*, 19:161). These acts and contents are initially given together as mine prior to the emergence of my determinate consciousness of a self. This awareness of the acts and contents of consciousness as mine is a " 'feeling of life' or 'self-feeling' " (*SW*, 1:340; *GS*, 19:161). At this level of awareness the sense of self is not the presentation of an "I think" but the awareness of the mineness of consciousness. Animals lack self-consciousness, but even "they have a reflexive awareness of what they possess, and they possess what they are reflexively aware of. Their feelings or desires are in them as their own" (*SW*, 1:339–340; *GS*, 19:161).

Every feeling is a reflexive awareness (*SW*, 1:339; *GS*, 19:160), a statement that cannot, however, be reversed to read that every reflexive awareness is also a feeling. Dilthey is not maintaining that reflexive awareness is some special kind of feeling. Indeed, the tension involved in any desire also includes reflexive awareness (*SW*, 1:339; *GS*, 19:160). It is then perhaps most accurate to say that reflexive awareness is entailed not only in feeling but also in volitional impulses. An indeterminate sense of self is given in consciousness through feeling and desire insofar as they entail reflexive awareness.[18]

Representational acts such as thinking and perceiving do not entail but may be accompanied by a reflexive awareness, and thus the awareness of self is not fundamentally of an intellectual subject. Dilthey does not begin with the intellectual intuition of a Cartesian cogito. Representational acts can, nevertheless, be accompanied by the reflexive awareness entailed in

18. Ineichen finds this position problematic, pointing out that Dilthey's formulation may lead the reader to believe that *Innewerden* is a feeling. If reflexive awareness is a feeling, it is an act that, like any other act, is differentiated from its object. In this case reflexive awareness would not have the pre-reflective character Dilthey maintains for it. Cf. Ineichen, *Erkenntnistheorie*, p. 111. Perhaps this problem is solved by understanding that the claim that all feelings entail reflexive awareness is not reducible to the claim that reflexive awareness is a feeling.

the feelings and impulses involved in intellectual states. However, this reflexive awareness of representational acts is the most derivative of the three levels and will be described last (*SW*, 1:342–343; *GS*, 19:163–164).

At the second level, self-consciousness becomes more determinate through the reflexive awareness of the differentiation of a sphere of mineness defined by spontaneity and feeling from a not-me of resistant things. Whereas acts and content were indeterminately mine at the previous level of awareness, the reflexive awareness of volitional impulses and emotional facts as mine involves their distinction from things. "The reflexive awareness of impulses of the will and facts of feeling allows what we experience about things to separate a sphere of our feelings and spontaneity from a sphere of objects," Dilthey notes (*SW*, 1:340; *GS*, 19:161). The resistant things remain mine as volitional object or obstruction, but they emerge, due to their own resistance, as a more determinate not-me. This is not an inner-outer distinction between a thinking subject and a representational object but one between mine and not me which is tied to the reflexive awareness of feelings and will: "It is not merely something-in-us and something-outside-us that we distinguish in this act. What we call 'ours' receives its stamp from this reflexive awareness of feeling, longing, and states of will" (*SW*, 1:340; *GS*, 19:161).

The feeling of self, then, becomes more determinate along with the growing awareness of the world as other. It is "the reflexive awareness of our psychic state, as the latter is conditioned by the world" (*SW*, 1:340; *GS*, 19:161). Indeed, a determinate awareness of self arises only through the reciprocity of the inner life of feeling and willing and the world, and it appears in different degrees in different psychological acts (*SW*, 1:341; *GS*, 19:162). The changing determinations of the feeling of self are grounded in emotional fluctuations, whereas its more constant ground is found in volition (*SW*, 1:341; *GS*, 19:162). But in any case, the feeling of self, because it involves the reciprocity of the environment and inner life, is most prominent in those individuals constantly confronted with environmental and interpersonal resistance (*SW*, 1:341; *GS*, 19:162).

In the essay "Beiträge zur Lösung der Frage vom Ursprung unseres Glaubens an die Realität der Aussenwelt und seinem Recht" (Contributions to the solution of the problem of the origin and the validity of our belief in the reality of the external world) (1890), Dilthey elaborated on the awareness of the body in this differentiation of the inner life from the world in reflexive awareness. As explained in the preceding section, the structure of psychic life is given as a purposive nexus of feelings, volitions, and instincts that are mediated by thought processes (*GS*, 5:96). Every stream of sense perceptions and thought processes has an inner side of volitions, feelings, and instincts that are separable only through reflection (*GS*, 5:96). The body forms the exterior of this private, inner life (*Eigenleben*) of instincts, feelings, and volitions. It is from the *Eigenleben*, which is spatially oriented by virtue of its reference to sense perception, that the differentiation of self from world arises (*GS*, 5:96). It should be emphasized, however, that this lived spatial orientation is not the abstract space of the natural sciences. At this level of awareness, the external world is given as a predominantly volitional and evaluative fact through the reflexive awareness of intention and resistance, whereas the natural sciences present a spatially ordered field of surfaces.

According to Dilthey, vision is always given with a focal point: "The planelike visual field is given to us in a definite relation to our spatial orientation. It is distinguished from the subject, and decreases in clarity from the point of sharpest focus on the retina" (*SW*, 1:365; *GS*, 19:183). Visual objects stand in a relation of decreasing clarity from this reference point. This visual field is always correlated with a sense of our body's position through the feeling of pressure on the skin and our ability to change the relations in this field through movement (*SW*, 1:365; *GS*, 19:183). Prior to the conception of an absolute, essentially mathematical space, there are, as it were, lived relations of our corporeal situatedness in the world.

Thus Dilthey's analysis of our lived spatiality anticipates, albeit crudely, Merleau-Ponty's corporeal interpretation of our Being-in-the-World, and a brief discussion of Merleau-Ponty's analysis of perception and spatiality may help clarify this still vague aspect of Dilthey's conception of the life-nexus. Like Dilthey, Merleau-Ponty concentrates on overcoming the metaphysical dualisms of inner-outer, subject-object, and mind-matter, which for him takes the form of a rejection of Descartes's theories of the subject, matter, and sense perception. Within the Cartesian system, sense perception, although arising from the interaction of body and mind, is a uniquely mental occurrence. Perception, as a property of mind, completely excludes body. Accordingly, these perceptions serve only to represent the material world. For Merleau-Ponty, the material world is corporeal, not essentially mathematical or pure extension as for Descartes, and the perceiver is thrown into the midst of this corporeality. Perceivers are their bodies, and their bodies are the seat of their perception. Hence, perception is the corporeal reflection of the object in the flesh of the subject. In Merleau-Ponty's words, "Sensation is literally a form of communion."[19]

Just as the body is enmeshed in the corporeal world, so too is it enmeshed in its corporeal spatiality. Space is not the aperspectival nexus of relations between objects constructed from the outside by the Cartesian geometer but rather is "reckoned from me as the zero point or degree zero of spatiality. I do not see it according to its exterior envelope; I live in it from the inside; I am immersed in it."[20] Each of the senses is spatial, because space is the contour and the shape, the direction and the distance, of each thing, as corporeal, in a corporeal place, in relation to my flesh. For example, visual space is the phenomenon of one thing occluding the visual presence of another. Vision brings us, in our corporeal perspective, each thing in its own place. Merleau-Ponty cites the example of viewing the tiles of a pool through the water lying between these tiles and the perceiver.[21] The refractions are not deceptive tricks of vision but the presence to me from my perspective of the tiles through water. Vision is always spatial, and space is always perspectival.

For Dilthey, as for Merleau-Ponty, the geometer's space is not an a priori condition for this original visual and tactile experience. Rather, the conception of an absolute space is a construction that arises from this original experience, and geometry is the intellectual analysis of this representational construct (*SW*, 1:365; *GS*, 19:183–184). Natural scientific knowledge situates sense objects in an idealized, geometrical space. In lived experience, however, objects of outer perception are oriented around the volitional and emotional focal point of inner life, not absolute space.

Thus, within lived experience, the inner life of instinct, feeling, and will is given along with the spatial surroundings as a differentiated yet continuous whole. The body is given within this spatiotemporal whole as the boundary of the inner life, for it is only within the limits of the body that arbitrary, unmediated movement is possible (*GS*, 5:106).[22] Voluntary

19. Maurice Merleau-Ponty, *Phenomenology of Perception*, trans. Colin Smith (New York: Humanities Press, 1972), p. 212.

20. Maurice Merleau-Ponty, "Eye and Mind," in *The Primacy of Perception*, ed. James M. Edie (Evanston: Northwestern University Press, 1964), p. 178.

21. Ibid., p. 182.

22. In the "Berliner Entwurf," Dilthey characterizes the relation of the body to inner life as *Zugehörigkeit*: "The relation between one's body and one's inner life is given in experience as a *belonging-together* [*Zugehörigkeit*]" (*SW*, 1:468; *GS*, 19:309).

movement is accompanied by sense impressions in muscles, joints, and skin, whereas such impressions are absent in movements observed beyond the body. As Dilthey states, "The area of this body is demarcated from an environment within which impulses to move produce a movement only indirectly, an external movement that lacks then the internally accompanying sensation in muscles, joints, and sensitive surfaces" (*GS*, 5:106). Further, movement beyond the body may arise from volition only indirectly, insofar as our arbitrary movements of limbs mediate the movement of external objects by acting on them as another body.

The volitional impulses to move, which arise from the drive to satisfy a need and are always accompanied by sensual impressions, meet with resistance. Movement is always accompanied by pressure on the skin, muscular contraction, and the bending of joints. Resistance is experienced within the self or inner life, which reflects a hindrance of intention by something beyond the self. Within some of the facts of consciousness themselves is a mediated experience of otherness relative to consciousness through resistance. The conative self is differentiated from resistant things in the world within consciousness (*GS*, 5:102–103).

Heidegger praises Dilthey for his analysis of "the phenomenon of resistance" but laments that "he is kept from working out the analysis of this phenomenon correctly by the epistemological problematic of Reality" (*BT*, 253; *SZ*, 209). This epistemological problem Heidegger characterizes as a concern about the existence of extra-mental reality—especially the possibility of proving its existence and knowing it in itself. According to Heidegger, Dilthey claims that extra-mental reality is given as a volitional, not a cognitive, object. This presupposes, argues Heidegger, a prior disclosure of the world as such, since any resistance to our endeavors can occur only within a context of our involvements in the world. Dilthey thus overlooks the disclosive structure that is *Dasein* itself.

But Heidegger misreads Dilthey here. Dilthey's analysis of resistance is not so much an expression of the problematic of reality as it is an attempt to find a way to philosophize beyond it. Not concerned with bridging the mental and the extra-mental through will rather than intellect, Dilthey seeks to unearth the primordial ways in which we are situated within the world as lived. Like Heidegger, Dilthey looks to disclose the ways in which we are in a world prior to theoretical formulations of I or world. Resistance does not function so much to bridge mental and extra-mental as to characterize the pretheoretical world as such.

The awareness of our intellectual and perceptual acts as our own is the final level of reflexive awareness. This appropriation of intellectual states is not, however, essential to intellectual acts as such. In other words, reflexive awareness can accompany intellectual and perceptual acts, but it is not entailed in them (*SW*, 1:341; *GS*, 19:162). Only insofar as the acts and contents of perceiving and thinking are accompanied by reflexive awareness am I aware of them as mine; otherwise, the sense of self is submerged in the intellectual or perceptual absorption in the object.

Involved even in our perceptual and intellectual acts are impulses toward thinking or perceiving, the strain of attention, the feelings of organs, the feeling of certainty, and a play of intellectual feelings (*intellektuelle Gefühle*) (*SW*, 1:341; *GS*, 19:163). Because feelings and volitional impulses always entail a reflexive awareness, a perceptual or intellectual act is given with a sense of mineness only insofar as it is accompanied by such a feeling or impulse. "A perception that is noted without that concentrated attention which makes itself felt subjectively in consciousness simply confronts me as a thing, without my noting any feeling of my self as perceiver" (*SW*, 1:342; *GS*, 19:163).

Representations have an "inner reality" to the extent that they are related to our feelings or the will as something active beyond us: "It is the reflexive awareness of pressure on feeling and of resistance to the will that reveals an activity outside of me. All the representations in consciousness have such reality when they stand in such a relation to the feelings and the will" (*SW*, 1:342; *GS*, 19:163). In other words, only the feelings and the will, with the reflexive awareness entailed in them, reveal to us a resistant other, one that at the same time reveals the self to us. Without this relation to the will and the feelings, a representation has only a kind of *"dead and passive objectivity"* (*tote Gegenständlichkeit*) and the feeling of self recedes (*SW*, 1:342; *GS*, 19:163).

The intellect works together with the senses to distinguish perceptions of external objects from subjective states, thus giving rise to the mediated experience of the inner and outer, self and object. Strictly speaking, the inner-outer distinction is a more derivative awareness than is that of mine from not-me found in the second level of reflexive awareness. It is brought about through the mediation of thought when we are confronted with the unexpected, whereas the experience of resistance is immediate. Whenever a perception given to one of the senses is neither matched by the other senses nor repeatable for the same sense, "an inference corrects the perception and interprets it as a subjective state of the self, which is delimited by the boundaries of the body" (*SW*, 1:343; *GS*, 19:164). In the face of unsuccessful attempts at sensual verification, thought construes this sensual experience as located in the corporeally delimited self as opposed to the external world. In those cases of successful sensual verification, "my perception is confirmed by an inference" (*SW*, 1:343; *GS*, 19:164). The intellect judges sensual repetition as corroboration and, on the basis of this, situates the perceptual representations in the external world as profiles of objects.

What is originally given in reflexive awareness as an undifferentiated part of a whole is presented as the mediated perceptual experience of something external to a subject, as Dilthey notes: "What we have a reflexive awareness of in feeling and exertion is perceived by the sense of touch as something external" (*SW*, 1:343; *GS*, 19:164). But just as the intellect and the senses present this perceptual content as objective, reflexive awareness presents this content as related to a perceptual act of a self, as belonging "to a subjective act of perception" (*SW*, 1:343; *GS*, 19:164). This awareness of a self of representational acts defined over against objective representations is the most determinate yet most derivative sense of self provided by reflexive awareness. That is to say, the self is defined as a subject of representational acts situated within a body, and some of this subject's representations are shown to be subjective and others, objective. This awareness, however, occurs only after the mediation of thought. The reflexive awareness of the correlation of act-content and of impulse-resistance found at the first two levels is always already entailed in these lived experiences.

In summary, the awareness of the I-world relation emerges gradually in three levels of reflexive awareness. The most primitive level provides an indeterminate awareness of the correlativity of the acts and contents of consciousness prior to any distinction between subject and object. A self of volitional impulses is differentiated from a world of resistant things at the second level, which is characterized by the reflexive awareness of the juxtaposition of our impulse to move and the resistance to this. Conative and emotional impulses are located in my body as mine and differentiated from a resistant not-me, but the inner-outer distinction remains as yet unmade. The inner and the outer are delimited in the final stage of reflexive awareness. Perceptual representations are judged to be objective or subjective on the basis of sensual verification or the lack thereof, and reflexive awareness presents these representations as related to a subject of corporeally located representational acts. The traditional representational subject and object are not epistemological or metaphysical starting points but products of a life process.

Dilthey's genetic analysis demonstrates that life is a network of relations which continually articulates itself. Life's dynamism is expressed not only in the reciprocal interaction between organism and world but also in the increasing complexity of the relations inherent in the life-nexus and the increasing determinacy of the awareness of these relations. This self-articulation of life should not, however, be equated with a dialectical unfolding of ideal relations. Reflexive awareness never brings life to intellectual clarity. Indeed, it could not do so without distorting life, because the relations of the life-nexus are not exhaustively intellectual. Because it is a volitional-evaluative-representational nexus, life remains unclear for the intellect but is given with vitality in reflexive awareness. Dilthey's later writings suggest that the articulation of life's unfolding involves the formation of a narrative.

The Sociohistorical Interpretation of Life

In Dilthey's twentieth-century writings, the transition from a psychological foundation for the human sciences to a hermeneutic approach coincides with a development of the notion of the life-nexus. With the shift of emphasis away from psychology, Dilthey's reliance on the organism-environment metaphor gives way to a contextual conception of life as objectified human spirit. In the psychological writings, Dilthey construed the world primarily as the counterpart of our volitional and instinctual inner lives; he does not reject this psychological component of the I-world relation in his later writings. We certainly still have desires and emotions, and the world is always given in relation to these. But in the later writings, Dilthey comes to a fuller appreciation of the way in which the world we live in is always already shaped by and provides meaning for human praxis.

In the *Aufbau* Dilthey insists that life is constituted by life-relations (*Lebensbezüge*). Nothing exists for consciousness merely as a neutral representation. Whatever is there for us stands in a life-relation to us (*GS*, 7:131), that is, it in some way determines the self, places limitations on or increases capacities, or enhances life. Everything—things, events, actions, written expressions, and other humans—stands in a life-relation to the self. As Dilthey writes, "There is no human being and no thing that is just an object for me and does not entail oppression or promotion, the goal of a struggle or a commitment of will, importance, a demand for consideration and inner closeness, or resistance, distance, and strangeness" (*GS*, 7:131). Life as lived is a structural nexus of evaluative, purposive, and volitional relations between the subject and world. Life-relations surround and determine the self. Things stand in relation to the self in much the same way as described in the first section of this chapter, although the organic language has been dropped. They are "close" to or "distant" from the self as goals, limitations, or enhancements of life. That is, for Dilthey, "the life-relation . . . makes these people and objects into carriers of happiness for me, sources of the expansion of my existence and heightening of my strength; or in this relation they limit the scope of my existence" (*GS,* 7:131).

Michael Ermarth indicates that life-relations "are not formal or logical relations," and he claims that such relations are "perceptual ones, originating in the whole mind as a perceiving, willing and thinking consciousness."[23] Although these relations are certainly not exhaustively logical, to claim that they *originate* in the mind is somewhat misleading. It is perhaps more accurate to say that in lived experience the subject is the crossing-point of these structural relations. As we have seen, self-consciousness emerges from the reflexive awareness of the correlativity of impulse and resistance; it emerges from the I-world relationship expressed by life-relations which is always already given. To maintain that life-relations originate in the mind might lead one to believe that Dilthey's starting point is more subjectivistic than it actually is.

Our lived experience is in part constituted by our present life-relations. But as we saw in Chapter 1 with respect to the apprehension of objects, the structures of present lived experience link it with structurally related lived experiences of the past, thus creating a larger temporal whole. In the same way, we come to an awareness of the course of our own lives by virtue of recalling past lived experiences in their connections to one another and to our ongoing lives. That is, "As what is experienced with the passage of time continually increases and recedes ever further, the memory of the course of our own life arises" (*GS,* 7:132). This awareness of the course of life is, as it were, a view of our life-relations over time, or in other words, the way in which we as psychophysical units interact with our changing circumstances of people and things. The same is the case in my understanding of the lives of others. Dilthey writes, "Similarly, memories of their circumstances and existential images of different situations are formed from the understanding of other persons. That is, in all of these memories the persistence [of these persons] is always linked with

23. Ermarth, *Dilthey: The Critique of Historical Reason,* p. 125.

their milieu of external facts, events, and persons" (*GS*, 7:132). Although Dilthey does not explicitly claim that this awareness of the course of life is narrative in form, his insistence that biography and autobiography, which are themselves narrative in structure, are methodical amplifications of our everyday reflection on the course of life suggests that it is (*GS*, 7:200).[24] The extended analyses of the temporal structure of the awareness of life and the contextual function of sociohistorical systems in the following chapters will make this increasingly clear.

On the basis of this everyday narrative, we form general statements about the values, purposes, and rules by which life is conducted which Dilthey calls life experience (*Lebenserfahrung*). We arrive at these generalizations in a manner that is "equivalent to induction" (*GS*, 7:132) and revise them continually on the basis of further lived experience. These generalizations have a sort of pragmatic validity, but because they "are not methodically derived," they never achieve the universal validity of scientific propositions (*GS*, 7:132). The life experience derived from reflection on the course of our own lives may be one-sided because it is derived from the narrow perspective of the course of our own lives, it is "corrected and broadened in general life experience" (*GS*, 7:132–133). That is, reflection on communal life also yields general statements about "the course of life, value judgments, rules for the conduct of life, and the determinations of purposes and goods. Their defining trait is that they are creations of communal life" (*GS*, 7:133). General life experience allows us to see the rules, values, and purposes governing our own actions as components of more encompassing and perhaps enduring social practices.[25]

---

24. Carr makes a very similar point in *Time, Narrative, and History*, pp. 75–78.

25. The *Annales* school rejects the narrative approach to history because of its presumed assertion of the primacy of the individual and its focus on events as isolable points in history. Instead of producing biographies of great, world-shaping individuals and analyzing watersheds such as battles, the *Annales* school emphasizes enduring structures, trends, and cycles. From this perspective, histories of individuals or events are superficial and tend to obscure the deeper history of long social trends and the history of groups and institutions. But as his claim that general life experience corrects and fills out individual life experience indicates, Dilthey sought to show that the study of the individual is not the study of isolated events at all. On the contrary, understanding individuals is in large part a function of reckoning how their actions embody the longer trends of the historical contexts within which they are immersed. (We shall return to this point in Chapter 4.) Marc Bloch and Lucien Febvre are considered the founders of the *Annales* school. See Bloch, *The Historian's Craft*, trans. Peter Putnam (New York: Knopf, 1953), and Febvre, *Combats pour l'histoire* (Paris: A. Colin, 1953), p. 7. This brief discussion, however, is drawn primarily from the

This emphasis on the meaning-constituting function of social systems marks the most important turn in Dilthey's view of life. In the *Aufbau*, Dilthey comes to emphasize that from the perspective of the human sciences, the milieu within which the psychophysical unit is situated is always already shaped by human praxis—in his words: "These manifestations of life . . . are embedded in the system of nature, as it were. This great external reality of spirit always surrounds us" (*GS*, 7:146). The life-nexus is still a practical milieu, but it is now also a common meaning context, or more precisely, a plurality of contexts, as well. Actions and expressions make sense because they are contributions to established systems of practices such as business enterprises, political parties, educational institutions, language, and religion. Human consciousness itself becomes conditioned by the world that it shaped.

A brief comparison of Dilthey's life-nexus and Husserl's life-world makes this last point clear. Husserl argues that all sciences are grounded in a pre-predicative, pretheoretical stratum of consciousness which he calls the life-world. In *The Crisis of European Sciences and Transcendental Phenomenology* he writes, "Science is a human spiritual accomplishment which presupposes as its point of departure, both historically and for each new student, the intuitive surrounding world of life, pregiven as existing for all in common."[26] Nevertheless, this surrounding world remains a function of transcendental subjectivity, and consciousness remains the final context for all analysis. Dilthey's conception of the life-nexus also serves as the pretheoretical ground of science. Dilthey, however, views the life-nexus as a matrix of more encompassing sociohistorical contexts within which subjects are woven. The life-nexus is not, as is the case with the life-world, a layer of the consciousness of a transcendental subject.

For Dilthey, consciousness itself is already immersed in a world that

writings of Fernand Braudel. See, for example, his "La longue durée," in *Ecrits sur l'histoire* (Paris: Flammarion, 1969), pp. 41–83; "The Situation of History in 1950," trans. S. Matthews, in *On History* (Chicago: University of Chicago Press, 1980), p. 11; and *The Mediterranean and the Mediterranean World in the Age of Philip II*, 2 vols., trans. Sian Reynolds (New York: Harper and Row, 1972–74).

26. Edmund Husserl, *The Crisis of European Sciences and Transcendental Phenomenology: An Introduction to Phenomenological Philosophy*, trans. David Carr (Evanston: Northwestern University Press, 1970), p. 121. For a definitive discussion of the function of the life-world in Husserl's theory of history, see David Carr, *Phenomenology and the Problem of History: A Study of Husserl's Transcendental Philosophy* (Evanston: Northwestern University Press, 1974).

includes the praxis of contemporaries, the influences of these and one's own actions, and the expressions of predecessors preserved in matter. These actions, influences, and preserved expressions are not, as for Husserl, a less primordial stratum of consciousness layered on more primordial strata. They form systems—unified by purposes and rules—that are a fundamental part of the life-nexus. Although the awareness of these systems emerges only gradually in the analysis of the life-nexus, their existence and their historicity are not secondary to or derived from the subject. Sociohistorical systems have their own structure, their own principles of development, and a relatively independent status. Individuals are then "crossing-points of systems which permeate and exist through them but which extend beyond their life" (*GS*, 7:135). Ermarth aptly expresses this thought, writing that "individual life is not closed upon itself but merges with wider coherences up to the level of humanity as a whole."[27] That is to say, life, viewed structurally, is a nexus of real, evaluative, volitional, and intellectual relations between I and world. But the individual is not merely the crossing-point of a multitude of relations with individual things and persons. Individuals are also involved in social systems which are more encompassing and which survive the death of any particular individual. Our activities involve us in larger contexts of life-relations, such as cultural systems and political organizations.

As we saw above, our everyday reflection on the course of this communal life results in generalizations about the rules, purposes, and values governing our lives. This prescientific reflection on life is rigorously pursued by the human scientist, who methodically traces the development of specific social practices; these, in turn, serve as sociohistorical contexts or settings within which the unfolding of particular human lives can be understood. Dilthey's critical task is to provide for the historian the conditions for the possibility of the construction of historical narratives from which generalizations about historically developed forms of life can be drawn. In Chapters 3 and 4 I shall show how Dilthey's reflections on time and sociohistorical systems perform precisely this function.

In summary, we have seen that Dilthey's conception of the life-nexus developed from an organic to a sociohistorical model. Through 1894, Dilthey's work continually returned to the role played by the psychological processes of the individual in ordering the world according to values and purposes. Indeed, Dilthey conceived of this relation between purpo-

---

27. Ermarth, *Dilthey: The Critique of Historical Reason*, p. 125.

sive, psychophysical individuals and the world organized by them as an internally related whole that is life itself. Life is, then, an organized whole or context, but it is not a fundamentally rational totality. Thought arises only in the service of the individual's adaptation to the world. Further, Dilthey's earlier conception of life includes a genetic description of the awareness of the self and the world. That is, life is a whole whose parts become distinguished in our awareness only step by step. The life-nexus is at first given as an indeterminate whole within which the acts and contents of consciousness are undifferentiated correlates. Next, a sense of self arises from the resistance of the world to our conative impulses. The awareness of subject and object emerges from this primordial unity only in the final stages of this genetic account.

The genetic account thus resists Helmut Johach's characterization of Dilthey's philosophy as a philosophy of the subject.[28] Though Johach is quite correct to point out that Dilthey's epistemology owes more to the transcendental than to the empirical tradition, it would not be completely accurate to characterize life primarily in terms of subjectivity. Self-consciousness is always a correlate of the consciousness of the external world. The self is always and only given in relation to the world. In Dilthey's words, "Without a world we would have no self-consciousness, and without self-consciousness there would be no world present for us. What transpires in this act of contact is life" (*SW,* 1:330; *GS,* 19:153). As Dilthey shows in his genetic account, the subject-object distinction is derivative, not foundational. Subject and object emerge from a primordial life-nexus (*Lebenszusammenhang*) characterized by Rudolf Makkreel as "a relational nexus . . . a structure that always relates something outer to something inner."[29] Subjectivity presupposes the distinction between subject and object, and this distinction by no means occurs at the most primordial level of awareness; rather, it is the most derivative awareness of the relation between the self and the world, that is, life.

After 1900, Dilthey increasingly used "life" to refer to sociohistorical, human life in exclusion of nonhuman animal life. This does not mean that he rejected his earlier view that thought serves the exigencies of life. Rather, he more fully developed this view by articulating the sociohistorical, communicative function of human thought and action. In his late

28. Helmut Johach, "Diltheys Philosophie des Subjekts und die Grundlegung der Geistes- und Sozialwissenschaften: Zur Aktualität der 'Einleitung in die Geisteswissenschaften,' " *Dilthey-Jahrbuch* 2 (1984): 93.
29. Makkreel, "The Feeling of Life," p. 102.

writings, Dilthey continued to view the world as the object of our volitional, emotional, and perceptual operations, but he also came to understand it as a plurality of systems of historically developed and developing human practices in which we always participate. In other words, his later analysis of the life-nexus is broadened to include consideration of the sociohistorical determinants of life's meaning. Indeed, this sociohistorical reflection forms a larger context within which our volitional relation to the environment makes sense. In both the earlier and the later writings, life is portrayed as a multiplicity of dynamic relations whose coherence is achieved in the process of living itself. There is no stable subject or ego to anchor or center the flux. A meaningful structure must be carved out over time. In the next chapter, we will turn to the problem of shaping the multiplicity of lived experiences into the coherent whole we call a particular, individual life. In Chapter 4 we then explicate more fully the notion of a sociohistorical context and how individual lives derive meaning from participation in such contexts.

Chapter Three

Temporality and the Narrative Coherence of Life

In the preceding chapters we saw that Dilthey's revised transcendental project seeks to trace the categories of historical understanding to structures inherent in the life-nexus. For him, the fundamental category of all life, hence of all historical understanding, is temporality. Individual and communal life alike can be analyzed diachronically precisely because of the temporal structure of the life-nexus. But making the course of life intelligible involves more than the production of a chronology of events. Dilthey himself repeatedly chose biography as a historiographical genre, and as Carr has indicated, Dilthey viewed the narrative structure of biography and autobiography as an articulation of the structure of life itself.[1] Thus, when Dilthey says, "Temporality is contained in life as its first categorial determination, fundamental [*grundlegend*] for all others" (*GS*, 7:192), he means that life unfolds as a story that can be told and followed.[2]

Although temporality applies to communal and individual life alike, in this chapter I concentrate primarily on the temporal structure of individual lives and leave the discussion of sociohistorical systems for Chapter 4. Accordingly, we must turn our attention to the transcendental underpinning of biography and autobiography. Because biography and autobiography assume narrative form, narrative structure itself must be at least implicit in the life-nexus or the truth of narrative accounts of life is out of the question. This puts Dilthey's position at odds with contemporary theorists, such as Mink and White, who have argued that narrative structure is imposed by interpreters on the lives of those they seek to understand, whether they seek to understand others or them-

---

1. Carr, *Time, Narrative, and History,* p. 78.
2. For a discussion of the phenomenology of following a story, see Gallie, *Philosophy and the Historical Understanding,* especially chapter 2.

selves.[3] Life as lived would not, from this perspective, have a narrative structure, which is achieved only through reflection on life. Although Dilthey agrees that life becomes a narrative only with reflection, analysis of the temporal structure of life makes it clear that narrative is an articulation of structures immanent in life, not an external imposition of a narrative form on the content of life. Dilthey readily admits that the narrative coherence of life is a reflective achievement, but he denies that narrative structure is a form imposed on the content of life from without.

A more grave threat to the Diltheyan approach is Derrida's attack on analyses of temporality in general. Whereas Mink and White blur the historiography-fiction distinction by focusing on the role of judgment and imagination in the writing of history, Derrida suggests that any analysis of time is inextricably linked to a concept of the simple present, a concept that is itself untenable. Life cannot, from Derrida's perspective, have a narrative structure, as narrative structure presupposes an account of time. Accordingly, narrative historiography—and autobiography in particular—cannot be said to be true. So, before proceeding with Dilthey's argument, it is important to survey briefly Derrida's position on this point, as it may seem to undermine the relevance of Dilthey's approach.

Time and Autobiographical Truth

In the essay "Otobiographies," Derrida takes up the question of autobiography and its relation to life by way of a discussion of Nietzsche's *Ecce Homo*.[4] For him, *Ecce Homo* redefines the relation between the life and the autobiographical text in a way that transforms our very notion of the author's identity.[5] We can begin only with the author's name, and Derrida argues for a sort of a priori relation between any name and its bearer, writing, "Only the name can inherit."[6] The signature, like any written word, escapes the intention of the author. We are accustomed to the so-called misunderstandings to which the written word gives rise, the unintended meanings read from texts once these texts have left the

3. Mink, "History and Fiction," pp. 541–558; and also his "Narrative Form," pp. 129–149; White, "The Value of Narrativity in the Representation of Reality," especially p. 23. In addition, see White's article "The Historical Text," pp. 41–62, and his *Metahistory*.

4. Jacques Derrida, "Otobiographies: The Teaching of Nietzsche and the Politics of the Proper Name," trans. Avital Ronell, in *The Ear of the Other: Otobiography, Transference, Translation*, ed. Christie V. McDonald (New York: Schocken, 1985).

5. Ibid., p. 8.

6. Ibid., p. 7.

author's grasp. The signature, like other words, becomes detached from its author. But the signature is a word like no other, for the signature is involved with the identity of the author. Thus, the detachment of the signature from the signer releases the identity of the author from the signer's control. So, when we say in answer to, Who is Nietzsche? that he is one of the philosophical sources of Nazism, we are crediting (or debiting) Nietzsche with an effect that was impossible for the signer of *Ecce Homo* at the time of signing. But Derrida is not just reiterating Danto's point that narrative descriptions involve the transformation of the meaning of an earlier event from the perspective of a later event. Danto's position would suggest only that Nietzsche's identity is transformed by subsequent events. Derrida, by contrast, argues that the identity of the author is an effect of the signature. This seems paradoxical, since presumably my identity precedes and authenticates the signature.

But Derrida inverts the signer-signature relation, such that "who" or identity is given the name only after the name itself is inscribed. As he says elsewhere of the signers of the Declaration of Independence, "The signature invents the signer."[7] The subject is constituted by the signature, but as something that is not present at the signing but only after the fact of the signature. In Derrida's view, Nietzsche neither describes an already given coherence nor transforms the events of his life in retrospect. He anticipates a coherence to life in the writing of *Ecce Homo*. His identity "has passed to him through the unheard-of contract he has drawn up with himself. He has taken out a loan with himself."[8] Nietzsche does not write *Ecce Homo*, his life story, on the basis of an authority derived from the self-presence of a subject but does so by extending himself a line of credit. The credit that Nietzsche extends himself is the unity of his own life, a unity not yet made but assumed at the signing. Nietzsche's life is a text that is always yet to be written. With *Ecce Homo* Nietzsche projects a certain reading, a certain unity, to his life. He neither records nor discovers it.

In the essay "Declarations of Independence," Derrida displays this structure of the proper name using the text of the Declaration of Independence. His strategy there is to show that the declaration itself entails an indispensable "undecidability" necessary for its effect as a declaration of independence, namely, "One cannot decide . . . whether independence

7. Jacques Derrida, "Declarations of Independence," trans. Tom Keenan and Tom Pepper, *New Political Science* 15 (1986): 10.
8. Derrida, "Otobiographies," p. 8.

is stated or produced by this utterance," whether "to declare" is consta-tive or performative.[9] That is, if the declaration is genuinely a perfor-mance, then it constitutes the people of the United States as an indepen-dent people authorized to sign such a document. But at the same time, the representatives signing the declaration could be authorized to do so only by a previously existing, independent people. The paradox, then, is that the signatures create the people who authorize the signing of the document. Derrida writes, "They do *not* exist as an entity, it does *not* exist, *before* this declaration, not *as such*. If it gives birth to itself, as free and independent subject, as possible signer, this can hold only in the act of the signature."[10]

Whether we speak of Nietzsche signing for himself or of Jefferson signing as a political representative, Derrida insists that this analysis of signing demonstrates the bankruptcy of the metaphysical analysis of time. The concept of time in its various manifestations comes again and again to rest on a concept of a simple present. But the inversion of the signer-signature relation illustrates the derivative nature of the present, because the signer's identity or self-consciousness, that is, one's presence to oneself, must precede the act of signing but can also only follow the act of signing. Accordingly, presence is always derived from elsewhere. Der-rida thus displaces the metaphysical analysis of time, which is character-ized by "the domination of presence,"[11] with différance as a kind of temporalizing.[12] Différance is at once a differing and a deferring which is not derived from but is already at work in any presence. The temporaliz-ing of différance is a kind of deferment that constitutes presence itself. As Derrida writes, "In this sense, *différance* is not preceded by the originary and indivisible unity of a present possibility that I could reserve, like an expenditure that I would put off calculatedly or for reasons of economy. What defers presence, on the contrary, is the very basis on which pres-ence is announced or desired in what represents it, its sign, its trace."[13] The deferring and differing of the act of signing is a kind of temporaliza-tion. In the case of the declaration, the people sign through their repre-

9. Derrida, "Declarations," p. 9.

10. Ibid., p. 10.

11. Jacques Derrida, *Margins of Philosophy*, trans. Alan Bass (Chicago: University of Chi-cago Press, 1982), p. 63.

12. Différance actually functions in a number of ways. See Rodolphe Gasché's discussion in *The Tain of the Mirror* (Cambridge: Harvard University Press, 1986), pp. 194–205.

13. Jacques Derrida, *Positions*, trans. Alan Bass (Chicago: University of Chicago Press, 1981), p. 8.

sentatives, whose authority as representatives is itself a product of sign-ing.[14] Their authority to sign is deferred until after they have signed. The everyday sense of deferment refers only to a presence that happens at the moment not to be present or is kept present elsewhere to be made present here at another moment in the future. On this interpretation, Nietzsche's *Ecce Homo* could be viewed as the revelation of an identity that Nietzsche has hidden from his contemporaries but that had been present to him all along. The everyday sense of deferring is, then, dependent on presence. Derrida insists that presence is first made possible by differing and defer-ring. Whatever is present always contains within it the trace of "what it absolutely is not."[15] This does not mean that the present is derived from the past and the future as moments *in time*. These, for Derrida, are deriva-tive from the present, the now. Temporality—the relation of past, present, and future—is derived from différance as temporalizing. Temporal struc-ture—and thus narrative structure—is not, then, an original structure of life but is itself a sort of achievement.

If this were indeed the case, Dilthey's project would be seriously com-promised. Recall that his transcendental project is to trace the categories of historical understanding back to the life-nexus. Temporality is for him the fundamental category of historiography, and any narrative account of life presupposes that temporal structure is really embedded in the life-nexus. As I will show in the following section, Dilthey is able to argue at once for the reality of time as a life-structure and for a concept of time which recognizes the dependence of the present on the other dimensions of time. In other words, we may accept Derrida's assertion that the pres-ent is derivative without drawing the further conclusion that all analyses of time are hopelessly misguided. On the contrary, it is still possible to show that our narrative accounts are rooted in the real temporal struc-tures of our lives.

The Temporal Structure of Experience

Dilthey's conception of time is at once an appropriation of and a depar-ture from Kant. Following Kant, Dilthey turned to an analysis of inner

14. As Derrida writes, "In signing, the people say—and do what they say they do, but in differing and deferring themselves through (*différant par*) the intervention of their represen-tation whose representativity is fully legitimated only by the signature, thus after the fact or the coup (*après coup*)" ("Declarations," p. 10).

15. Derrida, *Speech and Phenomena*, p. 143.

perception for his analysis of time. But whereas Kant's analyses of outer and inner sense, that is, space and time, are parallel, Dilthey insists that inner perception requires its own analysis. The analysis of outer perception requires differentiating its mentally imposed form from the content provided by external stimuli (*SW*, 1:369; *GS*, 19:196). This approach is not, however, appropriate to the analysis of inner perception. Dilthey writes, "In inner experience, one cannot divide up the given in this way; everything, qua inner fact, is real in the same sense" (*SW*, 1:369; *GS*, 19:196). In other words, the spatial manifold is phenomenal, but the manifold given in inner perception is real. Further, the connections between facts in outer perception are imposed from without, but the facts of inner perception are always already interconnected in real temporal relations. Everything given in inner perception has the same sense of reality, including the temporal relations between the events of life.

Dilthey thus agrees with Kant that time is an a priori form of the manifold of inner states but balks at Kant's view that time is an ideal form of intuition (*SW*, 1:384; *GS*, 19:216). Time is a priori insofar as an awareness of inner states as atemporal is inconceivable. Volition, for example, cannot be thought except as a projection of an unrealized possibility: "For the will extends from remembered states, which are to be reinstituted, to the object-representation belonging to the future" (*SW*, 1:382; *GS*, 19:213). In volition, that which has passed from the present is recovered and linked purposively with the future. But time must not be interpreted as a form divorced from its content. Kant conceived of time as a pure form within which natural events occurred. But the individual events that compose the content of life are not separable from the flow that constitutes their form. Time is not externally imposed on life but is its real passage. Dilthey viewed Kant's failure to recognize the reality of time as the form of our psychic lives—that is, his "extension of the concept of appearance to inner experiences"—as the fundamental shortcoming of his view (*SW*, 1:383; *GS*, 19:216).

In his positive analysis of time, Dilthey begins by broadening Kant's purely intellectual approach to time. Time is not, in Dilthey's view, given solely to the intellect but also to the representational, emotional, instinctual, and volitional totality of psychic life as the flow of this very life itself: "Time is given in the totality of our self-consciousness and is not merely a fact of the intellect" (*SW*, 1:384; *GS*, 19:217). Kant's one-sidedly intellectual analysis of time led him to construe time as an abstract, representational continuum. Without reference to the other dimensions of consciousness, Kant was unable to differentiate past, present, and future qualitatively. The abstract ideality of time entails that it is an infinite continuum from which any particular time must be differentiated. Time is a totality of nows or presents (though not necessarily static now-points), and past and future can be determined only as nows that are no longer present and nows that are not yet present. By rejecting time's ideality, Dilthey also rejects the view that it is an infinite now. Human temporality is always finite, and each dimension of time is qualitatively distinct from the others. Thus past and future cannot be said to derive from the present.

Dilthey argues that the most distinctive attribute of our pre-reflective experience of time is the constant advancement (*Fortrücken*) of the present: "What is present recedes into the past. . . . From the composite processes which constitute the present, something is lost drop by drop, as it were, into the sea of the past. Ahead, something expected, something from the future, becomes present" (*SW*, 1:381–382; *GS*, 19:211). The present is not a simple, self-contained point. It always already refers beyond itself; indeed, it would not be what it is without reference to past and future. The content of the present ceaselessly drains off into the past, and the future constantly flows into the present. Dilthey anticipates Husserl's and Heidegger's discontent with any model that views time as only a succession of now-points that are themselves atemporal. Such a model could differentiate past, present, and future only by their relative position on a timeline, but it fails to account for the experience of time's passage.

In our pre-reflective experience, the present has a kind of duration. It is more like a continuous transition than a changeless moment. For example, the line between successive tones of a melody is hazy (*GS*, 19:215). They all seem to be present: "Lived experiences gradually recede by degrees, as it were, into memories" (*GS*, 19:215). Dilthey also used the example of hearing a rolling wagon: "The sequence of a continuous sound, such as that of a rolling cart on the street beneath me, is not composed of one indivisible, unextended moment that is present and others that are past. Rather, the sequence is to be found in our actual perception" (*SW*, 1:385; *GS*, 19:218). Dilthey's point here seems to be something like Husserl's analysis of protention and retention. Protention and retention are extensions of the now, and their contents are always given along with the now. The givenness of any object includes the contents of protention and retention, which are not representations of the past and future but the given extensions of the now.[16] Dilthey departs from Husserl's emphasis on the present as the fundamental dimension of time, however. Husserl views the now as the source of the contents of protention and retention, whereas Dilthey thinks of the now as a focal point for the future and past such that all these aspects of time are equiprimordial in constituting the living present.[17] With respect to this deemphasis of the role of the present, Dilthey more closely resembles Heidegger than Husserl, but their agreement is not complete. Heidegger gives the future priority over the other two dimensions of time and derives the present from the past and future.

Again anticipating Husserl, Dilthey distinguishes this pre-reflective awareness of past and future within the living present from reflective representations of past and future. Although the contents of protention and retention (to use Husserlian language) are given, reflection actively represents experiences that are no longer or not yet given and relates them to the given present. In reflection, "past and future are formed only by means of representation" (*SW*, 1:387; *GS*, 19:221), according to Dilthey; in our reflective lived experience, past, present, and future "are distinguished qualitatively from each other as states of consciousness" (*GS*, 19:214). The present, composed predominantly of feeling and volition, is not a representation but the given reality. It is "nothing other than a living state which manifests itself in attention, feeling, and willing" (*SW*, 1:382; *GS*, 19:211). Memories constitute the past, thus the living experiences of the present are distinguished from the resurrected experiences of the past. "As a state of consciousness the past is distinguished from the present by all the traits which distinguish memories from lived experience" (*SW*, 1:382; *GS*, 19:211). The future is "indeterminate merely in terms of imaginary representations," which are like "fogbanks" forever trying to overtake us (*SW*, 1:382; *GS*, 19:211). Yet to be realized possibilities in the form of fears and hopes constitute the future, "but these possibilities are images connected with the attitude of expectation" (*SW*, 1:382; *GS*, 19:211).

16. Edmund Husserl, *Husserliana*, vol. 10, *Zur Phänomenologie des inneren Zeitbewusstseins*, ed. Rudolf Boehm (The Hague: Martinus Nijhoff, 1966). Translated by James S. Churchill as *The Phenomenology of Internal Time-Consciousness* (Bloomington: Indiana University Press, 1964), sections 11–14.

17. For a detailed comparison of the Diltheyan and Husserlian conceptions of time, see David Carr, "The Future Perfect: Temporality and Priority in Husserl, Heidegger, and Dilthey," in *Dilthey and Phenomenology*, ed. Makkreel and Scanlon, pp. 125–137.

Dilthey's insistence that the present is the only reality may seem to involve him in a contradiction. That is, his analysis of the pre-reflective awareness of time demonstrates that there is no simple given present that may be distinguished from past and future as representational reproductions. The lived present is already an intersection or production of a past and future which cannot be reduced to the present. To this extent, then, Dilthey's analysis of the pre-reflective experience of time arrives at a conclusion quite similar to that of Derrida's, namely, the present itself is not an original. To say that we are related to the past and future only through representations or reproductions of something originally given in the present cannot suffice to distinguish these dimensions of time when we are forced to admit that there is nothing original about the present. But it is possible to read Dilthey's discussion of the reflective experience of time without reference to the metaphor of original versus reproduction, thus without involving him in this contradiction.

Dilthey does not resort to a simple given present, for along with descriptions of the present as "the reality of our self" and as "existence [*Dasein*] as given in experience," Dilthey makes use of expressions such as "fulfilled totality of life" and "fulfilled self-consciousness" (*SW*, 1:387; *GS*, 19:221). Accordingly, a case can be made that he continues to view the present, this "fulfilled" reality, as an intersection of past and future, not as a given from which the other two are derived. Even in abstraction from their contents, past, present, and future are qualitatively differentiated. The temporal positions filled by this content are "not equivalent to one another like the points on a line" such that only the vividness or liveliness of the content distinguishes past, present, and future (*GS*, 19:212). Rather, these positions are distinguished by means of the intentional structures of remembering, perceiving, feeling, and expecting. These psychic acts are themselves qualitatively differentiated, and it is these processes that reveal the reflective temporal structure of life. The intentional structures, as well as the contents of past and future, are realized within the present. Considered reflectively, the present is a "fulfilled" reality in that it completes the past as end to means, as fulfillment (or disappointment) of expectation. But it is also open to the future to *be* fulfilled or completed in precisely this way. The present becomes the dynamic crossing-point of past and future, and life entails a double "sense of an ending," to borrow and to transform Frank Kermode's phrase.

Dilthey's analysis of time need not, then, be construed as metaphysical, that is, as dominated by presence. This may seem a strange claim because Dilthey clearly uses the language of "presence" and links the present to reality. But Dilthey's conservative language obscures a radical strain in his thought. That is, Dilthey's claim that the present is a "fulfilled reality" is an acknowledgment that the present is what it is by virtue of what is *not* present. At one level Dilthey certainly refers here to the future and past as presences that are expected and remembered rather than perceived. In this sense, he does make use of "presence" to understand the past and future. But, even so, these are not simple presences. Each dimension of time is what it is only by virtue of its relation to and difference from the others. Indeed, life is not a static, present thing. It is a differentiation, an integration, an appropriation that produces the metaphysical oppositions of subject-object, inner-outer, cause-effect, and so forth. Time is the way in which life makes itself present, a structure that emerges from life by which, as we shall see, life can make itself reflectively articulate. But there is always a surplus. Life is unfathomable, and its pre-reflective depths make reflection possible but can never be exhausted by it.

Dilthey, like Kant, links time to self-consciousness, but his conception of self-consciousness differs significantly from Kant's. Inner states can always be accompanied by reflexive awareness and thus have a sense of mineness. Although the awareness of the appropriation of these states may vary in degree, there remains the sense that they "belong to my consciousness. Specifically, I have a reflexive awareness of this ego as being the same throughout the changes in its states" (*SW*, 1:369; *GS*, 19:196). There is a reflexive awareness of the identity of the subject throughout the changing states because these inner states are connected through a sense of mineness. Dilthey does not, however, posit an unchanging 'I think', be it logical or substantive, to which this flow belongs.

Self-consciousness is not the product of an intellectual intuition or spontaneous representation of an unchanging 'I think' but is itself presented as a flow in the reflexive awareness of our inner states. "The ego is ordinarily not given to me separate from processes. The individual process contains only a reflexive awareness that it belongs to the same consciousness as other processes," Dilthey notes (*SW*, 1:370–371; *GS*, 19:197). An "I" is never presented as separate from the flow of consciousness. Every psychic state is accompanied by a sense of mineness, by virtue of which it is pre-reflectively connected to all others. This awareness of self, then, is an indeterminate, appropriative awareness entailed in the flow of inner states; thus it fluctuates in its determinations with the fluctuation of the determinations of our states. Indeed, this flow of states is none other than the flow of my life: "It is the life-course of a self" (*SW*, 1:371; *GS*, 19:198). All lived psychic states are given not merely as present but also as being under way from and toward something. The unity and coherence of these states with one another is itself something fluid, and the higher-level coherence of this temporal flow, which we could call the meaning of life, must be carved out by reflection.

Before proceeding to a more detailed discussion of life's reflective unity, it is important to forestall a misunderstanding that could arise from Dilthey's conservative terminology. His distinction of inner from outer perception leaves the impression that each contains its own manifold— psychological states and spatial objects, respectively. The contents of inner perception are characterized by their direct relation to and modification of the subject. Outer perception spatially relates facts of the external world to other facts of the external world. Or, in Dilthey's words, "The hallmark of inner perception consists in the reference of a fact to the self; that of outer perception in the reference to the world" (*SW*, 1:374; *GS*, 19:202). But, that inner perception is the flow of my life does not entail that things in outer perception are excluded from inner states. The circumstances of the external world can be subsequently related to the inner states of the self, not merely as hypothetical causes, but as part of the overall situation that makes up the states. "That which is given in the senses, i.e., that which is referred to the external world, can subsequently be apprehended as a modification of my self. It is then shifted from outer to inner perception" (*SW*, 1:375; *GS*, 19:202). Whenever conditions in the external world are related to the emotional and volitional life of the individual, they are objects of inner perception. In other words, inner perception does not order facts spatially; rather, facts of the external world are related in inner perception according to the purposes and values of the volitional and emotional components of psychic life. Things of the external world can be objects of inner perception insofar as they can be means or ends, represent failure and success, and so on. Awareness of our lives includes, then, an awareness both of psychological states and of the surrounding world that conditions these states (*GS*, 19:203).

Selfsameness and Accountability

As we have seen, the unity and coherence of life must themselves be construed as historically developed. Life contains no stable point that unifies its flow. Mere self-equality does not suffice to express the historical subject's identity, for it does not allow for development. Dilthey thus introduces the category of *Selbigkeit,* or selfsameness. In "Leben und Erkennen," Dilthey maintains that through selfsameness, "an experienceable unity, which can be expressed by no concept, holds together everything different and all changes in a living unity" (*GS,* 19:362). Rather than an abstract concept, selfsameness is a category that expresses a fact of lived experience. The unity of human existence cannot be logically derived from selfsameness. On the contrary, "it is expressed in the consciousness of responsibility for something past" (*GS,* 19:363). Selfsameness articulates that unity of the different moments of life which arises from the consciousness of responsibility for past deeds or consequences of deeds. Characterizing this unity of an individual life, Dilthey writes, "In this precisely he who now judges himself is another from he who acted yet knows himself as the same" (*GS,* 19:363). What I am now is different from what I was or have done, but these changes and acts belong to me in that I feel a sense of responsibility for them. Unfortunately, Dilthey says very little about this sense of responsibility; what he does say, however, is highly suggestive.

Selfsameness is "the expression for the way in which continuous life feels itself in a certain manner in . . . the succession of its changes [and] for which there is indeed no description and no formula except the appeal to self-consciousness" (*GS,* 19:363; cf. *GS,* 7:247). The unity of life is not at first given to the intellect as a theoretical fact. The awareness of the unity of life is more like a feeling that ultimately refers back to the fact of our own self-consciousness. Self-consciousness is composed in part by reflexive awareness. Recall that reflexive awareness always entails a sense of mineness. Responsibility also entails a sense of mineness, and it is difficult to believe that it is mere coincidence that Dilthey refers selfsameness, which contains an appropriative sense of responsibility, back to self-consciousness, which contains an appropriative, reflexive awareness. Indeed, Dilthey's method is characterized by bringing an initially indeterminate awareness to a sharper focus. Thus it is not unwarranted to suggest that the sense of responsibility at the core of selfsameness is arrived at by bringing the originally primitive sense of mineness entailed in reflexive awareness to a more determinate level.

Reflexive awareness initially presents acts and contents as correlates. Both are given as facts of my consciousness. The ways in which they are mine have not been distinguished, and the way in which the contents of consciousness are not me has not been determined. But this sense of mineness is only adequate for an indeterminate unity of consciousness, not the coherent, determinate unity of the course of an individual's life. As we saw in Chapter 2, self-consciousness arises in the pre-reflective awareness of resistance in which self and world are differentiated as correlates. Selfsameness describes the higher-level reflective activity of articulating this self's sense of identity. Responsibility is the appropriation of my deeds as my life. It is a more determinate, reflective articulation of the initial sense of mineness found in reflexive awareness. Selfsameness refers to a reflective unity of representations.

Responsibility presupposes the experience of our own volitional spontaneity and intentionality. That is, the resistance that serves to bring about the emergence of self-consciousness involves the opposition of the spontaneity of our will to move and the world's hindrance of this. In this way, then, we are able to see our acts as products of our own authorship. This is not to say that the meaning of our actions is reducible to our intentions, only that these actions continue to relate to us as something we have made. Further, responsibility refers to our involvement in a community, that is, we are responsible to others. Dilthey insisted that individuals must be understood in relation to and in divergence from concrete sociohistorical circumstances. As we shall see in detail in the next chapter, individuals are always involved in a number of groups and institutions and thus are always accountable to others for their actions. Others construct stories about our behavior, and we are called to "account" for ourselves by offering our own story. Being a part of a community means in part being called on by others to provide a coherent account or narrative of ourselves. Alasdair MacIntyre has made the point more clearly than Dilthey: "To be the subject of a narrative that runs from one's birth to one's death is . . . to be accountable for the actions and experiences which compose a narrative life. It is . . . to be open to being asked to give a certain kind of account of what one did or what happened to one."[18]

Finally, the sense of responsibility also contains a certain sense of my own deeds no longer being me. I continue to possess past deeds but as *transcended.* In the judgment of my past deeds I preserve them, bearing them with me into the present and future, but in the manner of reflec-

18. Alasdair MacIntyre, *After Virtue* (Notre Dame: University of Notre Dame Press, 1981), p. 202.

tively standing outside them. The identity of the individual's life is described as an ongoing process of negating yet preserving the past by reflectively transcending it. In "Descriptive Psychology," Dilthey further discusses principles of the development of psychic life which account for the way in which life forms itself into a coherent temporal whole.

Purposiveness and the Temporal Coherence of Life

In "Descriptive Psychology," Dilthey emphasizes the categories of value and purpose to describe the development of psychic life, but he does not explicitly link these categories to temporality, as he will do in his twentieth-century writings. What he achieves in this work that both the discussion of our experience of time and the analysis of *Selbigkeit* leave largely unarticulated is a framework for construing life as a temporally developed and constantly developing structural whole. Thus, Dilthey characterizes development as "the unity, constancy and determinacy of goal" ("Descriptive Psychology," 95; *GS,* 5:214).

Dilthey describes the temporal coherence of psychic life by making use of an organic conception rather than a metaphysical conception of development, beginning with the claim that psychic life exhibits an immanent-subjective purposiveness. Psychic life is purposive insofar as its interaction with the environment is always governed by "the desire to produce or maintain a state of fulfillment of our drives and of happiness" ("Descriptive Psychology," 95; *GS,* 5:215). But Dilthey takes care to distinguish the subjective immanent purposiveness of psychic life from the biological objective hypothesis of purposiveness. The latter is based on observing purposive activity in outer perception (hence as objective). These activities are then explained by referring to instincts not accessible to the senses for the preservation of the self and the species. That is, the biological, objective hypothesis of purposiveness "issues from the relation between emotional-instinctual life and the preservation of the individual and the species" ("Descriptive Psychology," 88; *GS,* 5:207). A hypothetical connection between something inaccessible to outer perception (i.e., instincts) and the facts given in outer perception (e.g., aggressive or defensive responses to stimuli) must be presumed to construct a coherent whole from the givens of outer perception.

In contrast, the subjective-immanent purposiveness of psychic life is given as a fact in inner perception. As Dilthey states, "It is subjective because it is given to us in inner experience as a lived experience. It is immanent because it is grounded on no other conceived goal, which would be external to it" ("Descriptive Psychology," 96; *GS*, 5:215). Purposiveness, here, describes the relation, as given in inner experience, between the driving agency of feelings and instincts and the intellectual and volitional life of the individuals within their milieu. It does not refer to our telic attraction to a goal beyond ourselves or to the actualization of a preestablished form. Rather, purposiveness refers to the manner in which the interrelation of the psychic components—instinct, feeling, representation, and volition—promote an increasing articulation of the relation of individuals to their environment for the sake of enhancing or sustaining the value of life.

The value of life, although intimately involved with feelings, is not reducible to them. Indeed, Dilthey explicitly rejects the utilitarian tendency to reduce all values to the feelings of pleasure and pain. In the "Poetics," Dilthey differentiates six spheres of feeling and relegates pleasure and pain to a sphere that reports physiological processes but has no representational content and no relevance to aesthetic value (*SW*, 5:79; *GS*, 6:150). What we feel as the value of life is "the fullness of life which we experience, the richness of living reality which we dimly realize, the vitality of what is in us, which seems to us to be the value of our existence" ("Descriptive Psychology," 97; *GS*, 5:216). This suggests that Dilthey has in mind the fifth sphere of feeling, which he associates with an appreciation of the meaning-content of an artwork. These feelings result "from the particular *material impulses* which pervade the whole of life and whose entire content is possessed in a reflexive awareness obtained through feelings" (*SW*, 5:83; *GS*, 6:154). The hindrance or furtherance of our impulses (such as drives for nourishment, self-preservation, procreation, and love of offspring) by the milieu gives rise to these feelings. Those of pride, shame, honor, envy, and vanity are all involved with the obstruction and furtherance of our basic impulses. Purposiveness, then, may be now more fully understood as the preservation, development, and increase of the values of life. Moreover, the purposiveness of the psychic nexus gives rise to an "increasing articulation of psychic life" ("Descriptive Psychology," 97; *GS*, 5:217). To further adapt to and gain control over the conditions of life, feelings and instincts utilize impressions. A general representation of the workings of the world is formed on the basis of the interest in transforming this world or ourselves for the sake of fulfilling our volitional-instinctual lives: "Typical images are formed which represent the external conditions in a useful manner; thoughts concerning the relations of similarity and causality of the external world are developed" ("Descriptive Psychology," 97; *GS*, 5:217).

As we have seen in the analysis of time-consciousness, past experiences do not simply recede from the present. Here, Dilthey attempts to provide a psychological underpinning for the reflective coherence of the past and its connection to the present. Our continual adaptation to the environment involves the formation of a semiconscious psychic nexus composed of representations of regularities in the surrounding world and their internal relations to our values and purposes. This acquired psychic nexus (*erworbener seelischer Zusammenhang*) functions as a context within which the present is situated. It exercises "sovereignty over the particular conscious processes" ("Descriptive Psychology," 98; *GS*, 5:217) by allowing events in the environment to be seen as parts of a larger natural process or expression of a natural law, by placing our reaction to our circumstances into a larger system of values, and by situating momentary desires into the framework of long-range goals. Dilthey stresses that the acquired psychic nexus is a structural, interrelated whole composed of internally related volitional, emotional, and representational acts and contents. All the contents of the acquired psychic nexus are parts of a holistic structure and derive their significance from their place in this whole.

The acquired psychic nexus structurally represents the personal history of an individual. Makkreel points out the unifying function of the acquired nexus, stating that "the term 'acquired' indicates that the nexus . . . is not abstract and inferred, but concretely 'possessed' through the individual's life history. The nexus is thus a system which is historically acquired and reveals the structural ordering of past experience."[19] This psychic nexus is the product of the individual's evaluative, purposive interaction with the environment and is continually brought to bear on the evaluation of the present and future for the sake of praxis. All the moments and periods of development are bound into a whole by virtue of the fact that all the processes of psychic life work together for the establishment of a stable psychic nexus ("Descriptive Psychology," 100; *GS*, 5:220). That is to say, the life history of an individual's development is structurally retained in a nexus that in turn plays a controlling role in the evaluation and cognition of further experience and development. Ac-

19. Makkreel, *Dilthey, Philosopher of the Human Studies*, p. 98.

cordingly, the individual's life acquires a kind of structural unity over time. The past, then, is not merely a bygone flux but a developed structure as well. Because this acquired nexus both controls experience and is itself continually shaped by it, our past continues to develop with new experience and only rigidifies with old age.

Dilthey's use of the acquired psychic nexus to account for the developmental coherence of the individual's life may appear to commit him to the position, criticized by MacIntyre,[20] that the temporal coherence of life can be derived from psychological principles alone. But even in his psychological descriptions of individual psychic structure, Dilthey stresses that psychic structure is formed in the interaction of agents with their world. Because individuals are situated in a sociohistorical context and the acquired psychic nexus is formed through interaction with the milieu, the acquired nexus at least indirectly reflects the influence of such a context. MacIntyre's point, however, is that our own narratives require reference to specific social contexts, and the abstract claim that the acquired psychic nexus is a product of social influences is clearly not sufficient for linking events in our lives to specific social settings.

Death, Closure, and Narrative Coherence

Dilthey was keenly aware that life as it is lived remains incomplete. Although he does not thematize life as always ahead of itself in the way Heidegger characterized *Dasein*, Dilthey's analysis of temporality nevertheless makes the unrealized possibilities of the future an essential dimension of life. Accordingly, Dilthey stresses that life can be viewed as a whole only after death, such that birth and death naturally provide the beginning and ending necessary to view life as a narrative. But as Heidegger has demonstrated, using the death of others as the termination of their lives may provide us with a biological end point adequate for compiling an exhaustive chronology, but it provides no clue about how we may view our own lives as a coherent story whose meaning is derived from an end (*BT*, 281–285; *SZ*, 237–241). Death must be taken as my own, as the meaning-bestowing closure of my own life, in order to understand how I may construe my *own life* as a narrative whole while this life is under way. In fact, if the goal is to understand others' lives as lived, the

20. MacIntyre, *After Virtue*, p. 192.

mere biological termination of their existence is insufficient for understanding even the course of their lives. We must understand death as it
approaches us from within life itself.

For Heidegger, death is to be understood as an essential structure of
Dasein, keeping firmly in mind that *Dasein* is a being that is essentially a
"not-yet." Death is, in other words, a possibility. But, unlike other possibilities, death is not something that can be actualized. It is the possibility
that all the movement toward possibility, that is, *Dasein,* will be brought
to an end. Although he did not make death an explicit theme of his
analysis, Dilthey, too, recognizes the centrality of death to the experience
of life, which he says contains "the intuitions of the power of chance, of
the corruptibility of everything we possess, love or hate and fear, and of
the constant presence of death which omnipotently determines the significance and meaning of life for all of us" (*GS,* 8:79; cf. 140). Dilthey and
Heidegger each claim that the realization of the finitude of existence is
involved in moving beyond shallow existence and toward reflection on
the temporal coherence of our lives. For example, Dilthey asserts that the
depth of the religious genius derives from the confrontation with the finitude of life, "not a dream of something transcendent" (*GS,* 7:266). The religious genius does not succumb to "the forgetfulness of death" and "the
everyday forgetfulness of past and future" (*GS,* 7:266).

Heidegger argues that an analysis of authentic existence presupposes
an analysis of death: "The existential Interpretation of death takes prece-
dence over any . . . ontology of life" (*BT,* 291; *SZ,* 247). Death performs
the function of closure even as life itself is under way, and this closure
serves to turn reflection back on life as a provisional narrative whole.
Dilthey's characterization of death as life's corruptibility seems to have
led Heidegger to believe that he still viewed death as an event at the end
of life rather than an ongoing process. But life's corruptibility is not syn-
onymous with the final event of life's corruption. Rather, Dilthey seems
to have in mind here an ongoing awareness of our finitude which provides an indeterminate sense of closure. This indeterminate sense of closure allows, indeed compels us, to reconstruct our lives as narratives in
progress.

Kermode's example of a ticking clock illustrates well the way in which
an ending transforms the temporal flow into narrative or fictive time. The
"tick" and the "tock" are sounds provided by us to mark the temporal
interval with a beginning and an end. The duration between tick and
tock, understood as a meaningful interval, is a function of this beginning

and end: "The fact that we call the second of the two related sounds *tock* is evidence that we use fictions to enable the end to confer organization and form on the temporal structure."[21] Time is humanized by the imposition of this fictional form on it. Thus, we can repeat the ticktock accurately. But the interval between tock and tick cannot be reliably reproduced, presumably because it provides only succession. Novel-length fictions, to say nothing of our lives, are obviously more complex and extended than the simple ticktock. Even given this sense of closure, maintaining the temporal thread that holds the narrative together requires reflective strategies. Dilthey's account does not emphasize the experience of life coming apart at the seams, as it were. In crisis our lives can lose their coherence. Our worlds can be denuded of value; our purposes can prove hollow or illusory. Life can threaten to become a senseless succession of events rather than a coherent narrative. But Dilthey is aware that the coherence of life as a whole is a reflective achievement, and his analysis of the pre-reflective experience of time serves as a basis on which to view the reflective strategies used to shape and to maintain a coherent narrative of life as articulations of structures embedded in life itself.

Inherent in the dynamic structure of life is a twofold process of expansion and unification. Life unfolds in a multiplicity of lived experiences. Were this life's only tendency, it would be nothing more than a flow. But life is also characterized by the tendency to unify this multiplicity. Dilthey characterizes this dual impulse as implication-explication in his revision of the *Poetics* (1907–8): "Lived experiences are related to each other like motifs in the andante of a symphony: they are unfolded (explication) and what has been unfolded is recapitulated or taken together (implication)" (*SW*, 5:227; *GS*, 6:316).

Lived experiences are structural units composed of evaluative, representational, and volitional acts and their objects, and this structure differentiates and relates lived experiences. To illustrate his point, Dilthey says: "The death of a loved one involves a special structural relation to grief. This structural relation of grief to a perception or representation, referring to an object about which I feel grief, is a lived experience" (*SW*, 5:224; *GS*, 6:314). An object or event—the death of a friend—forms a focal point of feelings and representations that constitute a structural, ongoing whole. Grief and sorrow are mixed with memories of times together

21. Frank Kermode, *The Sense of an Ending* (New York: Oxford University Press, 1967), p. 45.

or images of the deceased to make up this particular lived experience. Characterizing the way in which it is distinguished from others, Dilthey writes, "This lived experience is delimited from other lived experiences by the fact that as a structural nexus of grief, of perceiving or representing what the grief is about, and of an object to which the perception refers, it constitutes a separable immanent teleological whole" (*SW*, 5:224; *GS*, 6:314). This structural connection is qualitatively differentiated from others by a shift in object, the kinds of feelings evoked, and their relation to the representational component. For instance, the grief over someone's death could evoke a sentimental coloring of one's memories of that person and times past. But if one had heard instead that this person had been convicted of molesting children, feelings of righteous indignation and shock might well combine with a suspicious reinterpretation of this person's past behavior.

Correlatively, structurally related lived experiences in the past are internally related to the present and affect lived experience in the present.[22] For example, we may visit a museum and be particularly struck by Dürer's *The Four Apostles*. Subsequent viewings of the work resume previous viewings: "The lived experience of the latest visit contains the fullness of the earlier visits. Past lived experiences have come together in a more powerful unity" (*SW*, 5:227; *GS*, 6:316). Present perceptions and feelings can serve as focal points that bring past lived experiences to a new unity. But the past experiences are not leveled down by being seen as the "same" experience. The differences of past and present experiences are maintained such that they may be viewed as variations on a theme. Thus, the qualitative distinction of lived experiences serves not only to divide the continuous flow into separate events but also to allow life to be seen as a unity of recurring themes. Although this kind of pre-reflective coherence is certainly not equivalent to the reflective narrative of biography and autobiography, it does provide a basis for viewing individual events as developments of continuing concerns.

Reflection, Temporality, and the Meaning of Life

For Dilthey, autobiography and biography are the literary articulation of the self-reflective tendency of life itself (*GS*, 7:200). This is not to say

---

22. Rudolf Makkreel also discusses the temporal structure of lived experience in "The Overcoming of Linear Time in Kant, Dilthey, and Heidegger," in *Dilthey and Phenomenology*, ed. Makkreel and Scanlon, pp. 153–156.

that we always seek a single golden thread, whether this be a value, purpose, or meaning, binding the many experiences of our lives. We do, however, construe our lives as recurring—sometimes consonant, sometimes dissonant—themes. Our life stories are neither absolute chronologies nor totalizations of all lived experiences. As any storyteller, we emphasize, de-emphasize, and omit events. The autobiographer "selects [*herausheben*] and accentuates the moments in his memory that he experienced as significant and allows the others to sink into forgetfulness" (*GS*, 7:200). The understanding of human life, both individual and communal, requires the capacity to view individual moments as part of a coherent temporal whole. In the *Aufbau*, Dilthey must clearly discusses the reflective strategies for producing this coherence in his application of temporality to the categories of meaning, value, and purpose, which are to be used to understand the connection of individual events to the temporal whole of life (*GS*, 7:201).[23]

We have seen that time is qualitatively differentiated into past, present, and future. Meaning, value, and purpose correspond to these "parts" of time. The category of meaning is an expression of the connection of individual moments of the past into a mnemonic whole: "By looking back in memory we grasp the connection of the passed parts of the course of life under the category of their meaning" (*GS*, 7:201). That is to say, the past is given as a remembered whole that forms a context for individual events. Though his reasons for doing so remain unclear, Dilthey maintains that the present is an evaluative moment and thus is expressed by the category of value: "When we live in the present, which is filled with reality, we experience its positive or negative value in feeling" (*GS*, 7:201), adding that "as we stretch ourselves out toward the future, the category of purpose emerges from this conduct" (*GS*, 7:201).

Each of these categories functions as a reflective device for drawing together the multiplicity of our lived experiences from a different perspective, and none may be reduced to the others (*GS*, 7:201). Nevertheless, meaning emerges as the category without which a diachronic whole is inconceivable. Neither purpose nor value suffices to express the internal unity of the individual moments of life. The category of value construes life as little more than a chain of evaluative moments: "Thus, from

23. The *Aufbau* represents a more mature formulation of the categories of life than that found in the earlier writings (1883–94) used to define the problem. Though value, purpose, and meaning are all found in "Leben und Erkennen," their connection with temporality is not fully explored there.

the perspective of value, life appears as an infinite plenum of positive and negative values of existence" (*GS*, 7:202). A serial aggregate of positive or negative now-points is possible, but no overall unity is presented. In Dilthey's words, "Each of these is a tonal structure that fills the present; but they have no musical relation to each other" (*GS*, 7:202). That is to say, each individual moment may be evaluated for its fullness of life. Moment after moment may be thus evaluatively lined up, one after the other. What is lacking, however, is the means to determine the relation between these moments beyond their mere succession or value relative to one another.

Because a goal is something *worth* achieving, "the category of purpose or good which understands life from the standpoint of the orientation toward the future presupposes that of value" (*GS*, 7:202). Dilthey's use of purpose does not usher in a teleological metaphysics, whether of nature or of history. Thus, the flow of life cannot be unified by the actualization of an immanent form or a single historical end. Life viewed under the category of purpose presents only a manifold of possibilities and the subordination of means to ends for the sake of these possibilities; no single, overarching purpose teleologically unifies the manifold. "The relations of purposes to each other are only those of possibility, choice, and subordination" (*GS*, 7:202). Value, then, appears to be immediately given, whereas purpose must first be placed in a volitional means-ends relation by an active projection on our part.

It is only upon reflection that life can be presented as a temporal whole; thus only with the category of meaning, which Dilthey links to the past, are all the moments of time—past, present, and future—given as a whole. Pre-reflectively, past, present, and future cooperate to produce an open-ended flow within any given moment, but no explicit connection to experiences beyond this living present is made. In reflection, the present is articulated as a dynamic intersection of the extended past and future. Individual events are viewed in relation to the whole of life under the category of meaning: "Meaning signifies the relation of the parts of life to the whole which is grounded in the essence of life" (*GS*, 7:233). Only in the past are the individual moments of life given in the context of a complete, though not completed, whole. Dilthey writes, "We have this connection only through memory, in which we can survey the past course of life" (*GS*, 7:233). Because the present incessantly becomes the past, this whole is constantly changing. But the past is presented in memory as a whole whose parts themselves may change in meaning as their relations to the developing whole change.

Although meaning is derived by virtue of the part-whole relation of the remembered past, it is not determined through an assessment of the part-whole relationships of the past in isolation from the other modes of time. A past event has "meaning through its connection to the whole, through the relation of past and future" (*GS*, 7:233). The meaning of the past is assessed with reference to its applicability to future activity. Dilthey insists that the past "is meaningful insofar as a commitment for the future takes place in it through a deed or an external event" (*GS*, 7:233). The meaning of the past is the ground from which purposes and plans grow, but at the same time, the way in which we construe the meaning of the past reflects the goals and plans we have: "Every life plan is the expression of an understanding of the meaning of life. Whatever we assign to the future as a goal conditions the determinations of the meaning of that which is past. The shaping of life which is realized acquires a standard through the assessment of the meaning of that which is remembered" (*GS*, 7:233). We reflectively shape our lives into coherent but developing stories. These stories shape and are shaped by ongoing concerns. There cannot be a single correct narrative, because the changing circumstances of life lead us to emphasize and de-emphasize different elements of our lives—in other words, to rewrite our lives. Nevertheless, the narrative structure that bestows coherence on life is an articulation of the temporal structures of life itself.

Dilthey always sought to understand individuals as a reflection of a concrete place and time without reducing them to a mere reflex of their sociohistorical context. The biographer "must find the standpoint from which the general historical horizon is extended [*sich ausbreitet*] and the individual resides [*bleibt*] in the middle point for a system of influences and meaning" (*GS*, 7:250). There are many reasons that compel us to trace the development of individuals within their circumstances. For example, psychologists seek the roots of abnormal behavior; criminologists try to uncover sources of criminal behavior; and families keep their own lineage alive in stories and reminiscences (*GS* 7:249). But only great historical figures such as poets or world and religious leaders articulate the interplay of the social forces of their times in a way that can typify the times themselves, "for only in [historical personalities] lies the force to form such a middle point" (*GS*, 7:250). This suggests that the temporality of individuals is integrally related to the historicity of larger social contexts. The structure and temporality of such systems will be discussed in the next chapter. But the question of the role of these social contexts in the formation of the narratives of our lives is important here. That is, it is important to determine the extent to which we shape these narratives of ourselves.

Dilthey's answer to this question is not explicit. But Heidegger addresses the problem with his conceptions of authentic existence and *das Man*. And because, as I have shown in the preceding chapters, he shares with Dilthey the view that human existence is always already situated in the world, Heidegger's analysis provides an instructive clue for developing Dilthey's position. According to Heidegger, our average everyday existence is largely given over to *das Man*. We passively receive our possibilities from others by fitting into prearranged social positions and understanding our lives with common, shopworn formulas. Authentic existence involves the individuation of our possibilities as our own, and this can occur only by confronting death as one's ownmost possibility. That is, the "who" of *Dasein* is not first an individuated transcendental ego or a self-identical "I" substance. In its everyday dealings, *Dasein* is at first an undifferentiated part of *das Man*, or the they: "Proximally *Dasein* is 'they', and for the most part it remains so" (*BT*, 167; *SZ*, 129). *Dasein* does not begin by taking responsibility for its own thrownness and standing out toward its own possibilities with resolve. Quite to the contrary, in day-to-day intercourse, *Dasein* plays the roles and conforms to the standards set up not by any particular individual but by all as anonymous parts of the they. "Dasein has been *dispersed* into the 'they'" (*BT*, 167; *SZ*, 129). *Dasein* lives the possibilities handed it externally by virtue of social position, job, and so on. In contrast, MacIntyre specifically rejects what he sees as Heidegger's claim that we are capable of self-authorship and links it to an extreme, untenable individualism exemplified by the Sartre of *Being and Nothingness*. Human intentions, argues MacIntyre, are unintelligible apart form the settings of an agent, and these settings are stories of which I am inevitably a part but which are not written by me. Accordingly, I may assume preestablished roles in ongoing stories, but I may not create a role out of nothing.[24]

But Heidegger's conception of authenticity is not radically individualistic. On the contrary, authenticity most broadly considered reintegrates

24. MacIntyre, *After Virtue*, pp. 192, 199. David Carr attempts to find a middle ground between MacIntyre's view and the view he criticizes, namely, that we are the authors of our lives. Carr construes our role in the formation of our life's narratives as that of a narrator. On this view, we may avoid the question of whether we create the narrative of our lives and settle for the more limited claim that we relate a story with which we are more familiar than are others. See *Time, Narrative, and History*, p. 85.

Dasein into the community. Just as the possibility of time is grounded in the temporality of *Dasein*, the possibility of history is based upon the historicity of *Dasein*. The description of how care is routed in temporality demonstrated that *Dasein* is not "in" time, but temporal*izes*. In an analogous fashion, *Dasein* is not "in" history, but histor*izes*. History is derived from historizing, which Heidegger characterizes as "the specific movement in which *Dasein is stretched along and stretches itself along* [between birth and death]" (*BT*, 427; *SZ*, 375). *Dasein*'s historizing, or historicity, is ultimately rooted in the temporal structures of care. The claim that *Dasein* is not in history is not a denial of *Dasein*'s historical character. It is, rather, a qualification of the manner of this historicity. *Dasein* is not to be conceived of as a "plaything of circumstances and events" whose choices are determined by sociohistorical forces (*BT*, 433; *SZ*, 382). Because the Being of *Dasein* is care and care is grounded in temporality, the historical character of *Dasein* must be found in this temporality. *Dasein* makes history in the projection of its possibilities from its situation and illuminates its past by reflecting on how these possibilities resided in the situation. But *Dasein*'s situation is not private, because *Dasein* is characterized by Being-in-the-world, thus by Being-with Others. Communities share a situation and possibilities, thus *Dasein*'s "historizing is a co-historizing" (*BT*, 436; *SZ*, 384).

Dasein is already in a world with others. Even though *Dasein*'s differentiation from the they occurs only with a grasping of the situation as its own and a self-conscious choice between the possibilities inherent in this situation, this differentiation from the they is not a detachment. A resolute acceptance of one's thrownness as one's own, as limiting one's own possibilities, does not exclude a reference to Others. "As thrown, *Dasein* has indeed been delivered over to itself. . . . It has been submitted to a 'world', and exists factically with Others" (*BT*, 435; *SZ*, 383). Reflection on one's thrownness reveals that it includes the history of one's family, state, community, and tradition. One's situation includes Being-with Others who are practically engaged in their world and the world already made by the practical engagement of Others in the past. When *Dasein* accepts this thrownness as "a *handing down* to oneself of the possibilities that have come down to one," *Dasein* has a *heritage* (*BT*, 435; *SZ*, 383). Reflection on one's own mortality, the limitations of this heritage on one's possibilities, and the meaning of one's choices for the realization or rejection of these possibilities reveals *Dasein*'s fate (*BT*, 435; *SZ*, 384).

With the concepts of heritage and fate, Heidegger reinterprets the temporality of *Dasein* as historicity.[25] Our thrownness becomes our heritage when the past is understood as at once *Dasein*'s own situation and a shared history. The meaning of history is illuminated by the way in which it limits *Dasein*'s fate. *Dasein*'s historizing, that is, its standing out toward its fate from its heritage, is the condition for the possibility of historiography, because it is only with reference to *Dasein*'s possibilities that a heritage has a meaning. Heritage limits not only the possibility of each *Dasein* but also the possibilities of a group as a whole. Thus, just as one must take up one's own thrownness but still may be said to be sharing a heritage, so too one can reach out to one's fate as one's own while also reaching out as one among many to a people's destiny (*BT*, 436; *SZ*, 384).

So, Heidegger's strategy for reconciling our claim to the authorship of our own narratives with the claim that we are parts of more-encompassing, ongoing stories is to provide a reinterpretation of the thrown-projecting movement of *Dasein* through use of the social categories of heritage and destiny. He does this by providing for our common experience of the world in his analyses of worldhood and Being-with. Dilthey, too, provides the ground for common experience, but he departs from Heidegger by turning to an analysis of enduring social systems for this purpose. Dilthey comes increasingly to emphasize that the meaningfulness of lived experience itself is a function of our situatedness within concrete sociohistorical systems.

In this chapter I showed how Dilthey lays the ground for narrative accounts of our lives by articulating the temporal structure of the life-nexus itself. In the posthumously published second volume of the *Introduction*, Dilthey's descriptions of the fundamentally temporal structure of lived experience portray the present as the dynamic intersection of past and future. This allows us to view the moments of life as unfolding from and toward other moments in a larger temporal framework. His later writings show that death provides the sense of closure necessary to shape life's temporal advance into a narrative progression, and they link the categories of life to the category of temporality to provide devices for

25. David Couzens Hoy offers an excellent discussion of Heidegger's conception of historicity in "History, Historicity, and Historiography in *Being and Time*," in *Heidegger and Modern Philosophy*, ed. Michael Murray (New Haven: Yale University Press, 1978), pp. 329–353.

reflectively carving a life narrative out of the myriad events and experiences of our lives. Even though this chapter is devoted primarily to the narrative coherence of individual lives, it is important to keep in mind that this represents a partial analysis of a larger I-world whole, namely, the life-nexus. That is, we have concentrated for the most part on the "I" and must discuss the "world" component to complete the analysis. Consequently, I now turn explicitly to the role played by sociohistorical contexts in the constitution of life's meaning.

Chapter Four

Sociohistorical Systems and the Formation of Life's Meaning

Even though the problem of the formation of the meaning of our lives has been approached thus far only from the perspective of the lived course of an individual's life, it would be a mistake to assume that the stories of our lives are shaped without reference to larger social and historical contexts. This is utterly contrary to Dilthey's view. Narrative categories were certainly derived from the dynamic structure of *Erlebnis,* and these could be applied to the study of the development of an individual for the purposes of writing biography. But biography serves as a cornerstone of Diltheyan historical scholarship, not as a psychological tool alone. For Dilthey, historiography integrates the various disciplines of the human sciences, including those devoted to the study of sociohistorical systems, in the process of understanding individual humans. Sociohistorical systems serve as the contexts or settings within which and by virtue of which any individual's narrative can occur. The task here, then, is to discuss how Dilthey frames such systems into contexts that shape the meaning of our lives.

As is the case with much of Dilthey's thought, his view of sociohistorical systems underwent important developments. Dilthey initially viewed sociohistorical systems as based on enduring psychic structures. In his later writings, however, he came to think of these systems as themselves fundamental conditions for the constitution of meaning rather than as reflections of psychological structures. Life's meaning thus comes to be a function of context, and sociohistorical systems, as meaning-constituting contexts, assume the hermeneutic function of limiting the range of likely interpretations.

The Study of Social Groups in the Introduction

In the *Introduction,* Dilthey maintains that the structure of social groups is closely connected to the psychological structure of individuals. Accordingly, the analysis of social structures requires an analysis of psychic structure. Although Dilthey speaks of individuals as the elements of history and society, he distinguishes his sense of element from the natural scientific conception of atoms. Atoms are hypothetical constructs arrived at through a process of analyzing external reality, by "decomposing things," and then used to explain the mechanics of this reality (*SW*, 1:80; *GS*, 1:29). In contrast, "in the human sciences, the subjects are real units, given as facts in inner experience" (*SW*, 1:80; *GS*, 1:29). That is to say, the human sciences begin with the psychophysical individual as given in lived experience.

Psychology—or anthropology, as Dilthey often called it—is the study of individuals. But although the only psychic facts for experience are those of the individual, it is *not* the case that the facts of the human sciences are all found in psychology. Dilthey insists that "psychology by no means contains all those facts that comprise the subject matter of the human sciences" (*SW*, 1:81; *GS*, 1:29). Psychologists study the psychic structure of the individual without reference to a particular sociohistorical situation. The individual, however, is always given as enmeshed in a social context. The ahistorical, pre-social, atomistic individuals posited by social contract theorists such as Hobbes and Locke are "a fiction of genetic explanation" (*SW*, 1:83; *GS*, 1:31).

Psychology, then, does not exhaust the study of the individual, for the full study of individuals places them within their concrete sociohistorical context. The subject matter of the human sciences "is the individual as a component of society" (*SW*, 1:83; *GS*, 1:32). Dilthey maintains that the task of psychology is to provide a neutral description of the characteristics of psychic life apart from any *particular* sociohistorical setting (*SW*, 1:82; *GS*, 1:30). It is important to emphasize, however, that although psychology separates the individual from any particular sociohistorical context, it nonetheless studies the individual as sociohistorical. Individuals are never construed as self-enclosed atoms; indeed, life is a reciprocal interplay between individuals and their world. Psychology explicates the ways in which psychic life as such is always related to sociohistorical settings, but its task is not to explore the specifics of any social, historical setting. In so doing, psychology demonstrates the internal relation between the agent and the setting crucial to the production of a narrative.

Descriptive psychology provides, then, a nonhypothetical foundation for the other human sciences. It "is the first and most fundamental of the particular human sciences. Accordingly, its truths constitute the base of the further formation of the human sciences" (*SW*, 1:84; *GS*, 1:33). But this means neither that social and historical phenomena are ultimately explained by psychological laws nor that the rest of the human sciences are derived analytically from psychology, forming a deductive system. Psychology provides only broad structures and developmental principles of psychic life referred to in other human sciences. But these structures and principles must be shown to be inherently related to concrete sociohistorical situations and thus must be filled in by the rest of the human sciences. Psychology's "truths reflect only a part of this reality, and therefore presuppose a reference to this larger reality" (*SW*, 1:84; *GS*, 1:33). In other words, psychology is the most elementary human science in that all other human sciences make use of concepts arrived at in the psychological description of individuals. Study of the individual cannot be completed through psychology alone, however. The individual is always involved in economic, cultural, social, and political systems, and understanding the way in which the individual is shaped and shapes this sociohistorical nexus is necessary to particularize the general structures and principles provided by psychology.

Dilthey refers to the neutral descriptions of psychology as first-order theories or concepts. As we have seen, these concepts apply to the individual and must be referred to in any sociohistorical study. Studies of social systems, however, are not limited to first-order concepts but must make use of what Dilthey calls second-order psychological concepts. These concepts apply to "phenomena, which are produced by the interactions of individuals" (*SW*, 1:163; *GS*, 1:114) and "presuppose the truths of anthropology" (*SW*, 1:92; *GS*, 1:41). But to say that second-order concepts presuppose first-order concepts is not to maintain that the former are logically derived from the latter. Rather, the use of second-order concepts makes sense only with reference to those of the first order. Second-order concepts "are in no way fully reducible to anthropological facts" (*SW*, 1:163; *GS*, 1:114). Political economy, for instance, requires the use of concepts such as need, work, authority, and satisfaction (*SW*, 1:163; *GS*, 1:114). These are concepts that apply to relations between individuals. Although they have reference to volitions, emotions, and intellectual operations found in individual psychic structure, they cannot be deduced from these.

In the *Introduction*, Dilthey recognizes three different kinds of sociohistorical systems, each of which has a different kind of structure and a different principle of unity: (1) the external organization of society, for example, the political system of a nation; (2) cultural systems such as religion, art, science, law, economy, customs, morals, language, and education; and (3) large ethnic groups or peoples. The study of these systems constitutes different yet interdependent groups of disciplines. Dilthey argues that the external organization of society, cultural systems, and different peoples are components of the same sociohistorical whole, so an understanding of history requires the cooperation of these disciplines: "As all three of these objects are only parts of real human life, none of them can be understood historically or treated theoretically without reference to the scientific studies of the others" (*SW*, 1:93; *GS*, 1:42).

Peoples are distinguished—and presumably united—on the basis of genealogy and geography. Ethnologists begin by studying "how the human race, on the basis of family ties and kinship, is naturally grouped into concentric spheres measured by degree of kinship, i.e., how in each narrower sphere, along with closer ties, new common characteristics appear" (*SW*, 1:91–92; *GS*, 1:40–41). Families and broader groups bound by kinship, such as clans, are the historical origins of peoples, and shared habitats and traits are components in the delineation of a people. Ethnology turns from the study of shared genealogy and habitat to the distinction of individual races, using geography as a device for differentiating sociohistorical traditions (*SW*, 1:92; *GS*, 1:41). Finally, ethnology studies the peoples that arise from the mixture of shared genealogical origin and historical deeds. A common origin and development form peoples into "living and relatively independent centers of culture within the social context of a time and . . . [into] bearers of historical movement" (*SW*, 1:92; *GS*, 1:41).

In contrast to either the people or the external organization of society, Dilthey refers to the cultural system as a purposive system (*Zweckzusammenhang*).[1] Cultural systems are matrices of human actions related by virtue of their devotion to a common purpose (*SW*, 1:94; *GS*, 1:43). Although such systems do not exist independently of the individuals engaged in actualizing the common goal, they are also enduring institutions that transcend the life of any single individual. Every purposive system is a nexus of the reciprocal acts of many individuals, but these activities are bound by a goal arising from a trait characteristic of all

1. For extensive discussion of purposive systems, see Helmut Johach, *Handelnder Mensch und objektiver Geist*, Studien zur Wissenschaftstheorie, vol. 8 (Meisenheim am Glan: Verlag Anton Hain, 1974), p. 84; Hodges, *Philosophy of Wilhelm Dilthey*, p. 177.

humans. The purposive system "rests primarily on the reciprocal interaction of individuals in society insofar as their interaction is based on a shared aspect of human nature and results in an integration of activities in which that aspect of human nature attains its satisfaction" (*SW*, 1:100; *GS*, 1:49). Purposive human action involves individuals in the reciprocal causal interplay of the sociohistorical world synchronically and diachronically. Many of the needs of life that give rise to action cannot be satisfied by a single individual and so each of us cooperates with our contemporaries and builds on the work done by our forebears in order to satisfy our needs. Thus, the synchronic and diachronic unity of cultural systems rests in part on the psychological fact of the universality of human needs and the tension between individuals' needs and the limitations on their capacity to fulfill these needs alone or in a single lifetime (*SW*, 1:94; *GS*, 1:43–44).

But cultural systems have another principle of unity—that is, not all the acts of the individual are merely transitory. Human praxis affects the material world, and matter preserves these expressions of human life. "The system receives its full reality and objectivity only through the capacity of the external world to preserve and to transmit in a more lasting or reproducible manner the achievements of individuals" (*SW*, 1:101; *GS*, 1:50–51). Cultural systems consist, then, not only of ongoing human activity and an enduring structure arising from human nature but also of objectified human activity preserved in matter. Objects of the external world, that is, artifacts, are invested with the values of a purposive system and act as objective standards of these values. Thus, the constant structure of human nature provides a bare, structural historical continuity of sociohistorical systems. The particular content, the flesh and blood, as it were, of these systems is provided by the activities of particular individuals. These activities are preserved in matter and provide an enduring yet evolving context within which the individual lives. The material preservation of praxis insures a kind of cultural inheritance, a basis from which later generations and ages can and must work.

Individuals are crossing-points of a multitude of cultural systems, and any single act can participate in several systems at once. Dilthey gives the following example: the publication of a scholarly work can be an event in a system of science, insofar as the work is related to a system of propositions. Insofar as the work is a product to be manufactured and sold, the author participates in the economic system. The contract between publisher and author involves the scholar in the legal system. Finally, the scholar may be furthering an academic career by building a publication record. "The writing down of each letter of the work is thus a component of all these systems" (*SW*, 1:101; *GS*, 1:51). Individual acts are oriented within and components of a network of cultural systems whose goals are a function within society as a whole.

Johach accurately summarizes Dilthey's conception of culture in two moments. Culture functions as a framework for directing and understanding praxis in that it is an objectification of our emotional, volitional, and intellectual psychic structure. But cultural systems also bind individuals into a greater sociohistorical unity insofar as these individuals are practically involved with the function of these systems.[2]

Dilthey thus begins to undercut the distinction between the inner and the outer, the private and the public in human action.[3] Purposive human action arises from needs, and these needs do not separate but join us. The commonality of our needs and the limitations of our capacities bring us together with our ancestors and our contemporaries in ongoing projects. Many actions that "I" undertake are actions that "we" undertake in important ways. The consciousness of the plurality of action is not necessary, however, for this plurality. Carr distinguishes between groups and communities.[4] The former, like the Sartrean series, is an unself-conscious unity produced from without, whether by a common object (e.g., a television or radio program) or an observer. The latter is unified specifically by virtue of the self-consciousness of a common objective or a common experience. Carr is interested in a social system as a "we," a social system as lived from within. He argues that the construction of a broadly accepted narrative of shared origins and destiny is crucial to the constitution of a community, and its continued existence depends on the enduring acceptability of this narrative or the ability of the community (or certain of its members) to revise the narrative in an acceptable way. For Dilthey, a narrative is not required to constitute the group. Purposive systems can be effected by our *realization* of our participation in them, and even the sketchiest narratives we shape of our own lives or the lives of others entail some realization of our involvement in social settings, but our actions will be taken up into larger groups regardless of our recognition of their communal dimension. Even though the purposive actions taken up into cultural systems are done freely by the individual, that is,

2. Johach, *Handelnder Mensch und objektiver Geist*, p. 65.
3. Schrag devotes the bulk of his energies to precisely this task in *Communicative Praxis*.
4. Carr, *Time, Narrative, and History*, especially his fifth chapter, "From I to We," pp. 122–152.

the purpose pursued is chosen, the individual's recognition of others as purposive agents with the same goal is not required for the unity of the group.[5]

This conception of the unity of cultural systems remains undeveloped in an important way, however. That is, Dilthey has begun to see that social systems are the basis for the commonality, hence the objectivity, of our experience. He has not, however, adequately worked out how these systems act to govern our communicative interaction, in large part because he derives the structure of social systems from aspects of individual psychic structure. Personal experience comes first, and commonality and communication only come second. Social systems and experience must be reconceived such that the latter is always already informed by the former.

In addition to our voluntary participation in cultural systems, Dilthey points to the family, tribe, and state as examples of structures into which we are born and in whose varying rules, customs, and traditions we have, at least at first, little or no choice about participating. Such institutions are examples of what Dilthey calls the external organization of society. Whereas the unity of a cultural system is based on a goal arising from a common human need, the external organization of society is a network of volitional or power relations. *"Viewed from the subject's perspective, lived experience* shows his will to be subject to a complex of external bonds—to relationships of power and dependence vis-à-vis persons and things and to communal relationships" (*SW*, 1:114–115; *GS*, 1:64–65). Individuals find themselves in a multitude of systems of relations of authority. The external organization of society rests on a twofold psychological foundation. First, it is based on "enduring feelings of belonging together," which Dilthey explicitly distinguished from a *"kaltes Vorstellen"* (cold representation) of social relations (*SW*, 1:99; *GS*, 1:47). There is a feeling of community or solidarity among the individuals involved in such institutions. These relations of authority are not based on or derived from this feeling of community, which is instead a reflection of the consciousness of a common heritage and geographical juxtaposition. Participation in these institutions promotes similarities in individuals and their tasks and goals which are reflected in this feeling of community or solidarity. Dilthey does suggest a capacity to dissociate ourselves from these institutions. In

---

5. Dilthey's view that recognition is not a necessary factor in the constitution of a group stands in stark contrast to Jean-Paul Sartre's analysis of the group-in-fusion in *Critique of Dialectical Reason*, trans. Alan Sheridan-Smith (London: NLB, 1976), pp. 363–373. The constitution of the group requires, in Sartre's view, our reflective capacities as third parties.

our associations there is "in some degree or other a feeling of community conjoined with them, provided that it is not canceled by an opposing psychic influence" (*SW*, 1:116; *GS*, 1:66). This does not mean, however, that these power relations are created and maintained by assent to or recognition of them.

The volitional relation of authority and subjection, "power and dependence among wills," is the second concept on which the analysis of the external organization of society relies (*SW*, 1:117; *GS*, 1:67). These are not, however, relations of absolute authority between individuals. Dilthey insists that "this relationship too, like that of community, is only relative" (*SW*, 1:117; *GS*, 1:67). These concepts are used in discussion of the authoritative structure of institutions. Individuals, insofar as they participate in the state, the family, the corporation, and so forth, have a specific status in that organization. In this institution the individual is, according to the rules and structure of the institution, subordinate to or in a position of authority over others to the extent that they act within the confines of this institution and the status or office as assigned by that institution. But such power relations are a function of the institution and exist between offices or stations of such institutions. These relations apply to individuals only in their capacity as a participant in these institutions, and no individual is completely immersed in any institution.

External organizations arise on the basis of "interests and compulsion" (*SW*, 1:98; *GS*, 1:47), that is, they arise for the sake of achieving some purpose. This can take the form of satisfying deep instinctual drives in the family; addressing needs or problems of a specific time and place in organizations, such as business concerns; or institutionalizing of cultural systems such as religion in bureaucratic organizations such as the Church. The purpose acts as the *Bildungsgesetz*, or the principle, for the formation and organization of associations, that is, the association's function and structure are derived from its purpose (*SW*, 1:121; *GS*, 1:71).

In concrete sociohistorical situations, cultural systems are often woven into the organizational fabric of social institutions. As Johach points out, the distinction between cultural system and external organization should not be viewed as "only a differentiation, but at the same time a setting-in-relation. In reality individual cultural systems are involved with each other and with certain social forms of organization in varying degrees."[6] Dilthey demonstrates the relativity of the distinction between cultural systems and external organization in his analysis of law.

6. Johach, *Handelnder Mensch und objektiver Geist*, p. 68.

Law can be studied from two perspectives. On the one hand, law is the "consistent meshing of particular actions of various individuals" (*SW*, 1:104; *GS*, 1:53). That is, law is a cultural system grounded on the individual consciousness of right and wrong "as a constantly operative psychological fact" (*SW*, 1:105; *GS*, 1:54). On the other hand, law is a social institution of external relations of authority. Individual volitions are ordered and judged according to the parameters of the justice system. To investigate right as a system is to focus on the "power of those volitional unities that have dominated history and produce a consistent action within society by means of the individual wills subjected to them" (*SW*, 1:104; *GS*, 1:53–54).

The rights accorded individuals and the relations of individuals to property are systems of laws which not only guide the volitions of individuals but are maintained and carried only by individuals. As Dilthey writes, "This purposive system of law is directed toward an external binding of wills into a stable and universally valid order by means of which individual spheres of power are defined in their relation to one another, to the world of affairs, and to the collective will" (*SW*, 1:105; *GS*, 1:55). The justice system is not in some way derived from the consciousness of right and wrong; the study of law is not exhausted by a study of the external relations established and maintained by the justice system. Rather, the two exist simultaneously and have a reciprocal relationship, or in Dilthey's words: "Both realities always exist only alongside one another, in conjunction with each other. To be sure, they are not connected as cause and effect, but each has the other as the condition of its existence" (*SW*, 1:105; *GS*, 1:55).

This view is later echoed in the "Descriptive Psychology." The external organization of society stands in a reciprocal relation with the volitional component of psychic structure, according to Dilthey.

> We will study the nature, laws and connections of our volitions in the external organization of society, in the economic and juridical order. We have here the . . . objectification of the system of our practical behavior. . . . The particular volition is in fact with the individual only the expression of an enduring tendency or orientation of the will which can fill the entire life without our being continually conscious of it. ("Descriptive Psychology," 72; *GS*, 5:190)

The jurist's decision regarding a case is clearly the judgment of a particular individual. But this judgment is made in accordance with the laws

prevailing at the time. Law is an objectification of the volitional component of psychic structure, and its concrete form is the historically developed system of laws and ordinances brought about through the praxis of
individuals. Individual acts are conditioned by the system, but the existence of the system itself requires the praxis of individuals within the
parameters of its structure.

Historiography brings together the work of all the individual human
sciences in an attempt to study the way in which social systems develop
and influence one another over time and the way these systems interre-
late at any one time. As H. A. Hodges puts it, history "must investigate
two kinds of relations: the relations between one state of society and
another which comes before or after it in time . . .; and the relations
between the different branches of social life and activity at any one moment in time."[7] Dilthey sees, to borrow Danto's term, that the historian
must be more than an "ideal chronicler." Historians are interested not
only in a chronology of events but also in a developmental analysis in
which the significance of events is derived only from later events. Dilthey
clearly wants to draw relations between historical events as if they be-
longed to a larger temporal system, but in the *Introduction* he does not
analyze the temporality of social systems. Accordingly, Dilthey remains
somewhat unclear about the kinds of relations to be drawn between
historical events in historical accounts. He does, however, reject two possibilities. Diltheyan historiography avoids the universal history of speculative philosophy of history and the reductionistic positivism of the
sociology of his day.

Philosophy of history, especially as it is found in Augustine, Vico, and
Hegel, is universal history. It attempts to discern a single formula according to which the movement of history takes place (*SW,* 1:142; *GS,* 1:93).
For example, Hegel views history as a dialectical unfolding of freedom as
the essence of spirit: "Universal History . . . shows the development of
the consciousness of Freedom on the part of Spirit, and the consequent
realization of that Freedom. This development implies a gradation—a
series of increasingly adequate expressions or manifestations of Freedom, which result from its Idea."[8] Freedom is not, however, reducible to
the autonomy of the individual. Rather, the individual is free only within

7. Hodges, *The Philosophy of Wilhelm Dilthey,* p. 160.

8. G. W. F. Hegel, *The Philosophy of History,* trans. J. Sibree (New York: Colonial Press,
1899), p. 63.

the state. Thus, history becomes for Hegel an ideal development in which universal and particular are reconciled. That is, the will of the individual, insofar as it is merely subjective and concerned with its own passions, is particular. But the essence of will is rational will, that is, the universal. Thus, the truth of every particular will is the universal. The laws of the state are the universal, and only in conforming to these laws do individuals actualize their essence: "For Truth is the Unity of the universal and subjective Will; and the Universal is to be found in the State, in its laws, its universal and rational arrangement."[9] Volition in its true, essential form is volition according to the laws of the state. Thus, only insofar as the will of the individual coincides with the will of the state is the individual free. "For Law is the objectivity of Spirit; volition in its true form. Only that will which obeys law, is free; for it obeys itself."[10] The state, then, is the end of history. Philosophy of history is devoted to tracing the development of spirit in time as it moves from state to state. Each epoch is a stage in spirit's self-actualization as freedom. When spirit reaches the highest possible level of self-knowledge in one state, it moves on to another. History is not just the cyclical growth and decay of states. Spirit emerges from each state at a higher level of self-actualization: "Spirit—consuming the envelope of its existence—does not merely pass into another envelope, nor rise rejuvenescent from the ashes of its previous form; it comes forth exalted, glorified, a purer spirit."[11]

Dilthey agrees with Hegel's emphasis on the spiritual meaning-content of historical events. But whereas Hegel understood this meaning-content as a single Idea that unifies individual nations and the movement of history as a totality, Dilthey remained suspicious of any monolithic interpretation of history. Dilthey also takes exception to Hegel's speculative methodology. Although Hegel contends that he proceeds empirically and avoids forcing the events of history into a preconceived mold, the idea of reason brought to bear on history was first conceived in his speculative metaphysics. Hegel emphasizes those aspects of history which support the metaphysical position that reality is the unfolding of reason. Thus, he selects empirical evidence as significant on the basis of his metaphysical position and in turn uses this evidence to support the metaphysics. The metaphysical formula is arrived at speculatively, not

9. Ibid., p. 39.
10. Ibid.
11. Ibid., p. 73.

empirically. Experience is not used for verification but for the demonstration of a speculative thesis already accepted as true. A historian following the Diltheyan approach would, in contrast, begin with the research of the individual human sciences and attempt to situate individuals within their concrete sociohistorical context. The way in which the individuals fit within this context would be used to understand both them and the historical nexus of which they are a part. Hypotheses regarding the overall meaning of history or formulas governing universal history are to be made only tentatively and at the end of the above research process.

Dilthey's empirical approach to spiritual meaning-content differs as significantly from Comte's positivism as from Hegel's speculative metaphysics. In his sociology or social physics Comte's attempts to discern the causal connections between the observable phenomena of society. Although Dilthey later accepted Georg Simmel's approach to sociology because it used psychological concepts to help clarify social relations (*SW*, 1:497–498; *GS*, 1:420–421), he criticized Comte's sociology for its rejection of psychology and its reduction of psychic facts to physiological phenomena. Comte divides sociology into two components: social statics and social dynamics. "Social dynamics studies the laws of succession, while social statics inquires into those of coexistence."[12] Viewing society on the model of a biological organism, social statics is a synchronic study of society which determines the reciprocal relations between the different parts of society. Social dynamics demonstrates the efficient causal relation between successive states of society, showing how each state of society is "the necessary result of the preceding." The causal laws governing complex social phenomena are ultimately dependent on the laws governing the simpler phenomena studied by astronomy, physics, chemistry, and physiology, even if the positivistic method must be adjusted to accommodate the complexity of society. Dilthey rejects Comte's approach because Comte reduces the purposive and evaluative structure of social interactions and the lived experience of purposes and values to effects of biological influences, which are themselves reducible to chemical and physical influences. This kind of reduction of psychic facts to physical causes is never given in experience and thus remains an unverified hypothesis.

According to Dilthey, the task of the scientific study of history is too

---

12. Auguste Comte, *The Positive Philosophy of Auguste Comte*, ed. and trans. Harriet Martineau (New York: Calvin Blanchard, 1856), p. 464.

great for any one discipline. Historians do not just set down a record of chronologically related facts but integrate the work of the individual human sciences in historical narratives (*SW*, 1:144; *GS*, 1:95). Dilthey would have model historians be involved in as many of the individual human sciences as possible and, at the very least, not fail to take account of any of them. They would study the ways in which the purposes and values of individuals are expressed in and shaped by the character of the cultural systems and political organizations of which they are a part, attempt to trace the development of cultural systems, and try to make determinate the ways in which cultural systems interact within the larger setting of a nation. After this interdisciplinary process, historians may venture hypotheses about historical laws, but the production of such hypotheses is by no means the culmination of human scientific research. Historical understanding, as I shall show at length in the final chapter, is precisely the production of a narrative within which the significance of events emerges. Historians make use of generalizations about psychic life or descriptions of causal connections to clarify the movement of the narrative at various points, but they do not seek to displace this narrative with a form of explanation which connects events by subsuming them under hypotheses. Narratives make events intelligible to us in a way that is not reducible to any covering law model of explanation, even though such explanations may serve to fill gaps in our narratives. Gallie suggests a similar point when he writes, "Ideally, a story should be self-explanatory."[13]

Social Structure and Meaning

In the *Introduction*, Dilthey viewed social systems largely as subject matter or objects of study, but in the *Aufbau*, he comes to see the structures of the sociohistorical world as the objective conditions for historical understanding itself. Dilthey's appropriation of the Hegelian term "objective spirit" is indicative of his new approach. Whereas Hegel had viewed objective spirit as a stage in the rational movement from subjective to absolute spirit, Dilthey strips the concept of its metaphysical interpretation and rejects its one-sided intellectualism. Objective spirit is no longer understood as a step toward the rational totalization of the real but as the finite, partly irrational product of human praxis. Objective

---

13. Gallie, *Philosophy and the Historical Understanding*, p. 23.

spirit does not form an ideal unity. It is a general term that refers to the plurality of human products, expressions, and systems of interaction, and it includes "language, custom, every kind of form of life, comprised by life-style just as much as family, civil society, state, and right. And even what Hegel distinguished as absolute from objective spirit falls under this concept: art, religion, and philosophy" (*GS*, 7:151). Objective spirit both shapes and is shaped by humans and structures our experience. Ranging from the fleeting expressions of individuals to enduring cultural achievements, objective spirit constantly surrounds us and provides a common framework of meaning.[14] "It is . . . the medium in which the understanding of other persons and their expressions of life comes about, according to Dilthey."[15] We are all born into a common meaning framework within which not only the expressions of others but also our own expressions derive their meaning.

The move toward viewing the historical world as an objective condition for understanding also signals an analysis of social structure which does not presuppose psychic structure. This does not mean that all talk of psychological individuals is now to be dismissed. Rather, psychic structure itself is now construed as a function of the structure of the sociohistorical world, and structure is construed as a meaning-constituting *context*. As Rodi has demonstrated,[16] Dilthey's initial concept of context was developed in his psychological writings of the 1880s and 1890s and was drawn from the physiological conception of structure. Structure was used to describe the psychic life of individuals as a network of internally related emotions, volitions, and representations. The concept of structure is an organic metaphor, and it is used to emphasize that psychic structure is not static but dynamic. This is demonstrated clearly by the concept of the acquired psychic nexus. The psychic structure of individuals is gradually developed in their relations to the surrounding world and becomes rigid only with old age.

The publication of Husserl's *Logical Investigations* greatly influenced

---

14. Johach points out that an appreciation of the development of the concept of objective spirit suggests that it has two functions. First, it provides sociohistorical order and continuity. Second, it makes historical knowledge of ourselves possible (*Handelnder Mensch und objektiver Geist*, p. 158).

15. Wilhelm Dilthey, "The Understanding of Other Persons and Their Expressions of Life," trans. Kenneth L. Heiges, in Dilthey, *Descriptive Psychology and Historical Understanding*, p. 126 (to be abbreviated as "Understanding Other Persons").

16. Rodi, "Dilthey's Concept of 'Structure'" in *Dilthey and Phenomenology*, ed. Makkreel and Scanlon, pp. 107–119.

Dilthey's work, and in two essays written around 1905 it had the effect of rigidifying his conception of psychic structure.[17] But with the *Aufbau* of 1910, Dilthey distances himself both from this rigid view of psychic structure and from the emphasis on consciousness as the most important context for understanding others. In the *Aufbau*, Dilthey turns to the objective, sociohistorical determinants of meaning—that is, sociohistorical systems such as language, religion, and art—and speaks of them as systems of influences (*Wirkungszusammenhänge*). Systems of influences are still understood as holistic structures. But, instead of emphasizing a psychological system of emotions, volitions, and representations, Dilthey in his later work focuses on systems of influences as "a *system of functions*, which is grounded *in the structure*" of the system (*GS*, 7:153; cf. 154, 169). These sociohistorical systems constitute meaning, produce values, and realize goals. They make human communication possible by providing a shared set of rules delimiting the range of meaningful communicative action. Successful interaction, whether artistic, economic, religious, or scientific, is achieved only by submitting to these common rules (*GS*, 7:154).

Systems of influences form coherent contexts for human communication by virtue of the fact that each system of influences is "*centered in itself*" (*GS*, 7:154). Certain ideas, values, or rules that direct human actions form the "center" of a system of influences. That is, the condition for participation in a system is the subordination of one's actions to this center. These actions are then related to others devoted to the same center and understood in context with these other actions. As Dilthey states: "Like the individual, every cultural system, every association also has a middle point in itself. The conception of reality, evaluation, and creation of goods are bound into a whole in these" (*GS*, 7:154). At the same time, then, a periphery of sorts is erected. Those actions not devoted to its "center" are excluded from a system of influences, and this system would be an inappropriate context for understanding such actions. The meaning of any action is a function of its place in its appropriate context or contexts, and it is the task of hermeneutics to determine these contexts.

Dilthey's introduction of the concept of *Wirkungszusammenhang* does

17. Wilhelm Dilthey, "Der psychische Strukturzusammenhang," *GS*, 7:3–23, and "Der Strukturzusammenhang des Wissens," *GS*, 7:24–75. See my discussion of these essays in Chapter 1. For a discussion of both the rigidifying and the dynamic phases of Dilthey's conception of structure, see Makkreel, *Dilthey, Philosopher of the Human Studies*, pp. 281, 298, 389.

not completely displace the analysis of the historical world into purposive systems and external power relations,[18] and it also does not set up a separate system of historical rather than natural causes. Rather, the "system of influences" is a more general concept meant to include purpose, power relations, and natural causes as part of a meaning-constituting context that contains its own principle of unity. The *Aufbau* contains explicit reference to the *Introduction*'s analysis of cultural systems. The *Introduction*, however, construed the unity of cultural systems narrowly in terms of purposes alone. In the *Aufbau*, the events and actions that constitute the components of cultural systems are considered meaningful "in that they are members of a system of influences by cooperating with other parts in the realization of values and purposes of the whole" (*GS*, 7:166–167). The unity of these actions and events is provided by a function inherent in the cultural system itself (*GS*, 7:166–167). Thus, Dilthey seems to distance himself from the earlier analysis that traces the unity of cultural systems to the universal psychological structures of individual humans.

Similarly, Dilthey's analysis of the external organization of society emphasizes this move toward the broader context of *Wirkungszusammenhang*. In a political organization a composite structure is introduced in which the relations of power and purposive systems are bound in a more encompassing unity: "Here community first arises from the interaction of cultural systems" (*GS*, 7:170). Conceived as a determinate structural unity of systems of influences, each nation derives its common character from the regularity existing in (1) the course of development of these systems of influences contained in it; (2) the relations of these systems of influences to one another; and by virtue of their value and goal-creating nature, (3) the relation between systems of influences, the production of values, the positing of goals, and the framework of meaning residing in the political organization (*GS*, 7:173–174). This multiplicity of systems of influences is congealed "into an independently effective unity" through the domestic authority exercised over the nation's own citizens and the external might exerted for protection from and aggression against other nations (*GS*, 7:174). Social systems are interrelated as parts of a larger

18. In this I am in agreement with Makkreel (*Dilthey, Philosopher of the Human Studies*, pp. 317–318) and differ with Peter Krausser. See his *Kritik der endlichen Vernunft: Diltheys Revolution der allgemeinen Wissenschafts- und Handlungstheorie* (Frankfurt am Main: Suhrkamp, 1968), p. 164. On this issue, see Jacob Owensby, "Dilthey and Husserl on the Role of the Subject in History," *Philosophy Today* 32, no. 3 (Fall 1988): 226–228.

whole, whereas "each of these is a relatively independent system of influences" (*GS*, 7:174).

It was apparently Dilthey's application of the life-categories of meaning, purpose, and value—categories first derived from *Erlebnis*—to systems of influences that prompted him to refer to them as "subjects of an ideal kind" (*GS*, 7:135). And even though Dilthey stresses that these ideal subjects "are not psychological" (*GS*, 7:282), this manner of speaking has led a number of commentators to criticize him for modeling the unity of sociohistorical systems on the unity of psychological individuals.[19] For example, Hellmut Diwald argues that Dilthey recognized no principal difference between the unity of the course of an individual's life and historical continuity.[20] This results, according to Diwald, in the reduction of history to anthropology.[21] All problems of history would, from this standpoint, be reduced to the problems of human existence. But, as we have seen, cultural systems and political structures are relatively independent systems of influences, centered in themselves according to the function that they perform. They may be understood according to the categories derived from the analysis of *Erlebnis*, because these categories describe the life-nexus as an I-world relation, not merely a psychological subject. Systems of influences are experienced by individuals and shape the interactions between individuals, but it does not follow from this that they can be understood only by modeling them after the individual. The use of life-categories to understand systems of influences is not an application of psychological categories to history; rather, it is a framing of the sociohistorical world as the practical field of human endeavor as lived.

Dilthey conceives of the historical world as the ongoing product of communal human activity. Studies of social systems and history as a whole must always have reference to human goals, values, and meaning. One must never lose sight of the fact that systems of influences are composed of the influences of individuals, and the study of exemplary individuals as crossing-points of such systems is extremely useful. This does not mean, however, that history is limited to the study of individuals or

---

19. It is not surprising that this point in Dilthey's argument should attract so much attention. As Ricoeur indicates in *Time and Narrative*, the transition from the individual to the group is the central difficulty for narrative theory (p. 130).

20. Hellmut Diwald, *Wilhelm Dilthey: Erkenntnistheorie und Philosophie der Geschichte* (Göttingen: Musterschmidt, 1963), p. 81.

21. Ibid., p. 135n.

social systems viewed as individuals. Rather, the function and development of a system of influences can be studied *through* individuals qua
members of such larger systems.

Hans Michael Baumgartner also maintains that Dilthey univocally applies the categories to individuals and universal history. Because the individual is the model for Dilthey's organization of the historical world into
systems of influences, "the problem of historical continuity is reduced to
the question concerning those constitutive elements of the course of the
individual's life which ground its continuity."[22] The course of history is
reduced to the course of individual lives, that is, history is constructed
from the lives of individuals and ultimately reducible to *Erlebnis*. Baumgartner is certainly correct that it is impossible to view the historical
nexus as a system of lived experience. The continuity of history cannot be
readily reduced to the continuity of an individual's life, "in any event it
cannot be understood from the structure of lived experience and the continuity of the course of the individual's life indicated in it."[23] Dilthey is,
from this point of view, left with the choice between limiting historical
continuity to the course of individual lives or altogether forsaking *Erlebnis* as the foundation of historical continuity.

Surely Dilthey refers to systems of influences as ideal subjects, and the
categories derived from the analysis of *Erlebnis* are applied to the understanding of such systems. It is not the case, however, that they are so
modeled after the individual that historical continuity is reduced to the
continuity of individual lives. Systems of influences, though composed
of the effects of individual praxis, transcend the life of any single individual and indeed the lives of generations of individuals that actively participate in them. As we have already seen, these systems of influences do
not merely pass away from moment to moment but are preserved in
matter. This realm of objective spirit forms the cultural, intellectual foundation on which any further advancement, thus a continuity of past and
present, is made possible.

Johach best sums up the problem this way. Dilthey must adequately
conceptualize the transindividual social units in a way that does not
psychologize them.[24] But if these social systems are not psychological
individuals, the application of categories derived from lived experience
to these "ideal" subjects is problematic. Such ideal subjects do not them-

22. Hans Michael Baumgartner, *Kontinuität und Geschichte: Zur Kritik und Metakritik der
historischen Vernunft* (Frankfurt am Main: Suhrkamp, 1972), pp. 110–111.
23. Ibid.
24. Johach, *Handelnder Mensch und objektiver Geist*, p. 147.

selves have lived experience, are not born and do not die, and are not self-conscious of their own temporality.[25] As a result, Johach concludes that the categories of life are to be applied to these "ideal" subjects "only in an indeterminate analogy."[26]

This analogy is not, perhaps, as indeterminate as Johach suggests, however. Psychological individuals and social systems are internally related parts of the same overarching life-nexus. The categories of life are derived from an analysis of the life-nexus as experienced from within or as lived, not from an analysis of individual consciousness in isolation. The correlativity of I and world is the starting point, not a later development. Thus, the life-categories are not first derived from a psychological subject and then transferred to social systems. The study of systems of influences is the study of the life-nexus from a perspective other than that of descriptive psychology, but from a perspective with the same common ground.

Diwald and Baumgartner seem to presuppose that sociohistorical systems are *objects* to be observed from without. It is possible to argue, however, that Dilthey is not trying to analyze these systems as something to be viewed from the outside but as something lived through from the inside. Surely *Wirkungszusammenhänge* are objective structures. But this does not mean that they stand over against me. I am woven into the structure of objective spirit. I belong to it. As a result, the goods and values to which I relate are also social products. Systems of influences are best thought of, then, as principles of the commonality of our lived experience, not merely as objects in that experience. To put it in terms of narrative elements, systems of influences are settings, not characters. They are the settings in which the actions of characters can make sense. As MacIntyre puts it: "Without the setting and its changes through time the history of the individual agent and his changes through time will be unintelligible. Of course one and the same piece of behavior may belong to more than one setting."[27]

The Problematic Metaphor of Structure

Dilthey's use of the metaphor of structure to frame his concept of contexts has led Derrida to link the Diltheyan concept of context with the

---

25. Ibid., pp. 147–148.
26. Ibid., p. 148.
27. MacIntyre, *After Virtue*, p. 192.

static view formulated by structuralists such as Claude Lévi-Strauss.[28] Accordingly, Dilthey's view may be thought to succumb to the Derridean criticisms leveled against the structuralists. That is, the stability of meaning is dependent on the stability of contexts and the ability to agree on a limited set of contexts used in the production of meaning. Derrida argues from the internal inconsistency of the metaphor of structure itself that neither of these conditions can be met. Such limits on meaning are arbitrary and function only to stifle interpretation. Broadening contexts and bringing new contexts to bear in the interpretive act serves to open texts to infinite reinterpretation.

But Derrida's liberation of interpretation from artificial constraints appears to undermine the hermeneutic approach to excluding meanings from texts. Contrary to the view suggested by Derrida, Dilthey's conception of context anticipates the poststructuralist rejection of rigid parameters of meaning. As I shall show, the Diltheyan notion of context, though it makes much use of the metaphor of structure, departs significantly from structuralism. Contexts are dynamic, and the metaphor of structure is used in conjunction with the metaphor of "horizon" to construct a genuinely historical conception of context, which at once continues to provide both limits to interpretation and space for continued reinterpretation.

In *Writing and Difference*, Derrida characterizes "structure" in Lévi-Strauss by using precisely the central-peripheral model we find in Dilthey. He then attacks the notion of a center to undermine the concept of structure itself.[29] The focus on structure amounts to a vain search for a fixed foundation for meaning which only obscures the dynamic process by which meaning is constituted by context. The notion of a "center" has been introduced into this process of meaning-production as a way of placing limitations on it; Derrida states that "the function of this center was not only to orient, balance, and organize the structure . . . but above all to make sure that the organizing principle of the structure would limit what we might call the *play* of the structure" (*WD*, 278). Because a structure can be thought of as a whole that is composed of parts, any part derives its meaning from its relation to this whole or, more precise, from

28. Jacques Derrida, *Writing and Difference*, trans. Alan Bass (Chicago: University of Chicago Press, 1978), p. 160 (to be abbreviated as *WD*). Derrida's classification of Dilthey seems vindicated by Dilthey's own frequent use of the term "structure," particularly in bold phrases such as "Structure is everything" (*SW*, 1:439n; *GS*, 19:446n).

29. Cf. Gasché's discussion of Derrida on structure in *The Tain of the Mirror*, pp. 142–154.

its "play" with the multitude of "parts" with which it has been associated. This play is constrained in two ways by the notion that the system has a center. First, the "parts" with which any "part" may be associated are limited by the "periphery" of the structure. Nothing beyond the periphery or margin may enter into the meaning-constituting play of the system. Second, the play of "parts" within the structure is also regulated by the center. That is, the position of the center is not relative to any other of the system's parts. Its position is fixed. So, although the meaning of any part is relative to its position in the whole, the relativity of the play of parts stops with the absolute presence of the center. Structure allows, then, only a *controlled* play by assuming an absolute foundation for such play. According to Derrida, "The concept of centered structure is in fact the concept of a play based on a fundamental ground, a play constituted on the basis of a fundamental immobility and a reasoning certitude, which itself is beyond the reach of play" (*WD*, 279). In other words, the rules governing the play of parts are themselves *not* products of or susceptible to play.

But such a center, and accordingly such a structure, contains a contradiction: "The center is at the center of the totality, and yet, since the center does not belong to the totality (is not part of the totality), the totality *has its center elsewhere.* The center is not the center" (*WD*, 279). In other words, the "center" of the system *transcends* the system. To be a part of the system means to have only a position relative to other parts. This is not adequate for the stabilizing center. Its position cannot be relative, only absolute. Accordingly, the center must not be within the structure. The structure is then centered *outside of itself.* But this is obviously absurd, as is the notion of a stable center.

Because the structure has been de-centered, structurality must be rethought. "Henceforth, it was necessary to begin thinking that there was no center, that the center could not be thought in the form of a present-being, that the center had no natural site, that it was not a fixed locus but a function, a sort of nonlocus in which an infinite number of sign-substitutions came into play. . . . The absence of the transcendental signified extends the domain and the play of signification infinitely" (*WD*, 280). This de-centering removes the dual restraint of the center. First, with the destruction of the center comes the loss of the periphery. Previously delineated contexts, whether sociohistorical periods or contemporaneous systems of discourse such as art, religion, philosophy, and science, do not exclude one another except in an arbitrary fashion. Texts or actions once thought to belong to different, unrelated contexts are no longer restrained from interpretive interplay. Second, no context or set of contexts may be viewed as indispensable or definitive for understanding the meaning of a text.[30]

Derrida turns to this second point specifically in *Spurs: Nietzsche's Styles*.[31] He claims that the appending of Nietzsche's note "I have forgotten my umbrella" to *The Joyful Wisdom* is "a monument to hermeneutic somnambulism" (*Spurs*, 125). Derrida contends that the possibility always exists that the "appropriate" context could perhaps be found for the fragment. But the possibility also remains that there is no greater context for the fragment. Derrida continues, "For it is always possible that the 'I have forgotten my umbrella', detached as it is, not only from the milieu that produced it, but also from an intention or meaning on Nietzsche's part, should remain so, whole and intact, once and for all, without any other context" (*Spurs*, 125). This "I have forgotten my umbrella" is not a fragment because fragments presuppose a larger, totalizing context. It is a *non*fragment. The point here is not merely that some writings are difficult to authenticate or that their proper context is difficult to determine. The very idea of a proper context is called into question. This possibility of never knowing the context must be accounted for and in so doing "would withdraw [this nonfragment] from any assured horizon of hermeneutic question" (*Spurs*, 127). The nonfragment is a "forgotten text" (*Spurs*, 131). Such a text has no "appropriate" context and yet is graftable to an infinite series of contexts: "Because it is structurally liberated from any living meaning, it is always possible that it means nothing at all or that it has no decidable meaning. There is no end to its parodying play with meaning, grafted here and there, beyond any contextual body or finite code" (*Spurs*, 132–133).

The hermeneut would, so Derrida argues, abandon the decoding of such nonfragments because their meaning cannot be determined. Derrida insists that this is the wrong conclusion to draw. On the contrary, the decoding should be taken to an extreme (*Spurs*, 133). The idea here is not that nonfragments are contextless in the sense that they can be situated in no context. They are contextless in the sense that they are limited by no

30. Jonathan Culler underscores the boundlessness of context for Derrida in *On Deconstruction: Theory and Criticism after Structuralism* (Ithaca: Cornell University Press, 1982), pp. 123–124.

31. Jacques Derrida, *Spurs: Nietzsche's Styles*, trans. Barbara Harlow (Chicago: University of Chicago Press, 1979), to be abbreviated as *Spurs*.

particular context. They can be grafted onto and transform an infinite series of other nonfragments.

Not only the nonfragment "I have forgotten my umbrella" but also any of Nietzsche's texts could be considered as such "forgotten texts," texts bound to no particular context. It is possible "that there is no 'totality to Nietzsche's text,' not even a fragmentary or aphoristic one" (*Spurs*, 135). This calls into question not only the common hermeneutical practice of viewing the writer's corpus as one of the definitive contexts for determining the meaning of his or her texts; it also undermines the notion of *any* definitive context. Texts are not forever bound to any context or group of contexts as definitive. They may be situated within any context, and new meanings are opened with each new context. But to limit a text to any single context or set of contexts is an arbitrary limitation on the play of meaning. This results in at least two positive consequences. Texts are opened again and again to new and vital readings, and space is made for voices that have been previously placed at the periphery of discourse or excluded altogether. However, it also appears to have the unappealing effect of undermining the hermeneutical standards for the limitation of interpretation.

Dilthey's hermeneutics has anticipated much of Derrida's attack on the static notion of structure and the concept of totalization. Like Derridean poststructuralism, Diltheyan hermeneutics involves making different voices audible. Indeed, difference, whether historical or cultural, makes the hermeneutic task necessary. Certainly, the hermeneuticist views meaning as a function of context, and the hermeneutic notion of "context" serves to exclude certain interpretations. Hermeneutics, however, does not view contexts as static and rigid, and they are not self-enclosed. They cooperate in the constitution of meaning by both merging and conflicting. For the hermeneuticist, as for Derrida, there is a constant play of meaning, a play without the pretense of ultimately arresting such play forever. Thus, the interaction of meaning-giving contexts does not terminate, for the hermeneuticist, in a totalization that directs or constrains this interaction itself.

Derrida's "de-centering" is addressed to a rigid structure with a fixed center, and this may pose serious problems for structuralists like Lévi-Strauss. But, Diltheyan hermeneutics is not structuralist in this rigid sense; it is not driven by what Derrida calls the *"structuralist* demand," namely, the demand that "leads to the comprehensive description of a totality, of a form or a function organized according to an internal legality in which elements have meaning only in the solidarity of their correlation or their opposition" (*WD*, 157). Indeed, Diltheyan hermeneutics is equally if not more fully driven by what Derrida calls the "*genetic* demand," which "is the search for the origin and foundation of the structure" (*WD*, 157).[32] Dilthey's life-philosophy maintains that the "source" of all structure is the pre-reflective depths of life. All structure is not only *developed* structure but also develop*ing* structure. Thus, although Dilthey may be said to derive meaning from context, his notion of context differs from the static notion of structure attacked by Derrida.

In his concept of systems of influences, Dilthey offers a notion of contexts that are *dynamic* in two senses. First, they have a diachronic dimension (*GS*, 7:169). Systems of influences should be understood precisely as temporal structures. Second, systems of influences can merge in the production of meaning. They "are woven into broader sociohistorical contexts such as nations, ages, historical periods" (*GS*, 7:154). Systems of influences are not self-enclosed structures. They are made wholes (*ergänzt*) not by excluding other contexts but by interacting with them. A system of influences "first completes [*ergänzt*] its own peculiar life [*Eigenleben*] *through something other*" (*GS*, 7:154–155; emphasis added). Contexts are not static geometric shapes; they undergo constant transformation in that the limits they place on the play of the parts of the contextual whole are themselves developing. There is no fixed center that guides or restricts this development. Nevertheless, contexts may still be thought of as centered in themselves and forming a whole in a certain way.

Generation, age, and epoch are diachronic divisions of systems of influences into historical periods according to characteristic tendencies in the interaction of their components, whether these components are human individuals or larger social groups such as cultural systems. Such divisions of history do not, however, result in a conception of history as entirely isolable, merely juxtaposed periods or in a view of history as a unitary ascent toward a single end. These divisions are neither absolute breaks in history nor stages in the unitary progress of history but somewhat relative demarcations made by the human scientist to signify either the duration of a dominant unifying tendency in a system of influences or a characteristic way in which the parts of a larger sociohistorical whole interact. Because any period retains the past and contains the possibilities

---

32. Derrida portrays Husserl as torn between these two demands and Dilthey as driven by the former.

of the future, the transition from one period to another is a gradual development rather than a discrete leap. Thus, precisely where the temporal divisions are to be drawn is to some degree a function of the human scientist's judgment.

In the *Aufbau* Dilthey does not dwell on his conception of generation but refers to his discussion of the topic in his 1865 essay on Novalis (now found in *Das Erlebnis und die Dichtung*, or Lived experience and poetry)[33] and his 1875 essay "Über das Studium der Geschichte der Wissenschaften vom Menschen, der Gesellschaft und dem Staat." In the latter essay, Dilthey defines the term "generation" as "a signification for a *relation of the contemporaneity of individuals*. We refer to those who to some degree matured concurrently, i.e., had a common childhood, a common adolescence, whose period of adult capacities in part coincided, as the same generation" (*GS*, 5:37). Those who are children and adolescents at roughly the same time are members of the same generation. Were this the only defining characteristic of a generation, it would be a disappointingly arbitrary historical division because no naturally occurring, objectively measured temporal gaps between one group of infants and another can usually be found. That is, if a generation were determined only by using a particular calendar date to designate its beginning and end, diachronic order would not emerge from common elements in the development of the lives of those said to be part of the same generation. Rather, individuals would be grouped together without reference to shared values or purposes by virtue of the fact that their birth dates lie close together on an objective timeline. Exclusion from and inclusion in this temporal context would then be a function of the interpreter's arbitrary selection of beginning and ending dates for the generation.

But generations are not characterized merely by the accident of contemporaneous birth. The characters of the members of a generation are developed within shared cultural circumstances. Dilthey groups the multitude of influences on a generation under two broad headings. The first major influence is the intellectual climate at the time of a generation's education: "The hold of the intellectual culture emerges as it is found at that time in which this generation begins to be seriously educated." Second, a generation is conditioned by the sociohistorical situation as a

---

33. Wilhelm Dilthey, *Das Erlebnis und die Dichtung: Lessing, Goethe, Novalis, Hölderlin*, 15th ed. (Stuttgart: B. G. Teubner; Göttingen: Vandenhoeck & Ruprecht, 1970), p. 188 (to be abbreviated as *ED*). Cf. *GS*, 5:37–38.

whole when it tries to make progress on the basis of the already acquired knowledge or the worldview formulated by previous generations. That is, individuals find themselves under the influence of "the surrounding life, actual relations, social, political, infinitely varied circumstances" (*ED*, 188; cf. *GS*, 5:37–38). This does not mean, however, that the character of a generation can be deduced from its sociohistorical milieu. Rather, the generation is a way of tracing the unfolding of a characteristic mode of interaction between social systems and individuals which concentrates largely on individuals and their confrontation with sociohistorical conditions (*ED*, 189–190).

Although Dilthey repeatedly uses the image of the structure to characterize sociohistorical systems, he also returns repeatedly to the metaphor of a "horizon" in his discussions of the diachronic analysis of systems of influences into age, epoch, and *Zeitgeist*. The term "age" describes a period in the development of a system of influences which serves as the overall context or framework for the development of less encompassing systems of influences.[34] The image of the structure is still evident here. As Dilthey states, "The structure of a certain age proves itself to be then a system of particular partial systems and movements in the great complex of influences of a time" (*GS*, 7:185–186).

But it is clear that an age is not a fixed structure that restricts the interactions of the systems of influences within it. This interaction itself produces an inner structure that is gradually articulated and finally dissolved. As Dilthey states, "Thus the whole system of influences of the age is immanently determined through its nexus of life, its mental world, its value formation, and its ideas of purpose. . . . It forms the temporal horizon, and ultimately the meaning of each part in this system of time is determined through it" (*GS*, 7:186). The interactions between the systems of influences open up a temporal horizon broader than any of these particular systems which in turn determines the meaning of the systems of influences within it. This temporal horizon, however, serves only as a most indeterminate cutoff point between one age and another. The seeds of a new age can emerge and the remnants of an older age can remain in the midst of the predominant tendencies of a time. The systems of influences contained within an age develop at their own rate. They are not synchronized by virtue of their membership in a larger whole. This be-

---

34. On the distinction of age, epoch, and *Zeitgeist*, see Makkreel, *Dilthey, Philosopher of the Human Studies*, pp. 396–399.

comes especially clear in Dilthey's discussion of epochs and spirit of the times, or *Zeitgeist*.

These temporal categories are not at first clearly differentiated. Dilthey speaks of both as life-horizons that form a temporal boundary according to the life-relations of the people of that time to the modes of thought, feeling, and willing of that time: "A spirit of the times is spoken of in this sense. . . . At the same time, this means that each such epoch finds a limit in a *life-horizon*. By this I understand the limit within which men of a time live in relation to their thinking, feeling, and willing" (*GS*, 7:177–178). It may well be that the occurrence of a new epoch marks the emergence of a new *Zeitgeist*, but epochs are more specifically moments in the overall developmental unity of individual systems of influences, especially cultural systems such as art and religion (*GS*, 7:185). Systems of influences differentiate themselves synchronically by the rules exhibited in them according to their function. Diachronically, individual systems of influences will exhibit a different epochal development according to this rule. One may say "that every system of influences bears its law in itself, and that according to this its epochs are quite different from those of others" (*GS*, 7:185).

Zeitgeist characterizes the unity of a time period according to the predominant tendencies that run through it. The manner in which values are given and goals are posited and the standards of life of a certain time form an indeterminate meaning framework for the individual, the course of development, and the community (*GS*, 7:177).

> It is the *concentration* in itself of the whole culture of a time period, so that the standard for judgment, esteem, assessment of persons, and tendencies is located in the conferring of values, the positing of goals and the rules of life of a time, which gives a certain time its character. The particular, the tendency, the community have their meaning in the whole according to their internal relation to the spirit of the times. (*GS*, 7:177)

This is not to say that individuals, artistic schools, or political movements are merely a reflex of a monolithic Hegelian *Volksgeist* or that tensions and contradictions between systems of influences are overcome in a totalization. Systems of influences always exhibit their own developmental unity. A system's "relation to the spirit of the times" is not its expression of a more or less determinate idea but rather its relation to a matrix of regular interactions between a multiplicity of systems of influences (*GS*, 7:177). The temporal horizon Dilthey calls a *Zeitgeist* is, then, a network of influences within which different individuals and large sociohistorical systems are situated. As this network is always viewed from within and *produced* from within, there is neither an absolute perspective from which to view it nor an absolute center that organizes it. Different actions or texts can act as a focal point for a matrix of influences, and it is from these focal points that the interactions of influences must be interpreted.

It might be argued at this point that by making systems of influences *diachronically* self-enclosed, Dilthey still limits the play of meaning by deriving it from a fixed structure. That is, once an age has ended, it becomes a *static* thing of the past. It forms a context with fixed boundaries, and no contexts beyond this age may be brought to bear in interpretation. Accordingly, it becomes only a matter of time before a fixed and final meaning can be assigned to any event or expression of the age. For example, Dilthey claims that the system of the medieval world "has a *closed* [*abgeschlossenen*] *horizon*. Thus, an epoch is centered in itself in a new way" (*GS*, 7:155). But this interpretation is not completely correct. Past ages do form systems of influences with their own unity, and they will develop no further. They are brought to life again, however, by each interpreter, and no interpreter turns to the past in a completely disinterested way. We return to events or expressions of the past because of their life-relations to our current situations and projects.[35] That is, the focal point of an age is never fixed; it is always relative to the historical condition of the interpreter. This results, then, in the need for continual reinterpretation. Nevertheless, certain meanings *are* excluded, as the boundaries of the age and of the smaller systems within it remain intact. Accordingly, Diltheyan hermeneutics offers a middle way between the rigidity of structuralism and the apparent limitlessness of Derridean poststructuralism.

Structure, in Derrida's view, "refers only to space, geometric or morphological space, the order of forms and sites" (*WD*, 15). This spatial model of structure leads us to concentrate on the structure itself as if it were a stable object of study rather than the play of the meanings which is structurality itself. Indeed, it truncates and ultimately obscures struc-

---

35. Cf. Ludwig Landgrebe, "Wilhelm Diltheys Theorie der Geisteswissenschaften (Analyse ihrer Grundbegriffe)," in *Jahrbuch für Philosophie und phänomenologische Forschung*, vol. 9, ed. Edmund Husserl (Halle: Max Niemeyer, 1928), p. 345.

turality. "One risks being interested in the figure itself to the detriment of the play going on within it metaphorically" (*WD*, 16). But for Dilthey, the notion of structure is consistent with the metaphor of a horizon. A context is not a static morphē but a temporal life-horizon. Although the horizon is itself a spatial metaphor,[36] it escapes the rigidity of the geometric-spatial model. Gadamer's more explicit formulation of the metaphor of the horizon would be helpful here.[37]

Being within a horizon means to have a particular perspective on the world around us. Being within a horizon, however, is not to be limited to only what is closest to us. It is by virtue of being within a horizon that we have a world at all, that is, that things are more or less significant, "near or far, great or small" (*TM*, 269). But unlike geometrical figures, which are static and whose boundaries are precise, horizons are dynamic and indeterminately demarcated. To cite Gadamer, "A horizon is not a rigid frontier, but something that moves with one and invites one to advance further" (*TM*, 217).

Unlike the center of the morphologically conceived structure, the center of a horizon is not outside the horizon at all but precisely *within* the horizon, and it is *not* a fixed center. It is a movable (indeed, always moving) point of reference from which the play of whatever is found within the horizon occurs. This center does control the play of whatever occurs within the horizon insofar as the play is accessible only from a certain vantage point, but this vantage point changes and so does the play.

Gadamer departs from Dilthey, however, by concluding that this view of horizons entails that interpretation promotes a fusion of horizons. He argues that historically distant horizons are not hermetically sealed but are continuous with our own, stating that "the historical movement of human life consists in the fact that it is never utterly bound to any one standpoint, and hence can never have a truly closed horizon" (*TM*, 271).

36. It is interesting to recall that Dilthey's notion of spatiality is first practical. The geometrical view of space is an abstraction. See Chapter 2, above.

37. The metaphor of the horizon has been widely criticized as one-sidedly visual in its approach to hermeneutic experience and as bound to transcendental philosophy. Poststructuralism replaces the horizon with the text as the basic interpretive category and in the process distances the interpretive process from subjectivity. Calvin Schrag offers as an alternative to both these the metaphor of texture, arguing that texts and actions are each objects of interpretation and that texture is a fundamental structure underlying both. Texture has the advantage of applying to a broader range of experience (auditory and tactile as well as visual) and to the structures of texts. See his *Communicative Praxis*, pp. 23–25.

The prejudices that constitute a past horizon influence the prejudices underlying our own horizon and result in a larger, more comprehensive context for understanding.

Dilthey, as we have seen, would insist that past horizons can in certain ways be viewed as complete wholes. The fact that we understand other horizons from within a historical horizon ourselves does not necessitate a fusion of horizons. Rather, our own changing historical situation, values, purposes, and theoretical structures lead us to focus on different aspects of the past. These shifts of focal point change the interaction of the parts of this past whole but do not add to them. Thus, although the interpretation of the past must remain an unfinished task, the past itself imposes limits on our understanding of it. Whether such limits can provide for some kind of objectivity in historical understanding is a topic for the next chapter, where I turn to a closer analysis of the process of understanding itself.

Chapter Five

〜〜〜〜〜〜〜〜〜〜〜〜〜〜〜〜〜〜〜〜〜〜〜〜〜〜〜〜〜〜〜〜〜〜〜

Historical Understanding and Historical Consciousness

In the preceding chapters I demonstrated that human lives have a narrative structure and that these narratives are made possible by the matrix of dynamic sociohistorical settings within which these lives unfold. That is, we understand others by placing their expressions, words, and deeds in the broader context of their lives as well as in the larger sociohistorical contexts in which they are involved either consciously or unconsciously. But we who understand are also immersed in a finite sociohistorical context, and our very understanding is conditioned by our historical situatedness. Accordingly, understanding is facilitated, but also apparently complicated, by our situatedness in a limited sociohistorical context. Making use of our own context may seem a barrier to understanding persons and events of the past on their own terms, and in a certain sense it is. But this is not a shortcoming of historical understanding, for its task is not to capture a historically distant life as it was in itself.[1]

Historical understanding is inseparable from an understanding of the unfolding of our own lives, and thus we are never interested in the lives of others merely on their own terms. We understand others relative to the concerns of our own existence. Dilthey, however, repeatedly insists on the objectivity of historical understanding. This leads Gadamer to assess Dilthey's commitment to objectivity as an inconsistency best discarded altogether. In contrast, I will show that Dilthey went some way toward transforming the notion of objectivity in a way that is consistent with the historical character of human existence.[2]

1. Contemporary historians have largely abandoned the "noble dream" of objectivity. Peter Novick traces the declining fortunes of the notion of historical objectivity among professional historians in *That Noble Dream: The "Objectivity Question" and the American Historical Profession* (Cambridge: Cambridge University Press, 1988). But Dilthey's concern for objectivity should not be confused with the Enlightenment ideal rejected by many of today's historians.

2. Thomas J. Young has argued that Dilthey's theory of worldviews undercuts objectivism. He fails to point out, however, the ways in which Dilthey secures a transformed notion

This can be seen especially when we consider the importance of Dilthey's aesthetics for his theory of understanding.[3] For Dilthey, the poet's creative act not only best exemplifies the historical structure of human praxis but also serves to elucidate the very nature of *Verstehen*, or historical understanding, and its internal relation to lived experience. Dilthey's view of poetic expression underwent significant changes that are correlative to developments in his theory of understanding. His initial conception of poetic expression is systematically detailed in "The Imagination of the Poet: Elements for a Poetics" (1887), and his later position is sketched in his attempt to revise this work in "Fragments for a Poetics" (1907–8).[4] Rodi characterizes the development of Dilthey's aesthetics primarily in terms of a shift in methodology.[5] He maintains that Dilthey's "Poetics" contains a kind of morphology and that literary expressions are described in terms of fixed psychological types with reference to which variations among these expressions may be explained. Dilthey's later aesthetics, however, is more hermeneutical and historical; understanding, Rodi claims, assumes an existential character. Makkreel, although recognizing these shifts, has argued for more continuity in Dilthey's theory of understanding by correlating its development with the move from descriptive psychology to anthropological reflection.[6] I will go further by showing that this move provides a notion of historical understanding which belies Gadamer's well-known criticism that Dilthey's hermeneutics operates only at a methodological, epistemological level. As I shall show, Dilthey's hermeneutics also operates at a philosophical level as it analyzes the structures of life itself.[7]

---

of objectivity in his aesthetic writings. See his "The Hermeneutic Significance of Dilthey's Theory of World-Views," *International Philosophical Quarterly* 23 (1983): 125–140, especially p. 135.

3. By Dilthey's own admission, the aesthetic writings play an especially important role in the critique (*SW*, 5:35–36; *GS*, 6:108–109). Georg Misch briefly notes the importance of Dilthey's aesthetics for his conception of life; see his introduction to *GS*, 5:ix. Makkreel has made the most extensive use of Dilthey's aesthetics for the purposes of clarifying the notion of historical understanding. He also argues that historical judgment in Dilthey should be conceived in relation to Kant's reflective judgment as exhibited in aesthetic and teleological judgment. See Makkreel, *Dilthey, Philosopher of the Human Studies*, chapter 5.

4. *SW*, 5:29–173, 221–231. For convenience, I will abbreviate these essays as "Poetics" and "Fragments," respectively.

5. Frithjof Rodi, *Morphologie und Hermeneutik: Zur Methode von Diltheys Aesthetik* (Stuttgart: W. Kohlhammer Verlag, 1969).

6. Makkreel, *Dilthey, Philosopher of the Human Studies*, p. 380.

7. For Gadamer's distinction between traditional and philosophical hermeneutics, see *Wahrheit und Methode*, pp. 245ff., and *TM*, pp. 230ff. Frithjof Rodi confronts Gadamer's

The Psychohistorical Approach

In the 1880s and 1890s, Dilthey concentrated largely on the psychological processes involved in understanding and traced the understanding of others to apprehension in inner and outer perception. Understanding the other is a sort of inductive, analogical process. We first recognize in ourselves, through reflexive awareness, the connections between bodily gestures and psychic states. This is not to say that we intuit and then synthesize isolated psychic elements. They are given as internally related in our awareness of ourselves (*SW*, 1:388–389; *GS*, 19:223–324). Connections such as that between grief and tears experienced within ourselves are then projected in the understanding of other persons. That is, on the basis of our lived experience of the connection of our own bodily gestures and psychological states, we associate the gestures, given in outer sense, of other persons to general types, crying for instance. We then assess the degree to which the particular instance approximates the general concept ("bereaved person") and associate with this outer appearance an inner reality appropriate to the degree to which the outer appearance matches the concept (*SW*, 1:388–389; *GS*, 19:223–224).[8] The reproduction of these inner states may be more or less clear. The clearer and more comprehensive our understanding of the *context* of the inner state, the clearer the reproduction of this psychic state (*SW*, 1:389–390; *GS*, 19:224–225). Every state is determined by its place in the larger nexus of psychic life. As a result, I am able to broaden my understanding of the other's psychic life by situating the state in question within my own psychic nexus and then transposing it to his or hers.

---

claim that philosophical hermeneutics "overcomes" traditional hermeneutics by providing a "metacritique" of Gadamer's criticism of Dilthey's views of science and objectivity; see "Hermeneutics and the Meaning of Life: A Critique of Gadamer's Interpretation of Dilthey," in *Hermeneutics and Deconstruction*, ed. Hugh J. Silverman and Don Ihde (Albany: State University of New York Press, 1985), pp. 82–90. This is not to say that Dilthey failed to produce methodological advances in hermeneutics. See Thomas M. Seebohm, "Boeckh and Dilthey: The Development of Methodical Hermeneutics," *Man and World* 17 (1984): 325–346.

8. There are some parallels here with the analysis of our apprehension of the Other by Edmund Husserl in *Cartesian Meditations: An Introduction to Phenomenology*, trans. Dorion Cairns (The Hague: Martinus Nijhoff, 1977), pp. 112–116, and *Ideen zu einer reinen Phänomenologie und phänomenologischen Philosophie*, bk. 2, ed. Marly Biemel (The Hague: Martinus Nijhoff, 1952), p. 166. Both begin with our own experience of the compresence of psyche and body and move by way of analogy to the consciousness of the other. Unlike Husserl, however, Dilthey restricts his analysis to empirical rather than transcendental consciousness. See Chapter 1, above.

This analogical model seems of little help to a theory of historical understanding. It is devoted largely to accounting for our everyday understanding of the bodily gestures and facial expressions of those around us. Because our practical interests are often involved in such judgments, they are likely to be limited in their objectivity by our biases. Further, historians are only rarely contemporaneous with their subjects and do not generally seek to understand simple gestures and facial expressions. Dilthey does not, however, imply that bodily gestures and facial expressions are the fundamental data of historiography. Rather, he suggests that the same analogical method at work in everyday understanding is sharpened and formalized in historiographical study.

Dilthey brings this same analogical structure to his understanding of the poetic genius but provides further psychological tools to account for the social and historical determinants of meaning and moves to a more sophisticated object of study. In the "Poetics," Dilthey attempts a psychological explanation of the creative act and gives a central role in this explanation to the acquired psychic nexus. As we saw in Chapter 3, this acquired psychic nexus is a gradually developed and constantly developing structural whole that may be viewed as the continuing influence of the individual's past on lived experience. Like lived experience, the acquired psychic nexus is not composed merely of representations but is a tripartite structure in which perceptions and ideas always have an internal relation to volitions and emotions. Further, this acquired nexus consists not only of the contents of our past experiences, but as Dilthey states, "These connections are just as real as the contents" (*SW*, 5:72; *GS*, 6:143). Past experiences are not merely juxtaposed in memory. Rather, they are parts of an integrated whole of real relations acquired gradually over time. As present experiences fade into the past, they are related to other past experiences that exhibit similar structural relations between representations, emotions, and volitions. These structurally similar experiences form an organized system of typical relations between representations, feelings, and volitions. This structural nexus then affects the present by ordering stimuli according to these typical relations, acting as a kind of subconscious worldview composed of our past experiences (*SW*, 5:72; *GS*, 6:143). Because it is the product of the individual's evaluative, purposive interaction with the historical and natural environment, the acquired psychic nexus structurally represents the historical world as assimilated by a particular individual. Thus, through this acquired nexus, the historical world orders and structures our experience by providing the backdrop of prejudgments for knowledge, the context that gives our feelings significance in the whole of our lives, and the constancy of the system of ends required to ground our search for means.

The influence of the acquired psychic nexus on poetic creation is best illustrated by the image-forming process called completion. Through this process the poet transforms an image by presenting its internal relation to the private, inner life of feelings and will. Poets can complete an image in two ways. Either they animate an already given outer shape by filling in its effect on our emotional lives and the volitional response called forth by this effect, or they begin with moods and feelings and find outer shapes that adequately portray the stimuli which stirred such feelings and the overt behavior resulting from a volitional response (*SW*, 5:104; *GS*, 6:175). The former case is exemplified by Shakespeare's dramatization of historical events and Dickens's portrayal of life in London, and the latter, by Goethe's *Faust*. Poets draw these relations of feeling and willing to images from their own past experiences as organized in the acquired psychic nexus.

Unlike the British associationists, Dilthey did not view images as self-enclosed, changeless atoms but as parts of a mental whole. They are internally related to the rest of the psychic nexus, and their meaning is a matter of their position in this matrix of relations. Creation entails the transformation of images "in their nucleus" (*SW*, 5:104; *GS*, 6:175). This transformation is accomplished via an articulation of the ways in which the entire psychic nexus intersects in this image. The image is like a crossing-point where the diverse strands of the acquired psychic nexus are pulled together and brought to a sharper focus. This focusing tells us "what is essential about a state of affairs" (*SW*, 5:104; *GS*, 6:175). That is, the image is situated in its place in the psychic nexus, and at the same time, this nexus is made more articulate through the image.

Poetic images function, then, to articulate the unity of the individual's psychic life. An image acts as a focal point around which acquired experiences are gathered, as it were, and through which their internal relations are made determinate. The manifoldness of the individual's experiences is maintained, and at the same time these many experiences are unified by being brought to bear on the same image. It is important to keep in mind, however, that the nexus being unified is psycho*historical* in character.[9]

9. Makkreel and Rodi also stress this in their introduction to *SW*, 5:8.

The theory of understanding proposed in the "Poetics" is the correlate of this conception of poetic image formation. Understanding the poetic image is a matter of allowing it to excite the same processes in yourself as were active in the poet in the act of creation and that permeate the poetic image. Just as the image acts to draw together the strands of the acquired psychic nexus of the poet, it excites in the interpreter these same psychological processes and allows for a kind of reproduction by the interpreter of the acquired nexus of the poet. This is not to say that this reproduction is an exact replication. But Dilthey argues that at least some imaginative approximation of the other's acquired nexus is possible on the basis of the presumed universality of human psychic structure.[10] Because this acquired nexus is psychohistorical in character, this reproduction is not only an understanding of the individual's mental state but also of the way in which this individual was situated in the sociohistorical milieu.

This formulation of historical understanding, however, is unsatisfactory. According to Dilthey, the acquired psychic nexus is shaped by the individual's interaction with the historical life-nexus, and the poetic expression is the product of this acquired nexus. Thus the relation of the work to the historical life-nexus is always mediated by the psychic nexus of the individual. Although this may seem true from the standpoint of creation, it is most assuredly not the case from the standpoint of understanding. It is not necessary to use the individual's psychic structure as the intermediate link between the work and the historical world to understand the meaning of the work. To take an obvious case in point, the rules of grammar are always applied in the understanding of a linguistic expression, but it is not necessary to impose the author's knowledge of grammar between the work and the world to understand the work. Indeed, the expression's meaning is shaped by sociohistorical contexts and systems that were not operative in the poet's psychological creative process. Although Dilthey sought to provide a foundation for understanding the historical significance of poetic expressions, he initially narrowed the possible meanings of the expressions to those which can be arrived at by using the subject's psychological nexus as the definitive context. Defining the work's reference to the historical world through the acquired

10. Raymond Aron has referred to this as an analogical theory of understanding according to which understanding the other's expression is done on analogy with our own experience. See Aron, *La philosophie critique de l'histoire: Essai sur une théorie allemande de l'histoire,* 2d ed. (Paris: Librairie Philosophique J. Vrin, 1950), p. 79.

psychic nexus restricts the meaning of the expression to the psychological context of the poet at the expense of other significant contexts.

The Turn to Hermeneutics

In "The Rise of Hermeneutics" (1900), Dilthey turns from psychological description to the interpretation of written expressions. He asserts that the written expression is the most articulate form of life and hence the most promising object of human scientific research.[11] But this does not signal a complete abandonment of psychological analysis. It would be more accurate to say that in this essay Dilthey began to see the limits of the value of both descriptive analysis of the psychic structure of human life and the analogical analysis of action associated with it for the study of history. This is not to say that he utterly rejected these. Rather, he began to try both to find a method more adequately suited to historical research and to find the proper role for phenomenological analyses of psychic structure and action.

Dilthey does clearly call into question the capacity of descriptive psychology alone to grasp the individuality of others or even of ourselves: "Inner experience, in which I am reflexively aware of my own states, can never of itself [*für sich*] bring my own individuality to consciousness for me" (*GS*, 5:318). Phenomenological analysis cannot "of itself" deliver individuality, but this does not mean that it is not involved at all. Even in the *Introduction* Dilthey had recognized that psychological analysis provides only a structural framework and must be filled in by other forms of human scientific research. But, there, psychological analysis was thought to precede sociohistorical analyses. Now Dilthey insists from the first that a comparative psychological-historical analysis provides access to individuality: "Only in the comparison of myself with others do I pro-

11. Paul Redding argues that language serves a transcendental or universal function for Dilthey. See Redding, "Action, Language, and Text: Dilthey's Conception of Understanding," *Philosophy and Social Criticism* 9 (1982): 239. This is perhaps too strong, as it might suggest a linguistic turn similar to that of Heidegger, Gadamer, or even Karl-Otto Apel. For Dilthey, language remains a function of life. Redding's suggestion that understanding actions involves their textualization, that is, their linguistic articulation, is considerably more helpful. As Michael Ermarth remarks, "Dilthey emphasized the constitutive role of language in the formation" of objective spirit, but this does not mean that the human sciences became a "science of language." See Ermarth, "The Transformation of Hermeneutics: Nineteenth-Century Ancients and Twentieth-Century Moderns," *Monist* 64 (April 1984): 183; cf. his *Dilthey: The Critique of Historical Reason*, pp. 235–236, 278–280.

duce in myself the experience [*Erfahrung*] of the individual in me; I only become aware of that which diverges from others in my own existence [*Dasein*]" (*GS*, 5:318). Individuality is then clearly a matter of *individuation* from others, and only a comparative method captures this differentiation.[12] The analysis of psychic structure still plays some role in historical understanding, but it is now paired with hermeneutics in a largely unspecified way. In Dilthey's words, "Along with the analysis of inner experience appears that of understanding, and both together give proof for the human sciences of the *possibility* and *limits* of universal knowledge in them, insofar as this is determined by the way in which psychic facts are originally given to us" (*GS*, 5:320). Regardless of the questionable status of descriptive psychology, it is clear that Dilthey continues to seek some access to life as lived by individuals and continues to view the sensory manifestations of others as the embodiment of their psychological inwardness. Dilthey writes: "But alien existence is at first given to us from the outside only in sensory facts, in gestures, tones, and actions. We first complete the inner nexus [*das Innere*] through a process of reproduction of what falls within the senses in individual signs" (*GS*, 5:318). Psychological states can be understood through actions, gestures, and so on. The process of understanding, however, no longer begins with the interpreter's inner experience but with the interpretation of objectifications of psychic life. It is "the process through which we know something inner from signs that are given from outside in the senses" (*GS*, 5:318). Understanding others as well as ourselves works on the same model. We work backward from objects given in the senses to a psychological nexus from which they arose. "Thus we call understanding the process in which we know from sensibly given signs something psychical whose expression they are" (*GS*, 5:318).

Dilthey's reformulation of understanding in "The Rise of Hermeneutics" is a first step in overcoming the tendency found in his psychological writings to interpret human gestures and actions from the overly narrow perspective of the individual's psychological nexus. Dilthey retains the view that understanding, at least in its prescientific form, is a kind of practical, social activity.[13] He writes, "Our action everywhere presup-

12. Dilthey began working out this position in an essay on comparative psychology of 1896 (*GS*, 5:241–316).

13. This point is widely recognized. Cf. Redding, "Action, Language, and Text," pp. 234–235; Plantinga, *Historical Understanding*, pp. 90–91; and Stanley Corngold, "Dilthey's Essay *The Poetic Imagination: A Poetics of Force*," *Interpretation* 9 (1980–81): 305.

poses our understanding of others" (*GS*, 5:317). But he will from this point on focus increasingly on the objective conditions of understanding. That is, human interaction is often if not always a kind of communicative interaction that presupposes a common context. Dilthey will work this insight out more fully in the *Aufbau*, where, as we have seen in the preceding chapter, he comes to see the meaning-producing function of systems of influences. At this stage, this theory of understanding is confronted with two unresolved difficulties. First, because it is modeled on the understanding of contemporaries with a common context, it fails to account for understanding a historically distant agent in a different context. Second, linking understanding to the task of finding an "appropriate response"[14] in our communicative interactions involves the bias we often have as a result of our interest in the outcome of such interactions. In the continuation of the *Aufbau*, Dilthey will find it useful to distinguish forms of understanding in order to address precisely these problems. But in this essay Dilthey claims that the same process of *Verstehen* is involved in the full range of communicative action: "Understanding extends from the comprehension of childish babbling to that of Hamlet or the critique of reason" (*GS*, 5:318). Understanding is differentiated only by degrees according to the level of interest in the object (*GS*, 5:319). Lower interest results in lower attention, which further results in a lower degree of understanding. Only with a fixed objectification of life is the highest degree of attention, hence understanding, possible (*GS*, 5:319). Analysis of this type is properly called interpretation (*GS*, 5:319). There are, of course, many kinds of fixed expressions—architecture, painting, music, and so on. But because language brings human existence to its clearest articulation, literature holds a central position in the human sciences. "The immense significance of literature for our understanding of mental [*geistigen*] life and history rests in the fact that the inner life of humans [*das menschliche Innere*] finds its most complete, creative, and objectively understandable expression only in language. So, the art of understanding has its middle point in the exegesis or *interpretation of the remnants of human existence contained in writing*" (*GS*, 5:319).

Dilthey's well-known dictum that the human scientist is able "to understand the author better than he understood himself" (*GS*, 5:331)—commonly referred to as *Besserverstehen*—derives from his view that written expressions reveal more than introspection. This in turn requires a

---

14. Redding discusses this point very clearly in "Action, Language, and Text," p. 235.

theory of the genesis of expressions that accounts for their superiority to introspection. But in "The Rise of Hermeneutics," Dilthey says little more than that the principle of *Besserverstehen* is primarily a consequence of "the doctrine of unconscious creation" (*GS*, 5:331), which suggests that he is still largely influenced by Friedrich Schleiermacher's focus on the author as psychological nexus. As I shall show, Dilthey's later elaboration of the theory of expression leads him away from construing meaning as personal and psychological toward viewing it as an impersonal, socio-historically constituted structure of the expression.

Expression, Lived Experience, and Understanding

Dilthey distinguishes more precisely the kinds of expressions and the kinds of understanding correlated with each in his sketches toward the continuation of the *Aufbau*. Expressions are sensible objects that convey a spiritual meaning; they are the "expression of a spiritual meaning [*Ausdruck eines Geistigen*]" ("Understanding Other Persons," 123; *GS*, 7:205). Expressions are no longer viewed as *only* or even primarily the objectification of a personal, psychological nexus. They embody an impersonal, sociohistorically constituted meaning. Three classes of expressions exist.

First, there are purely intellectual expressions—the conceptual constructs that make up the component parts of science. Such expressions are completely abstracted from the lived experience in which they arose, and their meaning is independent of the life-context in which they occur. They can be transferred from one person or sociohistorical context to another without loss or addition of meaning. "The judgment is the same for him who asserts it and him who understands it; it moves, as if transported, unaltered from the possession of one to the other" (*GS*, 7:205; "Understanding Other Persons," 124). The understanding appropriate to such expression is at once the most complete and the most impoverished. Because this form of understanding focuses only on the intellectual content of the expression, it can attain a stable meaning, one that will not vary with context. This very characteristic of the intellectual expression, however, entails that nothing of the life-contexts of the one asserting the expression is opened up. "Understanding is here focused upon the mere thought-content, which is itself the same in every context, and so the understanding here is more complete than it is in regard to any other expression of life. At the same time, however, this understanding says nothing to him who apprehends about its relations to the dark background and the fullness of psychic life" (*GS*, 7:206; "Understanding Other Persons," 124).

Actions form the second class of expressions. According to Dilthey, actions are not communicative but purposive in their structure: "An action does not originate from an intention to communicate, but because of its relation to a purpose, this purpose is given through it" ("Understanding Other Persons," 124; *GS*, 7:206). There are, of course, actions that have communication as an intentional aim.[15] Dilthey, however, is referring to a class of actions whose primary function is achieving some end other than communication, such as driving a car, mowing the lawn, or operating a machine. Because actions occur in common contexts of equipment and ends, their purposiveness "is given through" the action—the action itself exhibits a purposive structure. Actions thus have a human or spiritual meaning insofar as they indicate an involvement in concrete contexts. Dilthey readily admits that the involvement of any particular action within any particular context or set of contexts cannot always be determined with complete certainty, so the connection of an action to a human meaning "allows for probable assumption" only ("Understanding Other Persons," 124; *GS*, 7:206). Understanding an action requires us to distinguish between the conditions of the psychic life of the agent and the larger context of the life-nexus which grounds this psychic condition. Actions express only one aspect of our existence. This one-dimensionality results from the fact that these expressions are determined by their participation in one or another social context. "Through the power of a determining motive, the deed moves out of the fullness of life into one-sidedness. However we may construe this, it accordingly expresses yet only one part of our essence [*Wesen*]" ("Understanding Other Persons," 124; *GS*, 7:206). The inner life of the agent is not revealed in its fullness, only to the degree that this action expresses a particular motive or need vis-à-vis the sociohistorical context.

The third class of expression Dilthey calls *Erlebnisausdruck*, or expression of lived experience. In Dilthey's words, "There is a special relation between it, the life from which it sprang, and the understanding which it brings about" ("Understanding Other Persons," 124; *GS*, 7:206). Such expressions bring lived experience to a more determinate focus than is

---

15. The work of Jürgen Habermas, Schrag, H. P. Grice, and John Searle (to name just a few) has been devoted in large part to communicative action.

available to self-reflection. "The expression can indeed contain more of the psychic nexus than any introspection can reveal. It raises life out of depths which are unilluminated by consciousness" ("Understanding Other Persons," 124; *GS*, 7:206). Unlike theoretical and practical expressions, expressions of lived experience can communicate life in its fullness. Dilthey works out this third notion of expression most clearly in his later aesthetics. In the "Fragments," Dilthey retains the same notion of the function of poetry as he presented in the "Poetics," that is, that poetry articulates life, but his view of the character of the nexus being articulated is dramatically altered. As a result, his conception of this articulation process and his theory of understanding are also revised. Central to Dilthey's new approach to poetics is his turn away from psychological explanations of the creative process in favor of an analysis of the value and meaning relations found in poetic expressions themselves. The creative act is no longer viewed as the articulation of the individual's acquired psychic nexus but as an expression of lived experience. The term "lived experience" receives a more precise and less subjectivistic definition than that found in the psychological writings and is defined structurally in relation to its objective expressions.[16] As Dilthey writes, "Lived experience generates its own expressions" (*SW*, 5:229; *GS*, 6:318). Expression is not merely an external representation of lived experience. It is a necessary part of the life process by which the relations inherent in lived experience are made articulate.

Lived experience is a component part of life. And, as shall be discussed more fully below, the term "life" itself no longer narrowly refers to the psychic nexus of an individual but to larger sociohistorical systems of influences (*Wirkungszusammenhänge*) as well. As parts of larger wholes, lived experiences are internally related to one another. Each lived experience thus may be viewed "as a function" of larger contexts of life (*SW*, 5:224; *GS*, 6:314). Correlatively, each lived experience is a "structural nexus" whose components—representational, volitional, and emotional acts and their correlative object—are understandable only with reference to that larger nexus; further, lived experiences are qualitatively differentiated precisely by the different way in which these structural components are related or intertwined (*SW*, 5:224; *GS*, 6:314).

---

16. For a detailed analysis of the development of the concept of *Erlebnis*, see Karol Sauerland, *Diltheys Erlebnisbegriff: Entstehung, Glanzzeit, und Verkümmerung eines literaturhistorischen Begriffs* (Berlin: Walter de Gruyter, 1972).

But the unity of lived experience is diachronic as well as synchronic. Lived experience "already contains in itself past and future within its consciousness of the present" (*SW*, 5:225; *GS*, 6:314). The past and the future reside in the present as representations of reality. But, these representations are not merely passive contents of lived experience. The past "is experienced as a force reaching into the present" (*SW*, 5:226; *GS*, 6:315). It is "drawn or incorporated into" the present as an effective "presence" (*SW*, 5:226; *GS*, 6:315).[17] Those past lived experiences structurally related to the present one are drawn into the present, thus creating a temporal whole. Perceptions and feelings in the present can serve as a focal point that brings past lived experiences to a new unity.

As we saw in Chapter 3, Dilthey contends that the relation between lived experiences is characterized by the dual impulse to expand the variety of experiences (explication) and to unify these experiences into recurring themes (implication) (*SW*, 5:227; *GS*, 6:316). Though not specifically stated by Dilthey, the existing text suggests that the poet's expression can be viewed as an extension of the life-impulse toward the unification of the diverse elements of lived experience. The poet's expression is a most articulate form in which the past is "drawn into" the present and life is made more determinate. Expressions can be seen as turning points or endings of a sort, that is, junctures at which prior lived experiences are brought into a unity. We may work backward from these points, interpreting lived experiences as leading up to them, as it were.

Dilthey's essay on Goethe in *Das Erlebnis und die Dichtung* clarifies the nature of expression as "implication" on the basis of another aspect of lived experience.[18] There, Dilthey claims that lived experience is constituted most primordially by what he calls life-relations (*Lebensbezüge*). The individual life is a crossing-point of a multitude of purposive and evaluative relations between I and world, and lived experience is the reflexive and reflective awareness of these relations. Lived experience is not a copy of these relations or something over against them but rather the process by which life-relations reveal themselves.

These life-relations link the poet to an objective network of more or less

17. This notion of presence is not fixed but dynamic. Thus, it has nothing to do with the concept of presence repeatedly criticized by Derrida.

18. Wilhelm Dilthey, "Goethe und die dichterische Phantasie," in *ED*, pp. 124–186; translated as "Goethe and the Poetic Imagination," in *SW*, 5:235–302. This essay originally appeared in 1877 and again in revised form in 1905 in the first edition of *ED*. The text referred to here is Dilthey's final revision of the essay for the third edition in 1910.

encompassing sociohistorical contexts or systems of influence, and expressions bring the interrelations of these systems in the life of the poet to a sharper focus. These systems range from the least encompassing—the individual human life—to the most encompassing—objective spirit. The latter is not a monolithic whole in which all smaller systems are totalized. On the contrary, these systems each develop at different rates and according to their own rules. Consequently, they can stand in tension with each other—for example, individuals can be out of step with their times. Objective spirit is best thought of as the broadest public context within which an expression may be situated. Thus, expressions may be said to articulate the relations between contrasting or conflicting systems without implying their totalization and without being a mere reflex of context. That is, these lived relations are drawn together by the poet: "Lived relations govern the poetic imagination and come to expression in it" (*SW*, 5:242; *ED*, 131). The poet already exists in a world of lived relations, and the creative act is one of bringing this world to a level of greater determinacy in language. "The poetic world is there before any particular event inspires the poet with the conception of a work and before he writes down its first line" (*SW*, 5:243; *ED*, 131). Not the externalization of something internal, the poetic expression is instead the articulation of a nexus of lived relations within which the poet is already situated but of which he is only indeterminately aware. But the life made articulate by the poet is not necessarily his or her own. Poetic experience is impersonal—the poetic imagination is capable not only of making more articulate the social and historical relations in which the poet is enmeshed but also of bringing together typical ways of living or life-relations in the unity of character, action, plot, and setting.

Thus, the poetic "implication" of lived experience, this drawing of the past into the present, not only makes individual human life, but also life viewed as more-encompassing nexuses, more determinate. "Every genuine poetic work accentuates some characteristic of life which has not been seen in this way before" (*SW*, 5:251; *ED*, 139). It presents a way of being situated within a life-world of values, meanings, means, and ends. Poetry, indeed any expression of lived experience, is more than merely the articulation of an individual's psychic life as was the case in the original version of the "Poetics." The articulation of the effective presence of the past in an individual's life brings to a sharper focus not only that individual's psychological nexus but also the typical ways in which individuals can stand in conflict or coalesce with larger sociohistorical systems. As a result, these systems are themselves made more determinate.

Elementary and Higher Understanding

In his sketches toward the continuation of the *Aufbau*, Dilthey continues to emphasize that understanding is rooted in our everyday social interaction with one another: "Understanding first arises in the interests of practical life. Here, people interact with one another. They make themselves understandable to each other. One must know what the other is up to" ("Understanding Other Persons," 125; *GS*, 7:207). As long as understanding is involved with actions and utterances in our own sociohistorical context, our interpretations will be guided by the assumptions that constitute this context and will be biased by our interests in the results of our own and the other's actions. Our everyday understanding of contemporaries remains largely driven by practical considerations; consequently, our understanding generally makes use only of contemporary assumptions and remains relative to our peculiar interests. But Dilthey seeks to show that in historical understanding we are capable of bringing to bear the contexts and assumptions of the past to determine the meaning of expressions in a disinterested way. His distinction between elementary and higher understanding is in part an attempt to show precisely this.

Elementary understanding involves the comprehension of "simple expressions," that is, single expressions such as words, facial expressions, gestures, and actions like swinging a hammer. In such expressions the sensory objectification of life and the spiritual meaning expressed in it "are completely fused into a unity" ("Understanding Other Persons," 128; *GS*, 7:210). This spiritual meaning says nothing about the individuality of the user of the expression, the particularity of her or his sociohistorical context, or the larger life-nexus within which this expression resides. In elementary understanding such expressions are taken to be regularly recurring types that occur in contexts common to both the user and the interpreter.

It is important to keep in mind that Dilthey's sketch of the meaning of simple expressions does not follow the Husserlian model of expression criticized by Derrida for its dependence on presence.[19] In the *Logical Investigations*, Husserl distinguishes expressions from mere signs. Signs indicate something that is not present, whereas expressions are signs bestowed with meaning by the intentional act of a subject. Meaning is

---

19. Derrida attacks the phonocentrism of Husserl's *Logical Investigations* in *Speech and Phenomena*. See especially pp. 70–87.

then ultimately a function of subjectivity.[20] In contrast, Dilthey traces the meaning of expressions to a shared group of practices, and this group of practices, and hence the meaning of expressions, is not reducible to subjective meaning-conferring acts. In elementary understanding, expressions are given as part of an established nexus of human praxis. Dilthey makes the point clearly with respect to the meaning of simple actions: "The crafts have developed in different lands definite procedures and definite instruments for attaining an end, and from these the end becomes understandable to us when we see the craftsman use hammer or saw. In every case, the relation between the expression of life and its human meaning is here established through an order within a shared context" ("Understanding Other Persons," 128; *GS*, 7:209). Dilthey's point is similar to Heidegger's claim that equipment always involves a totality of equipment. Picking up any tool involves us in a network of tools and tasks to be done which make this very tool what it is. Similarly, any expression and understanding at all is made possible by our situatedness in a common, historically developed context. "Before he learns to speak, the child is completely immersed in the medium of common contexts. And he learns to understand gestures and facial expression, motions and exclamations, words and sentences only because they confront him as being always the same, and as always bearing the same relation to that which they signify and express. In this way, the individual becomes oriented in the world of objective spirit" ("Understanding Other Persons," 127; *GS*, 7:208–209).

Understanding first becomes problematic and higher understanding first emerges with the introduction of difference: "The greater the distance between a given expression and him who understands, the more often uncertainties arise" ("Understanding Other Persons," 128; *GS*, 7:210). The most common and perhaps least problematic instance is a deviation in the common usage of gesture, deed, or word. When words and deeds stand in tension with each other or facial expressions belie words, we are brought up short, as it were. These expressions are no longer obvious in their meaning, and we have recourse to other expressions or the larger context in order to make sense of them.

But higher understanding is brought about not only by the negative experience of contradiction but also as a function of the exigencies of practical life. Our interactions with others in everyday life are not limited

---

20. Husserl, *Logical Investigations*, sections 7–9, pp. 276–281.

to the interpretations of isolated gestures, actions, or facial expressions. In work situations or friendships we must regularly assess "the character and capacities of the individual person" ("Understanding Other Persons," 129; *GS*, 7:210–211). We must regularly assess how much to trust others and gauge their reliability and integrity. Such judgments are made with reference to larger contexts of life, for example, family, profession, and the like, and they intersect in a single individual. "What we have in mind here therefore is an inductive inference from particular expression of life to the whole of the life-context. Its presupposition is knowledge of psychic life and its relations to milieu and circumstances" ("Understanding Other Persons," 129; *GS*, 7:211). We assume a purposive psychic context within which these larger contexts intersect. This interpretive process is never complete, and "certainty cannot be attained" ("Understanding Other Persons," 129; *GS*, 7:211). Because it arises from the requirements of interacting with contemporary agents in a shared context, this form of understanding is not appropriate for historical understanding. Although our communicative interactions with others are by the interest of determining the proper course of action in response to their actions, this is usually not the case for the historian. Further, this everyday, practical understanding is inevitably biased by our own subjective interest in the outcome of the interaction with the other person. Accordingly, Dilthey introduces disinterestedness in the understanding of expressions of lived experience such as dramas or lyric poems as the model for historical understanding.

Higher understanding has up to this point differed from elementary understanding only in its use of more particular contexts and of related expressions to help determine the meaning of an expression. Understanding expressions of lived experience is the highest level of understanding, and it consists of a *Nacherleben,* or re-experiencing, which involves the production and the reading of a narrative.[21] Dilthey cites the example of understanding a play. We understand by tracing the connections between characters, action, and setting as they fold together in the

21. Redding also characterizes historical understanding as a kind of reading, and on this basis he criticizes Dilthey's view for making the historian a detached observer of historical events: "The reader is removed from both the writer and that which is written about. . . . We relive the lives of others at the cost of the temporary suspension of our own" ("Action, Language, and Text," p. 242). But reading is not always detached as Redding suggests. Reading can bring the object written about close to and can affect the reader. We can all be quite stirred by action we read about. Also, the reading itself of *Nacherleben* leads to writing, namely, the writing of a historical narrative that is our own.

developing plot, not by referring to the mind of the playwright. Determining the meaning of simple expressions does not require that the interpreter explicitly refer back to a whole of which it is a part, even though understanding always presupposes a context. But in its highest form, understanding involves an imaginative reproduction of the temporal whole in which meanings develop. In *Nacherleben,* meanings and values are re-created by the interpreter in their living dynamism. We imaginatively animate the characters and their interactions with one another and their milieu. Words and deeds develop meaning and value as their significance in the unfolding narrative emerges ("Understanding Other Persons," 130; *GS,* 7:211–212).

The process of *Nacherleben* is modeled after the process of poetic expression. As we have seen, the poetic expression is the embodiment and articulation of the interaction of a number of sociohistorical, meaning-constituting systems. The poet provides us with an expression of "the most vivid experience of the interconnectedness of our existential relations in the meaning of life" (*SW,* 5:238; *ED,* 127). Most expressions are the product of the limited standpoint, interests, and prejudices of its time. Dilthey sees clearly that this leads to a certain relativism: "There is something frightful about this, since in the struggle of practical interests, any expression can deceive, and the interpretation can be altered by a change in viewpoint" ("Understanding Other Persons," 125; *GS,* 7:207). However, great works, so Dilthey claims, escape this relativistic play of interest by virtue of the disinterestedness of poetic experience. In such works "a spiritual meaning is set free from its creator"; they "say nothing whatever about its author" ("Understanding Other Persons," 125; *GS,* 7:207). Poets draw on the life-relations within which they reside, but they transform them imaginatively into structures of life which are not merely personal but universal, that is, impersonal. Thus, even though the creative process arises from the concrete life-relations of the poet, the lyric poem or the play presents more than an autobiographical portrait. It typifies a way of living in a certain age by articulating recurring patterns of human interaction in the concrete existence of an individual.

Nacherleben is thus not a passive appreciation; it is an active but disinterested production. Dilthey maintains that it retains the same property in historical understanding as well.[22] For example, on taking the reflec-

---

22. Dilthey thus anticipates Louis O. Mink's and Hayden White's analyses of the poetic dimension of historical understanding, but he diverges from their claim that historical narratives do not explicate the structures of real life. See Mink, "Everyman His or Her Own

tive position on the drama that it is an artistic creation, we can turn the direction of understanding toward the individuality of its author. Understanding the author's individuality, however, will require an imaginative reconstruction of the life-context of the author, setting it in motion such that the meaning of the play can emerge as an integral event in the unfolding of the author's life. The historiographical attitude takes poems, letters, official documents, secondhand reports, diaries, and so forth as artifacts to be used to understand the individuality of poets as a function of the concrete sociohistorical relations within which they are found: "Full appreciation of a poet would require us to define all the conditions, both within him and external to him, which influence the modifications of lived experience and understanding characteristic of his creativity" (*SW*, 5:253; *ED*, 141). Understanding first works in a backward direction, beginning with the termination of a series of actions and tracing them backward. Because expressions become significant as a function of the way the story unfolds after them, knowing the end of the story is necessary to weave the fabric of the narrative. *Nacherleben* then moves in the direction of life and re-creates the dynamic context of sociohistorical relations within which the poet's creative act took place and retraces this creative process. This is not just the re-creation of a nexus of psychological processes or of the actual experiences of the poet but primarily of a sociohistorical nexus within which a meaning is constituted. The author's life-relations to the sociohistorical systems of her or his time are not merely represented but also drawn together and made more determinate in expressions such as poems and dramas.

Nacherleben is the revitalization by the interpreter of life-relations embodied in the expressions used as data. It is to bring together again, using the individual as a focal point, a dynamic nexus of life-relations. Insofar as we transform the lives of historical figures into narratives, we are capable of understanding both their expressions in terms of the unfolding of their lives as well as the unfolding of their lives as embodiments of the development and interaction of more encompassing sociohistorical systems. Like that of the lyric poet, the historian's productive imagination is involved in the construction of this narrative world, and the imaginative process draws on the historian's concrete life-relations. But the historian's judgment is no more a mere reflex of these life-relations than is the poet's creative act. Historians imaginatively transform their own

Annalist," in *On Narrative*, ed. Mitchell, pp. 233–239, and White, "Narrativity in the Representation of Reality."

life-relations, but this imaginative production is guided by the structures of the expressions they seek to understand. Further, since historians' lives are not enmeshed in the life-relations of the narratives they create, their own personal interests are not involved in the storytelling. The historian's imagination is thus disinterested in the construction of this narrative world.

It has been objected that this view of understanding provides only a restoration of the past and presupposes that interpreters are capable of extinguishing their own historical situatedness for the sake of assuming a contemplative attitude toward a past meaning. Dilthey overlooks, so the argument goes, the necessity of applying the expression's meaning to the present context.[23] Dilthey does require that an expression's meaning be assessed by referring it to the context of life-relations within which it arose. This does not imply, however, that the meaning of an expression is in no way shaped by subsequent contexts, only that the nexus of life-relations embodied in the expression guides the re-creation of and limits the contexts within which this expression may be situated.[24] Expressions are the effective presence of the past in the present. Interpreters are not passive spectators of an already given past, but the past is also not merely the product of our contemporary assumptions. We actively re-create the historical influences that make expressions meaningful on the basis of the traces they leave within the expressions themselves.

23. In his correspondence with Dilthey, Yorck warned Dilthey of the aesthetic character of the comparative method but did not accuse Dilthey of associating aesthetic disinterestedness with historical understanding. See *Briefwechsel zwischen Wilhelm Dilthey und dem Grafen Paul Yorck von Wartenburg, 1877–1897*, ed. Sigrid von der Schulenburg (Halle a.d.S.: Max Niemeyer, 1923), pp. 192–193. Gadamer, however, charges Dilthey with precisely this kind of aesthetic detachment from historical influences (*TM*, 204–214). E. D. Hirsch's acknowledgment of Dilthey's influence on his own view of the possibility and necessity of reconstructing the "speaking subject" suggests that he, too, interprets *Verstehen* as a reconstruction of the past. See his *Validity in Interpretation* (New Haven: Yale University Press, 1967), p. 242. Commentators such as Hodges (*The Philosophy of Wilhelm Dilthey*, pp. 118–119) and Plantinga (*Historical Understanding*, p. 107) describe understanding as if it were a matter of restoration. By contrast, Johach argues convincingly that Dilthey's view of historical understanding is not reducible to a kind of restoration or conservation of the past. He further contends that Dilthey's hermeneutics is a sort of historical self-reflection that gains enduring practical principles from the past. I maintain that the results of this historical self-reflection are perhaps less systematic. We do not formulate clear principles of actions so much as gain a liberating appreciation of the one-sidedness of our own lives. See Johach, *Handelnder Mensch und objektiver Geist*, p. 145.

24. Makkreel makes a similar point when he shows that the style of the work limits the degree to which its meaning can be assimilated to a present context. See *Dilthey, Philosopher of the Human Studies*, pp. 414–416.

The aesthetic disinterestedness of historical judgment does not represent a complete divorce of judgment from the historical movement of life.[25] As we have seen, understanding the actions of contemporaries can always involve our own concern with the outcome of events for ourselves, and this can certainly entail a certain bias in judgment. Historical judgment, however, assesses the outcome of another's interaction with her or his milieu with the knowledge that this outcome will not affect the interpreter in the same way that interactions with contemporaries would. We are not called to respond in a communicative way with historically distant people. Nevertheless, our historical understanding of others is incorporated in our praxis.[26] Understanding the past can be a matter of situating oneself in a tradition. In this sense, our actions are oriented more richly within a temporal whole of meaning and purpose. The narrative of which we are a part is clarified, as it were. But it can also reveal the one-sidedness or impoverishment of our own existence, giving us at least the vague sense that there are other ways of living—an intimation of our own finitude.

It could be said, then, that understanding is a more or less articulate way in which we are affected by the past. "The reality of Luther, Frederick the Great, or Goethe receives increased energy and substantiality [*Kernhaftigkeit*] from their constant effect on our selves, thus from the determination of this self by the continually effective [*fortwirkenden*] wills of these forceful people who have drawn ever greater spheres [of influence] in history" (*GS*, 5:114). Understanding involves our submission to, resistance of, and revision of past tendencies as we take them into account in our own life stories. Understanding is our ongoing situation of ourselves in the historical world. Situating ourselves within a tradition is like understanding that our own story is part of a larger story of which I am not the sole author. So, Dilthey himself can write, "I merely adhere to the movement which, since the second half of the eighteenth century, has continued to negate metaphysics."[27] Historical understanding extends the narrative of ourselves as discussed in Chapter 3. Our actions and settings are then more clearly seen as components of a larger narrative.

25. Makkreel also discusses the disinterestedness of the poetic imagination. See Ibid., pp. 360–361.
26. Ilse Bulhof also stresses this point, arguing that interpreters appropriate the past in a way that affects their lives. See her *Wilhelm Dilthey: A Hermeneutic Approach to the Study of History and Culture* (The Hague: Martinus Nijhoff, 1980), pp. 60–61.
27. "Dilthey-Husserl Correspondence," p. 203.

But historical narratives need not incorporate our own life narratives. *Nacherleben* also broadens our horizons in another way not possible in everyday existence. As Dilthey writes, "Understanding opens up to [us] a broad realm of possibilities which are not available within the determination of [our] actual life" ("Understanding Other Persons," 134; *GS*, 7:215). Re-experiencing the past reveals the one-sidedness of the interpreter's life. Dilthey refers to his discovery of religious dimensions of life in the study of Luther, ones not available to his own experience.

> The possibility of experiencing the circumstances of religious life within my own existence is for me, as for most present-day men, very limited. When however I go through the letters and writings of Luther, the reports by his contemporaries, the documents of religious conferences and councils as well as his official correspondence, I then experience a religious process of such eruptive power and of such an energy (a matter of life and death!) that it lies beyond anything that a present-day man could possibly experience. I can however re-experience it. ("Understanding Other Persons," 134; *GS*, 7:215)

This is not to say that re-experiencing Luther's life would bring about a religious conversion.[28] But the historian does not remain unaffected by this *Nacherleben* as if in a clearly superior historical position.

Dilthey recognizes that the process of understanding is interminable. As historical, meaning is "something determinate-indeterminate, an attempt at determination, a process which will never come to an end, an interchange between part and whole" ("Understanding Other Persons," 144; *GS*, 7:227). Understanding seeks to make meaning determinate by situating expressions in their appropriate context, but this process is unending because of both the multidimensionality of historical meaning and our own changing historical circumstances, projects, and assumptions.

Thus, understanding the particular relations of individual persons in concrete sociohistorical settings is integrally related to the construction of our own narratives. But Dilthey also saw in understanding a philosophical dimension in that the structures unearthed there are structures of life itself. Just as the characters of a lyric poem or a play tell us not only about themselves but also about human life in general, so too does our histor-

---

28. As Bulhof has put it, "The historian does not 'go native.'" See *Wilhelm Dilthey*, p. 65.

ical analysis of significant figures open up for us universal structures of human existence. The question arises, however, as to how such universality is possible. As we have already seen (Chapter 1), Dilthey rejects the claim that metaphysics can arrive at universality. In its place, historical consciousness is to offer an insight into the universal structures of life which does not fix these structures as something lifeless.

Historical Consciousness and Relativism

Dilthey refers to the philosophical employment of historical understanding as historical consciousness. And it is by virtue of historical consciousness that Dilthey arrives at his philosophy of philosophy and his final criticisms of metaphysics. Historical consciousness reveals the metaphysical claim to rigorous science as a mere pretense. Metaphysical systems are, instead, worldviews—that is, their attempts to comprehend the world and human existence in a single theoretical, evaluative system are actually interpretations of life. Dilthey claimed that historical analysis demonstrates that these interpretive worldviews are always one of three types based on three limited perspectives on life. The first of these worldview types is naturalism. Humans are viewed as components of the material processes of nature. Our knowledge of these processes is derived from our senses, and we attain this knowledge for the sake of manipulating nature in a way conducive to the satiation of our passions. In subjective idealism, the second form of worldview, humans are construed as volitional agents whose free will confronts the forces of nature and who seek to transform the world according to moral ideals. Finally, objective idealism arises from a "contemplative, aesthetic, or artistic" attitude (*GS*, 8:114). Reality is appreciated or felt as a whole that is permeated with the highest ideals and values and within which we are harmoniously situated. Worldviews are also expressed in art and religion, but only in philosophy are they devoted to expressing the totality of life and world in a conceptual system.

This historical-philosophical approach led Husserl (among others) to classify Dilthey's *Weltanschauungslehre* (theory of worldviews) as historicist.[29] In "Philosophy as a Rigorous Science," Husserl characterizes his-

---

29. In his brief correspondence with Dilthey, Husserl denied linking him to historicism, but his own analysis of historicism casts considerable doubt on Husserl's sincerity on this point.

toricism as that approach which begins in facticity and results in relativism and skepticism: "Historicism takes its position in the factual sphere of the empirical life of the spirit. To the extent that it posits this latter absolutely, without exactly naturalizing it . . ., there arises a relativism that has a close affinity to naturalistic psychologism and runs into similar sceptical difficulties."[30] Drawing largely on Dilthey's discussion in "Die Typen der Weltanschauung und ihre Ausbildung in den metaphysischen Systemen" (The types of worldview and their development in metaphysical systems), Husserl accurately portrays the dynamic structure of life and recognizes that, according to Dilthey, art, religion, and metaphysics are cultural formations that arise from the developing morphology and the particular historical conditions of life.

Husserl has no quarrel with the claim that metaphysics, indeed any science, arises under particular historical conditions and motives. What he rejects is the skepticism and relativism that results from absolutizing this factical process as the ground of science. Relativists, Husserl argues, derive their skepticism from the de facto flux of systems of science and the conflict of scientific claims. "That an idea has validity," Husserl contends, "would mean that it is a factual construction of spirit which is held as valid and which in its contingent validity determines thought. There would be no unqualified validity."[31] The claim made by metaphysical philosophy to objective validity is thus made suspect, because the standards of validity are themselves cultural, historical products that are eventually transformed.

Husserl responds by insisting that historicism fails to discern the distinction between "fluid worth" and "objective validity," that is, the difference between historically variable standards and a priori, ahistorical validity. Even if there are difficulties involved in understanding the relation between the two, this distinction should nevertheless be maintained. Given this distinction, then, no empirical discipline can distinguish between "fluid worth" and "objective validity," for empirical disciplines deal only with the de facto connections between the components of cultural systems; they do not assess the validity of relations. Husserl continues, "The science of history, or simply empirical humanistic science in general, can of itself decide nothing, either in a positive or in a negative

30. Edmund Husserl, "Philosophy as a Rigorous Science," trans. Quentin Lauer, in *Husserl: Shorter Works*, ed. Peter McCormick and Frederick Elliston (Notre Dame: University of Notre Dame Press, 1981), p. 122.

31. Husserl, "Philosophy as a Rigorous Science," p. 125.

sense, as to whether a distinction is to be made between . . . historical and valid philosophy."[32] Historical and logical reasons are of two different kinds, and only the latter can be effective against the possibility of an objectively valid science.

Any philosophical criticism of previous or contemporaneous philosophical systems presupposes objective validity. "If there is something there whose objective validity philosophical criticism can refute, then there is also an area within which something can be grounded as objectively valid."[33] Accordingly, arguments for historical relativism that rest on critical analyses of the metaphysical systems of the past contain the contradiction found in absolute skepticism. Such arguments reject objective validity while appealing to objective validity to make their case.

For Husserl there is an unbridgeable gulf between *Weltanschauung* and rigorous science. The former is not scientific, according to Husserl. Its true aim is the development of a nonsystematic view of the world and of life whose purpose is to guide action. Worldviews are formed without waiting for scientific validation because the exigencies of life press us for a response. A worldview is, then, more properly thought of as the wisdom of the experienced or cultured person than as science. Rigorous science, on the other hand, is derived from a secure foundation and asserts no proposition without proper evidence. Accordingly, rigorous science must withdraw from the requirements resulting from our immersion in a particular time and place and allow itself to be guided by posterity, that is, by the regulative idea of an as yet unrealized system of objectively valid propositions. Worldviews are guided by an essentially different value than that guiding science. They are the accumulated wisdom, the accomplishments, of individuals and have only a fleeting worth. Science is an enduring body of objectively valid propositions accumulated by "generations of scholars."[34]

Husserl's essay initiated a brief correspondence between Dilthey and Husserl. In a letter dated June 29, 1911, Dilthey opens the exchange of letters with an expression of dismay that he has been portrayed by Husserl as a historicist. Dilthey insists that he, like Husserl, seeks a "universally valid theory of knowledge," that is, a foundational science.[35] But, at the same time, he underscores his difference with Husserl by repeating

32. Ibid., p. 126.
33. Ibid., p. 127.
34. Ibid., p. 143.
35. "Dilthey-Husserl Correspondence," p. 203.

his rejection of metaphysics and his incredulity toward any "attempt to conclusively express the world's coherency by using an interconnection of concepts."[36]

Dilthey's criticisms of metaphysics are by no means limited to historical accounts of the origin and conflict of various systems. Dilthey himself realizes that "the conflict between systems and the previous failure of metaphysics appear only as the historical facts which have brought philosophical thinking to the dissolution of metaphysics, and not as the proof for its impossibility."[37] The limits of metaphysics are drawn on the basis of the systematic principles of life-philosophy itself. All concepts, including those used in metaphysics, are expressions of and arise in the service of life. Accordingly, metaphysics must fail in two broad respects. First, the metaphysical attempt to capture all reality in a valid system of concepts must fail because all thought is a function of the volitional-emotional-representational whole of life and cannot, then, go beyond this ground to explain it. Metaphysics presents only a one-sidedly intellectual perspective on what cannot be reduced to reason. Second, the metaphysical drive to attain stable principles for explaining reality must also be thwarted, because life itself is dynamic. Metaphysical concepts arise in response to the practical demands for the fulfillment of life in the changing circumstances of human history. Thus, it is not the historical fact of the conflict of systems but the systematic account of concept formation that leads Dilthey to reject metaphysics as a rigorous science.

Husserl's formulation of the problem commits Dilthey to the view that all philosophy, including the historical consciousness of life-philosophy, is a worldview and that only because historical consciousness is a more adequate worldview may it criticize metaphysics. In contrast, Dilthey characterizes worldviews as "historical 'forms of life' " and explicitly differentiates them from "the universally valid sciences," apparently counting his doctrine of worldviews among the latter.[38] Nevertheless, Dilthey remained unclear on this point. Dilthey does classify philosophy, along with art and religion, as a kind of worldview. His depiction of philosophy in this context, however, more closely resembles the metaphysical consciousness he criticizes than his own philosophical analyses. That is, philosophy is the attempt to provide a valid conceptual account of life and

36. Ibid.
37. Ibid., p. 204.
38. Ibid.

world is characterized by an intellectual one-sidedness. In contrast to this, Dilthey also suggests a quasi-transcendental approach that is capable of uncovering the conditions and presuppositions underpinning worldviews while not being a worldview itself.

Husserl's deferential insistence "that there are no serious differences between us" is belied by the content of his own attempt to explain the closeness of his project to that of Dilthey's.[39] Objective validity, Husserl asserts, "refers to ideal, and thus to absolute ('absolute' in a certain sense) principles, to an a priori which, as such, is thus in no way limited by anthropological-historical facticities."[40] But it is precisely Dilthey's position that ideal constructs arise from the historical facticity of life. Dilthey cannot accept a division of the a priori from the historical such that, to use Husserl's phrase, the former is "the idea" and the latter "the dim form in which it appears."[41] "Objective validity" means for Dilthey something radically different from what Husserl has in mind. Dilthey's admission to Husserl that "Dear friend, you do not know, and it is natural that you do not know, how difficult it is . . . to penetrate into a world of such very different thought"[42] might equally be said of Husserl's failure at least to admit his vast differences with Dilthey. The question nevertheless remains, What sort of "objective validity" can be ascribed to historical consciousness such that it may assume a critical posture vis-à-vis metaphysics without succumbing to the very metaphysical constructions it criticizes?

In the *Weltanschauungslehre,* Dilthey links comparative historical analysis and a structural analysis of psychic life, thus suggesting that historical consciousness entails not only an inductive historical analysis and comparison of systems but also a phenomenological analysis of the historicity of human life.[43] Historical consciousness reveals the structures underlying the production of any worldview in a cooperative use of these two methodologies which is not made particularly clear by Dilthey himself. The function of historical consciousness is not to explain the factual historical conditions from which any particular metaphysical world-

---

39. Ibid., p. 205.
40. Ibid.
41. Husserl, "Philosophy as a Rigorous Science," p. 126.
42. "Dilthey-Husserl Correspondence," p. 207.
43. Tom Nenon argues to the contrary that Dilthey's approach is inductive and that this ensnares him in precisely the trap Husserl indicated. See his "Dilthey's Inductive Method and the Nature of Philosophy," *Southwest Philosophy Review* 5, no. 1 (January 1989): 121–134.

view arises but to bring to a focus the temporal structures of human life which make the construction of a worldview possible. It is also not the replacing of one metaphysical worldview by another but the quasi-transcendental uncovering of the ground of worldviews in general.

The question arises here whether on this interpretation Dilthey does not paradoxically view historical consciousness as ahistorical. That is, is the analysis of the historicity of life free from the one-sidedness and prejudices inherent in historicity itself? Does Dilthey's phenomenological analysis of the structure of life simply repeat a metaphysical strategy? Gadamer's discussion of Dilthey's historicism offers a widely accepted answer to this question. Gadamer himself clearly rejects scientific objectivism in Husserl's ahistorical sense and sees Dilthey's major shortcoming as his inability to disabuse himself of this notion. In Gadamer's view, historical relativism is a problem only with a theory of concept formation still linked to objective validity claims. Dilthey failed to recognize in his own life-philosophy the means for making relativism irrelevant rather than making it a problem to be solved. As I shall show, Dilthey's desire for objectivity can be read in an alternative way, but first I turn to Gadamer's criticism of Dilthey.

Gadamer argues for a central tension in Dilthey's thought, namely, that Dilthey realized that the historicity of humans makes history an issue for us. Dilthey's view of our historicity should have led him to the realization of the radical finitude of understanding. But, according to Gadamer, Dilthey remained obsessed with a natural scientific notion of objectivity. In other words, Dilthey maintains that historical understanding requires us to free ourselves of our own prejudices. Accordingly, Dilthey recognized the historicity of previous ages while forgetting his own. In Gadamer's view, "What his epistemological thinking tried to justify was fundamentally nothing other than the epic self-forgetfulness of Ranke. Only, instead of aesthetic self-forgetfulness there was the sovereignty of an all-round and infinite understanding" (*TM*, 204).

According to Gadamer, Dilthey viewed the finitude of the human mind as a subjective matter that could be overcome.[44] Historical consciousness overcomes this finitude precisely by recognizing it. To cite Gadamer, "For Dilthey the awareness of finiteness did not mean that

---

44. Commentators have followed Gadamer's lead on this. See, for example, David E. Linge, "Dilthey and Gadamer: Two Theories of Historical Understanding," *Journal of the American Academy of Religion* 4 (1973): 544–545.

consciousness was made finite or limited in any way; rather it bore witness to the capacity of life to rise in energy and activity above all limitations" (*TM*, 205). Human understanding is finite, then, only accidentally. There is no limit to its capacity to extend itself. All history is open to understanding because the structure of human life is the same in all ages. Comparison of oneself to other ages "fills out the fortuitousness of one's own experience" (*TM*, 205). Historical finitude is a merely subjective matter of preference and eradicable prejudice.

Dilthey's use of the comparative method to overcome these limitations is, according to Gadamer, a weak, if not the weakest, point in his analysis. Comparison commits Dilthey to a philosophy of the subject where the subject is free and "in control of both members of the comparison" (*TM*, 206). Following Graf Yorck, Gadamer classifies all comparison as aesthetic. In other words, the historian is construed as detached from the effects of history. Historical understanding is capable of transcending the limitations of its sociohistorical situatedness when comparing historical epochs.

Gadamer contends that Dilthey's notion of aesthetic detachment stands in tension with his own analysis of the reflexive character of life. Historical consciousness is able to transcend itself because it is a form of self-knowledge: "It adopts a reflective attitude towards both itself and the tradition in which it stands. It understands itself in terms of its own history" (*TM*, 207). So, we must turn to the question of how self-knowledge gives rise to a scientifically objective knowledge. Reflection is itself a structure of life. But such reflection is made possible only if "we distance ourselves from the context of our own activity" (*TM*, 208). Life's reflective self-image emerges naturally in cultural products and especially in great works of art. But such expressions are not expressions merely of the subjective peculiarities of an artist. They are expressions of objective spirit. Insofar as we are able to participate in the objective systems of culture, we transcend the particularity of our own subjectivity. Thus, Gadamer argues, Dilthey thinks he achieves an objectivity for historical knowledge analogous to natural scientific objectivity. As Gadamer states: "The nature of the experimental method is to rise above the subjective fortuitousness of observation and, with its help, the knowledge of the laws of nature is possible. Similarly, the human sciences endeavor to rise methodologically above the subjective fortuitousness of their own standpoint in history and above the tradition accessible to them, and thus attain the objectivity of historical knowledge" (*TM*, 208–209). By submitting ourselves to the structures and meaning-standards of objective spirit, we overcome our own subjective prejudices and adapt ourselves to a common standpoint.

This formulation saves Dilthey from relativism because he adopts a quasi-Hegelian view that the movement of history leads to totalization (without admitting the idealist postulate of a single unifying principle) and that the role of philosophy is to think this movement through. But Gadamer insists that what Dilthey should have realized is that this is not a solution of the problem of relativism; it is its dissolution. Objections to relativism arise from the very "intellectualism" that Dilthey's view of life and knowledge rejects. Gadamer traces Dilthey's inability to recognize this to a latent epistemological Cartesianism that stands in tension with his life-philosophy: Dilthey's "epistemological reflections on the basis of the human sciences are not really compatible with his starting point from life philosophy" (*TM*, 210).

Gadamer bases his argument largely on Dilthey's claim that "consciousness has shaken off authority and is seeking, through reflection and doubt, to attain to valid knowledge" (*GS*, 7:6; quoted in *TM*, 210). Cartesian doubt is applied here not merely to philosophical prejudices but also to the assumptions embodied in cultural systems such as religion, art, law, and the like. Such reflection is then no longer life's historical self-reflection on its own unfolding, which presupposes a surrender to objective spirit for its objectivity. This reflection is, like Descartes's, an autonomous reflection that rejects the authority of the tradition. According to Gadamer, scientific certainty is for Dilthey the highest expression of the pre-reflective certainty of life. Dilthey has failed to see, however, that these are utterly different kinds of certainty. The latter is a methodological certainty that allows of no doubt. Life certainty, on the other hand, is a factical certainty that exists always in balance with doubt. Life-philosophy and Cartesian science cannot be reconciled.

Although Dilthey was never explicit about the objective validity associated with historical consciousness, it is not the case that he slavishly appropriates the natural scientific model of objective, autonomous reason as Gadamer suggests. The objectivity of historical understanding does, as Gadamer indicates, derive from our participation in the common structures of objective spirit. But Dilthey does not completely lose sight of the finitude that this kind of objectivity imposes on understanding. Not only our subjective biases but also our historical movement and situatedness limit our understanding, and the latter are the conditions of understanding which cannot be somehow more deeply grounded. Gadamer's charges overlook a factical theory of concept formation that emerges, if a bit obscurely, in the *Weltanschauungslehre* and "Das Wesen der Philosophie."

Dilthey acknowledges that once philosophy incorporates historical consciousness, it is faced with an antinomy. The forms of human existence have changed over the course of history, and so too have the forms of thought. But as metaphysics, philosophy claims to offer a stable, objective conceptual system that fully represents life and world (*GS*, 5:365). How can a historical system provide ahistorical truths? For Dilthey, it cannot. This does not lead to a radical skepticism, however. Beneath the strife of various worldviews, Dilthey claims to find structures of life from which they arise. The antinomy is solved in that "philosophy brings to consciousness the connection [*Zusammenhang*] of the manifold of its systems with vitality [*Lebendigkeit*]" (*GS*, 8:8). This does not mean that the conflict between metaphysical systems could finally be brought to an end by offering an objectively valid metaphysics of life.

Metaphysics asserts the autonomy of its conceptual framework from the sociohistorical flux of life; and this is precisely the source of its self-contradictoriness (*GS*, 8:8). It is the function of historical consciousness to reconnect metaphysics, as well as any other worldview, to its roots in life. In doing so, it overcomes the antinomy of metaphysics. The antinomies in the systems of science "are grounded in the different origins in the functions of the structure" (*GS*, 8:8). The conflicts between metaphysical systems are accounted for by virtue of the fact that they are one-sided expressions of life's multidimensionality.

Dilthey's analysis of the structure of worldviews is more than an inductive generalization about art, religion, and philosophy. It can be read as an attempt to arrive at a theory of concept formation which escapes the double forgetfulness characteristic of metaphysics. First, metaphysics views reason as, at its best, independent of the vicissitudes of feeling and willing. The analysis of the structure of worldviews reminds us of the internal connections of these three aspects of psychic life and particularly aids in understanding how they cooperate in concept formation. Second, metaphysics asserts the autonomy of reason vis-à-vis the sociohistorical facticity of the individual metaphysician and in so doing arrives at a view of concepts that, when true, are fixed and dead. The analysis of worldview structure provides a key for understanding concepts as themselves dynamic and the truth involved with such concepts as something other than the reflection of a fixed reality by a fixed concept.

Dilthey outlines the structure shared by all worldviews, ordering them into layers. Underlying any worldview, though not actually a part of it, are the *Lebensstimmungen* (life-moods) of individuals of which pessimism and optimism are the broadest categories but which are actually expressed in a wide range of nuances (*GS,* 8:81–82). This focus on moods opens Dilthey to a charge of extreme relativism, because worldviews could be seen as ultimately grounded in the subjective states of individuals. There is some evidence, however, that Dilthey did not understand life-moods in a narrowly subjective way as psychological states. The life-moods are "the countless nuances of the relation [*Stellung*] to the world" (*GS,* 8:82). Moods are precognitive orientations in the world which reveal life, not merely subjective states.[45] At the bottom of all worldviews lies a *Weltbild,* a representation of the world derived from experience which finds its highest expression in theoretical formulations. On the basis of the representations of the world, a second layer is erected, namely, the system of our values and the meaning we assign to the people and things of the world around us. Finally, the third layer provides an overall volitional orientation. Based on our values, we erect a highest good or ideal that gives our actions a direction in an overall teleological scheme of life (*GS,* 8:82–84).

From this initial sketch of the tripartite structure of worldviews, it would appear that the representational structure is independent of the evaluative and volitional components of psychic life and that worldviews differ only in their fixed, conceptual foundations. Dilthey's analysis of the structure of the worldview is uncharacteristically rigid in this essay and may perhaps be explained by the influence exercised on him by Husserl. But in the later essay "Das geschichtliche Bewußtsein und die Weltanschauungen" (Historical consciousness and worldviews), Dilthey provides a more dynamic portrayal of the structure of worldviews and more clearly delineates the metaphysical worldview from the poetic and religious worldviews. There, Dilthey emphasizes that no worldview "can be deduced psychologically" (*GS,* 8:15). Worldviews are developed on the basis of psychological structure and the sociohistorical facticity of

---

45. Otto Friedrich Bollnow, in *Dilthey: Eine Einführung in seine Philosophie,* 2d ed. (Stuttgart: Kohlhammer, 1955), p. 8off., and to a lesser degree Makkreel argue that Dilthey's discussions of moods anticipate Heidegger, but Makkreel maintains that this is the case only in Dilthey's late aesthetic writings (*Dilthey, Philosopher of the Human Studies,* p. 367f.).

a time. Thus they are themselves dynamic. Psychic structure itself "is conditioned by the relation of the subject to the milieu" (*GS*, 8:16).

Representations are not given in isolation such that emotions and finally volitions can be derived from them. "Every impression contains, along with the image, a determination of the life of feeling and impulse" (*GS*, 8:16). Representations and evaluations of the world are always intertwined in concrete life, and they are only separated in intellectual abstractions (*GS*, 8:16). Makkreel has convincingly argued that Dilthey's analysis of metaphysical worldviews remains bound to the rigid schema outlined above precisely because metaphysics loses sight of its roots in life. Makkreel writes that "Dilthey's analysis of traditional philosophical *Weltanschauung* types does not move beyond this general constructionist schema built upon the *Lebensstimmungen,* because metaphysics lacks the experiential, dynamic base found in the spheres of religion and poetry."[46] Metaphysics is driven not only by the goal of capturing the world in a conceptual system but also by the desire to arrive at a fixed and final conceptual representation. Thus, the portrait of concept formation provided in the theory of worldviews is indicative of metaphysical intellectual one-sidedness, not Diltheyan life-philosophy. Dilthey's own theory of concept formation must more closely resemble that discussed in religious and poetic worldviews insofar as these are derived from a lived experience, represent an integration of the psychic structure, and maintain the dynamism of life.

The elements of the religious worldview—the world-image, the evaluative framework, and the volitional-purposive orientation—are all informed by the central focus on the relation of the individual to the "*Unsichtbar*" (invisible) (*GS*, 5:381). Values and purposes are derived from the requirement of devotion to this unseen, and the things we encounter in the world are infused with meaning as symbols, signs, or incarnations of the *Unsichtbar* or its designs. The religious orientation is grounded in a kind of religious life experience (*Lebenserfahrung*) that the highest value and goal of life is the relation with the *Unsichtbar* (*GS*, 5:382). This evaluative and purposive orientation, then, has the power to transform our image of the world. "There the great lived experience of an unconditioned, infinite, objective value, to which all finite values are subordinated, of the infinite life-value of communication with this invisible object determines objective apprehension" (*GS*, 5:390). Our percep-

---

46. Makkreel, *Dilthey, Philosopher of the Human Studies,* p. 354.

tual and conceptual grasp of the world is not merely the base on which evaluations and volitions are built. Determinations of value and purpose have the capacity to shape our image of the world. Concepts are internally related to feelings and impulses and are as a result more fluid than concepts abstracted from our volitional and emotional lives.

But the dynamism of the worldview is pushed to the limit by the poet. All forms of art bring to focus something universal in a particular, but poetry is in an especially privileged position to do so by virtue of its linguistic medium. Although the other arts rely on sensory presentation and are bound by the limits involved with this, poetry "has in language a mode of expression for everything that can appear in the human psyche" (*GS*, 5:392). Especially the lyric poet can present the typical life-relations between setting, motives, actions, consequences, and responses. But because the poetic imagination is disinterested, that is, it is not bound to reality by practical concerns, it is capable of opening up sides of life in the inner dynamics of characters and plot which are not derived from the senses. These insights into life can then change our view of the world. A dramatic "motif is precisely a relation of life grasped poetically in its significance. And in this motif an inner impulse is at work to adapt characters, events, and actions to each other such that each general trait is seen in the nature of things" (*GS*, 5:394). Like the structure of the religious worldview, the poetic worldview exhibits the internal relation of our conceptual world-picture to the totality of psychic life. But the poet's linguistic approach to life gives her or him a more all-sided approach than either religious or metaphysical genius. And it is this very multi-sided approach to life which works against the development of a fixed world-image and a stable worldview. "The more freely [the poet] creates from the experience of life, the more he stands under the power of life itself which always opens new sides to him" (*GS*, 5:397).

The life-philosopher and the poet converge on this point. Dilthey writes: "Life should be interpreted from itself. This is the great thought that links the philosophers of life to the experience of the world and to poetry."[47] The philosophy of life seeks to open up the many interpretations of life appropriate to its multidimensionality, not to build a stable worldview. Ilse Bulhof remarks that Dilthey does not specify whether the

---

47. *GS*, 5:370–371; "Das Wesen der Philosophie," translated by William Kuback and Martin Weinbaum as *Dilthey's Philosophy of Existence: Introduction to the "Weltanschauungslehre"* (Westport, Conn.: Greenwood Press, 1957), p. 31.

Mehrseitigkeit (multidimensionality) of life is a consequence of the limited perspective of the observer or a result of the dynamism and fecundity of life itself: "If their meaning is merely inexhaustible *for us* because of our limited reason, then *Mehrseitigkeit* is a regrettable condition; if, on the other hand, cultural objects and life themselves are *mehrdeutig* [that is, they exhibit a plurarily of meanings], this condition testifies to the depth and richness of life. Dilthey seemed inclined toward the first of these two interpretations." Dilthey falls victim to the Greek philosophical heritage, which "conceived of being as an eternal object to be contemplated."[48] But although Dilthey certainly concentrates on the historical finitude of our understanding, his theory of worldviews suggests that life is also to be seen as *"mehrdeutig."* Art, religion, and philosophy are not reducible to either of the other two worldview types, and they cannot be unified into a higher worldview. Each is an expression of life. For that matter, the naturalistic, subjective idealist, and objective idealist worldview types are also expressions of life which cannot be unified or reduced to a more fundamental worldview.

Historical consciousness is an appreciation of life's multidimensionality in a way that is appropriate to this multidimensionality. That is, historical consciousness does not provide a fixed conception of life derived from historical analysis. Nor does it even seek provisional conceptions of life guided by the regulative principle of a theory of life that is complete (even if such could never be actualized). It is, rather, a way of glimpsing the meanings of life as themselves incomplete.[49] It keeps life's vitality in the open. Life-philosophy does not, then, end in a finished conceptual system. It does not offer a canon, properly speaking. It is a way of philosophizing which entails pointing out the limitedness of every way of talking about our existence for the sake of enhancing this existence itself. The philosophy of life does not "ground" other sectors of culture—art, religion, or science—in the sense of providing a glimpse of the whole on which they give only partial perspectives. *Lebensphilosophie* seeks only to show that these cultural systems are modes of human interaction that spring from concrete sociohistorical circumstances and are, as such, always open to transformation.

48. Bulhof, *Wilhelm Dilthey*, p. 77.

49. As John Caputo says of radical hermeneutics, Dilthey's historical consciousness does not seek to make life easy by providing fixed truths. See Caputo's *Radical Hermeneutics*, especially the introduction, "Restoring Life to Its Original Difficulty," pp. 1–2.

Epilogue

Diltheyan hermeneutics seeks to provide a ground in lived experience for the objective truth of narrative history. In our postmodernist climate, this will seem to some a hopelessly misbegotten task. Philosophical foundations of any sort, and lived experience in particular, have undergone sustained attack. Perspectivism has relegated objectivity to the junk heap of discredited ideas, replacing it with the notion of a plurality of discourse communities vying for preeminence. Narrative structure is often thought of as a purely fictional organizational device. Indeed, truth itself has been portrayed as a game best left unplayed. These postmodernist contentions notwithstanding, the Diltheyan approach remains a viable position.

Dilthey's appeal to lived experience as a ground will lead some to link his project to Husserl's transcendental phenomenology and so to Derrida's criticisms of the same. At issue between Husserl and Derrida is both the transparency and the originary givenness of lived experience. In Derrida's view, Husserl's own analysis of the temporality of consciousness undermines the pure givenness he wishes to assign it. That is, Husserl contends that the present is constituted by not only a now but also protention, or primary expectation, and retention, or primary memory. The present is constituted by the non-present. There is then no simple present, no stable starting point for phenomenological description. The apodictic, purely given evidence so prized by Husserl as a stable foundation dissolves into a construct whose constitutive principles themselves always escape presence.

From a postmodernist perspective, this bodes ill for claims to narrative truth, because written narratives are true only if they meet two conditions. First, the events described in the narrative must have actually happened in the way described by the text. That is, agents must have undertaken the sequence of actions portrayed by the author. For obvious reasons, this can be quite problematic in the case of historically distant agents. Historical data can be scarce, fragmentary, misleading, or all of the above. The second condition for narrative truth claims is more central to the project of narrative history as such: the narrative structure within which these events are woven must itself be objectively real.

Narrative structure is a temporal framework that accounts for, bestows meaning on, the individual events of life. What may initially seem a disjointed sequence of events is made into a coherent whole when these events may be shown to culminate in, or even if we can anticipate that they will culminate in, some state of affairs—some achievement, comeuppance, joy, or disaster. If narrative accounts are true, the argument goes, then they must be copies of an original narrative reality. This original-copy relation is rejected for a number of reasons, the first of which arises from Derrida's denunciation of the originariness of lived experience. Lived experience is not itself an original. It is a simulacrum, a copy of a copy. With no original by which to verify the copy, those narrative truth claims that turn on the original-copy metaphor are rendered invalid.

White and Mink assert that narrative is a literary device, not a real structure of life. To say that any narrative text is true is to commit a category mistake, for narrative structure is a construct of our imagination, not the real order of human experience. It is, in other words, fictional. These claims are given philosophical teeth by the postmodernist appropriation of Nietzsche's eternal recurrence. The eternal recurrence undermines any sense of an ending, and without this principle of culmination, there can be no narrative structure. If all events lead ultimately only to infinite reiteration, they ultimately lead nowhere. Ascribing teleology of any kind to our lives, even the limited teleology of our personal narratives, would in this case be no more than illusion or self-deception.

Retrieving truth claims for written narratives requires first that we revisit just what "lived experience" means, and then we must recall just what Dilthey means by narrative truth. Lived experience is where all inquiry begins. But it is not by virtue of this an absolute starting point. It does not provide apodictic evidence on which all other scientific claims can be constructed. On the contrary, it is that point in the hermeneutical circle at which we begin and to which we inevitably return in order to understand our own lives. It is where we actually live our interactions with others, encounter joy and tragedy, sort through the banalities of everyday existence, and reflect on the meaning of all these things. Lived experience is not the inner of the inner-outer dichotomy. It is our situatedness in a life-nexus, a myriad of shared sociohistorical contexts.

For a Diltheyan, life as it is lived is where we begin because it is what we seek to understand. Although we must at times mistrust experience as it is initially given or need to move beyond given experience to clarify things that resist understanding, the Diltheyan impulse is to mistrust conceptual formulations that are in no way rooted in life as we live it. To claim that lived experience is constituted by principles that go beyond it—whether these principles appeal to atomic sense data, transcendental faculties, transcendent things-in-themselves, or différance—is to give priority to abstractions over the concrete sociohistorical relations from which they initially arose.

One may be tempted to argue here that Dilthey is content to accept the rules governing human interaction as they are found. As a result, he would be insensitive to the ways in which a culture's self-understanding obscures and distorts underlying sociohistorical realities. He appears unconcerned with what Herbert Marcuse called surplus repression, in other words, what our history is doing to us below the level of lived experience, as it were, and how we may extricate ourselves from its negative effects. This is not completely accurate. Although discerning the subconscious, oppressive constraints on human interaction is not the overriding interest motivating Dilthey's hermeneutics, life-philosophy clearly aims to go beyond a culture's self-understanding and can, in the process, ferret out the ways in which sociohistorical structures obstruct or debase life. Recall that *Besserverstehen* is a central tenet of life-philosophical hermeneutics. This is because the psychological and sociohistorical structures that constitute lived experience remain vague or implicit until they are made explicit in objectifications. When we interpret the written expressions of philosophers, artists, or religious figures, we are able to distinguish the historical and the psychological forces at work in their lives in a way unavailable to them through introspection. The interpreter is then in a position to see not only the conflicting demands that incongruent social institutions place on individuals but also the tensions between objective sociohistorical forces and subjective psychological needs, desires, and intentions. Accordingly, Diltheyan hermeneutics offers a way to explicate reflectively the life-stifling structures of our sociohistorical world.

As I have already indicated, recovering narrative truth from postmodernist criticism requires that we look again at the concepts "lived experience" and "narrative truth." Having considered the former, we can now focus on the latter. Postmodernist criticism rejects narrative truth largely as a form of correspondence theory. On this point, Dilthey would be in complete agreement. Historical narratives do not and are not intended to reconstruct a stable past as it was in itself. Historical understanding is not adequately captured by the metaphor of mind as mirror. Historical understanding is itself a historical process and as such requires a complete revision of what we mean by truth.

Nevertheless, written narratives can be true only if human life itself exhibits narrative structure. That is to say, Dilthey was fully aware that anyone's life lends itself to a plurality of valid interpretations. Beyond the verification of the facts of time and place and whether such and such an action was really undertaken, there always remains the question of the principle of the narrative coherence of a life. How, in the end, does it all hang together? Dilthey would not insist that there is only one correct answer to this question. Life itself is at once dynamic and multidimensional, such that the task of interpreting it is open-ended. What Dilthey does insist on is that the very structure of narrative is already implicit in our lived experience. It is not merely imposed on an incoherent flux.

Lived experience is a point of intersection, a crossing-point of future and past. This is the case pre-reflectively, as when we experience a melody. We experience time elapsing within the present. But the reflective use of representations, what Husserl would call secondary memory and secondary expectation, is also integrally involved in constituting the meaning of experience as we live it, such that the present can always be at once a provisional culmination of the past and an anticipation of an indeterminate ending in the future. For example, I read my son his bedtime story, a nightly dose of Tolkien's world of hobbits, dwarves, elves, and wizards. While I read, I remember my own childhood love of these tales and anticipate (more or less patiently) the quiet time my wife and I will have when this eldest child is finally asleep. This is all lived experience, and though certainly not yet a narrative, it contains the essential temporal structure of narrative.

As we read a story, we are involved in a continuous circular motion weaving from future to past and back again. We grant provisional meaning to events as we read them in the light of an anticipated ending or narrative conclusion, but we also understand these events as themselves pulling together the previous scenes in a way that allows us to see how they led up to them. In other words, present events act as focal points, providing a provisional coherence to past events. But what we are reading now is itself meaningful only with reference to an anticipated future, requiring at each step, then, a reinterpretation of the overall coherence of the story. It is precisely this circle from future to past and back again that Dilthey finds at the heart of lived experience.

Lived experience is the process of constituting temporal wholes. Writing historical narratives is a reflective extension of the life-process itself, and this is surely an important part of what Dilthey meant when he said that we can understand history only because we are ourselves historical. The temporal whole that we constitute first and foremost is our life. Our personal identity is an achievement, not a given. As Heidegger would later, Dilthey replaces the metaphysical question of "what" with the existential question of "who" when seeking the identity of the "I."

Our primordial narratives are then our own lives. The process of narration is less a recounting than an active formation. Crafting my life story is a matter of shaping my past into a meaningful whole by virtue of an anticipated future, a sense of an ending. Our expectations are often unfulfilled, contingency pervades human life. Our stories take unexpected turns, as it were. Accordingly, our narrative self-understanding is always provisional. The truth of such an account of ourselves has nothing to do with correspondence. It is, rather, a matter of what Heidegger would call authenticity. To put it briefly, we are truthful when we take ownership of our lives, and we are inauthentic when we passively receive our identity from the sociohistorical contexts in which we abide. Dilthey himself did not thematize authentic and inauthentic ways of being in the way made familiar by Heidegger. But he focused on the relation between our attempts as individual agents to form our own lives as coherent narratives and the social forces that shape us from without. Just as we are able to understand the conflicts between the social and the psychological in others by interpreting their objectifications, we are able to come to a clearer sense of our accommodations with, our resistance to, and our overcoming of the influences of our sociohistorical contexts via an interpretation of our own objectifications.

The question remains how such autobiographical truth relates to the biographical truth that is the more common domain for the historian. Indeed, if we take seriously the Diltheyan view that the past is always constructed as a function of our own lives, in the light of our own projects and ideals, then a serious problem arises. The past may always be nothing more than a fictional construct forged to suit our present purposes. After all, neo-Nazis appear to have no trouble denying the reality of the Holocaust. Americans often tell their national story as a unified narrative beginning with the *Mayflower* pilgrims, extending through the founding fathers, and culminating in a nation whose official language, should proposed legislation pass, is properly English. Such a narrative seems to discount the enslavement of Africans and the immigration of Hispanics and Asians as constitutive for our national identity. This story of American identity, many have argued, is really a reflex of the current white male power structure, issued in the interest of legitimizing and perpetuating this very power structure.

Were this only a matter of a number of specific cases of deliberate or even delusional distortions of the past—a past de facto obscured in these accounts but de jure accessible to the historian—it would not be a serious challenge. But the objection here is precisely that due to the historicity of the human knower, we are capable only of projecting our own self-understanding on others. Given the postmodern fondness for Nietzsche, I shall respond by formulating a Diltheyan response to Nietzsche on this subject.

Dilthey and Nietzsche contend that our constitution, hence our understanding, of the past is a function of life, but they draw radically different epistemological conclusions from this. Nietzsche construes the past as a fiction whose truth or falsehood is a matter of its facilitation or hindrance of praxis. Dilthey, by contrast, insists on a reciprocal relation between past and future that links the meaning of the past to our praxis but stops short of characterizing the constituted past as fictional. For Dilthey, the past itself constrains our interpretation of it. That is, for both Dilthey and Nietzsche, our interpretations are motivated by our interest in the fulfillment of life, and the past itself is a reflective achievement constructed on the basis of our own practical context. But whereas Nietzsche views our construction of the past as a form of fictionalizing, Dilthey argues that our interpretive transformation of the past is a matter of explicating the real, yet changing significance of past events in the ongoing narrative of our lives.

Nietzsche's genealogical approach to history is devoted primarily to liberating praxis from the oppressive influences of the past. Historical approaches that seek to understand the present as a function of the past subordinate the life of the present to the past, and as a result, "life becomes stunted and degenerate."[1] That is to say, a history devoted to recapturing the past as it was turns our attention away from what we are called to do. It seeks only to preserve life as it has already been devel-

---

1. Nietzsche, *Untimely Meditations*, p. 59.

oped. The internal connection between life and action means for Nietzsche that our interpretations of the past should serve the purposes of the future. Action is facilitated by a forgetfulness of the past, the past construed as a memory that possesses and oppresses us or as "a dark, invisible burden which [we] would like to disown."[2]

This is not to say that, according to Nietzsche, we are to disregard the past altogether. But in a life-serving historical approach, we seek to break from the past to establish new practices. Nietzsche writes that we "implant in ourselves a new habit, a new instinct, a second nature, so that our first nature withers away."[3] The past is an imaginative construct originally constituted to facilitate action. The past constrains action only when we elevate it to the status of unchanging fact and forget our capacity to re-create it. Nietzsche links life's fulfillment with our capacity to shape freely our ways of living, our life-forms. Reverence for established practices constrains the institution of new practices. Life can thus fulfill itself only by first deconstructively breaking the hold of the past on us. Genealogy asks what the past is doing to us, which established practices are lethal, in order to liberate us from an oppressive past. But this unhistorical deconstruction is capable only of producing ruptures. It leaves no room for explicating continuities.

In contrast to Nietzsche, Dilthey insists that the past itself constrains our interpretation of it, and thus he provides a foundation for explicating both breaks and continuities with the past. For Nietzsche and Dilthey alike, we construct the past as a framework for making action meaningful. That is, the past is always constituted in its relation to the future, such that our actions are given a coherent context. But each understands this quite differently. Nietzsche argues that the past is a fictional construct derived originally from our projects. This fictional past subsequently constrains action, as it becomes a sort of habit of thought. The genealogical task is then to facilitate a break from this past. In Dilthey's view, the significance of the past is always construed from the perspective of our possibilities. But there is a real, effective past that bears on our lives, and in our projects we can perpetuate the past, radically break from the past, or transform practices in a way that retains a connection to the past while moving beyond it. Thus the historian must seek both breaks and continuities.

2. Ibid., p. 61.
3. Ibid., p. 76.

Now, both positions contend that we act on the basis of our construction of a temporal horizon. So Nietzsche would have to admit that not only our own actions but those of other agents occur in such horizons. Even if those horizons are merely provisional and always in need of revision, or for that matter, even if they are delusional, they nevertheless do constitute the context of meaning within which the actions were intelligible for those who performed them. Contrary to the position he actually held, Nietzsche should have recognized, along with Dilthey, that the temporal life-horizons others constitute for themselves must form at least a minimal limit to the interpretations that can be given them subsequently.

It must be kept in mind that Dilthey's philosophy of history rejects an ultimate culminating narrative. Unlike Hegel, Dilthey awaits no final coincidence of the for-itself and the in-itself. There is no final, stable platform from which to observe the completed absolute. Our own self-understanding can always be clarified and made more explicit by those who come after us. But how can this result in anything like objectivity? In a certain respect, it simply cannot. Insofar as objectivity as a concept is bound to the correspondence theory of truth, there is no objectivity. But what Dilthey has in mind is something quite different. We cannot relinquish our historicity, so we cannot produce a narrative of historically distant lives without this narrative itself being told from the perspective of our own ongoing lives, our own provisional narratives. In this respect, then, historical truth is fundamentally hermeneutical. There is no final answer, there is no final best telling of the story. The story must be told and retold, made and remade. Objectivity in such a framework means the recognition that others told their own stories and lived their lives according to them. These are realities that we did not constitute ourselves. As a result, these lives constrain our interpretation of them.

Bibliography

Dilthey's Works

The standard German edition of Dilthey's works is the *Gesammelte Schriften*. 20 vols. 1914–90. Vols. 1–12, Stuttgart: B. G. Teubner, and Göttingen: Vandenhoeck & Ruprecht; vols. 13–20, Göttingen: Vandenhoeck & Ruprecht. The standard English translation of Dilthey's works is *Selected Works*. 6 vols. Edited by Rudolf A. Makkreel and Frithjof Rodi. Princeton: Princeton University Press, 1985–. Below is a list of other editions and translations of Dilthey's writings which I have used or consulted.

Der Aufbau der geschichtlichen Welt in den Geisteswissenschaften. Introduction by Manfred Riedel. Suhrkamp Taschenbuch Wissenschaft, 354. Frankfurt am Main: Suhrkamp Verlag, 1970.
Aus Schleiermachers Leben in Briefen, vols. 3 and 4. Edited by Wilhelm Dilthey. Berlin: G. Reimer, 1861, 1863.
"Briefe Wilhelm Diltheys an Bernhard und Luise Scholz, 1859–1864." Edited by Sigrid von der Schulenburg. Sitzungsberichte der preussischen Akademie der Wissenschaften, phil.-histor. Kl. 1933.
Briefe Wilhelm Diltheys an Rudolf Haym, 1861–1873. Edited by Erich Weniger. Berlin, 1936.
"Der Briefwechsel Dilthey-Husserl." With introductory comments by Walter Biemel. *Man and World* 1, no. 3 (1968): 428–446.
Briefwechsel zwischen Wilhelm Dilthey und dem Grafen Paul Yorck von Wartenburg, 1877–1897. Edited by Sigrid von der Schulenburg. Halle a.d.S.: Max Niemeyer, 1923.
"The Dilthey-Husserl Correspondence." Edited, with an introduction, by Walter Biemel. Translated by Jeffner Allen. In *Husserl: Shorter Works,* edited by Peter McCormick and Frederick Elliston, 198–209. Foreword by Walter Biemel. Notre Dame: University of Notre Dame Press, 1981.
"Diltheys Kant-Darstellung in seiner letzten Vorlesung über das System der Philosophie." In Dietrich Bischoff, *Wilhelm Diltheys geschichtliche Lebensphilosophie.* Leipzig: B. G. Teubner, 1935.

Descriptive Psychology and Historical Understanding. Translated by Richard M. Zaner and K. L. Heiges with an introduction by R. A. Makkreel. The Hague: Martinus Nijhoff, 1977.

Das Erlebnis und die Dichtung: Lessing, Goethe, Novalis, Hölderlin. 15th ed. Stuttgart: B. G. Teubner; Göttingen: Vandenhoeck & Ruprecht, 1970. First published in 1906.

The Essence of Philosophy. Translated by Stephen A. Emery and William T. Emery. University of North Carolina Studies in the Germanic Languages and Literatures, 13. New York: AMS Press, 1954. (Reprinted with permission of The University of North Carolina Press.)

Fragmente aus Wilhelm Diltheys Hegelwerk. Edited by Friedhelm Nicolin and Otto Pöggeler. Bonn: H. Bouvier, 1961.

Die grosse Phantasiedichtung und andere Studien zur vergleichenden Literaturgeschichte. Edited by Herman Nohl. Göttingen: Vandenhoeck & Ruprecht, 1954.

Grundriss der allgemeinen Geschichte der Philosophie. Edited and supplemented by Hans-Georg Gadamer. Frankfurt am Main: Klostermann, 1949.

Der junge Dilthey: Ein Lebensbild in Briefen und Tagebüchern, 1852–1870. Edited by Clara Misch, née Dilthey. 2d ed. Stuttgart: B. G. Teubner; Göttingen: Vandenhoeck & Ruprecht, 1960. First published in 1933.

Leben Schleiermachers, vol. 1. Edited by Hermann Mulert. 2d ed. Berlin: W. de Gruyter, 1922. First published in 1867–70.

Die Philosophie des Lebens: Eine Auswahl aus seinen Schriften, 1867–1910. Edited by Herman Nohl. Frankfurt am Main: Klostermann, 1946.

Texte zur Kritik der historischen Vernunft. Edited by Hans-Ulrich Lessing. Göttingen: Vandenhoeck & Ruprecht, 1983.

"Über die Einbildungskraft des Dichters." *Zeitschrift für Völkerpsychologie* 10 (1878): 42–104.

"Vier Briefe Wilhelm Diltheys an Erich Adickes: Winter, 1904–1905." *Deutsche Akademie der Wissenschaften zu Berlin, 1946–1956,* pp. 429–484. Berlin, 1956.

Von deutscher Dichtung und Musik: Aus den Studien zur Geschichte des deutschen Geistes. Edited by Herman Nohl and Georg Misch. 2d ed. Stuttgart: B. G. Teubner; Göttingen: Vandenhoeck & Ruprecht, 1957. First published in 1932.

Secondary Sources

Allison, Henry E. *Kant's Transcendental Idealism.* New Haven: Yale University Press, 1983.

Aron, Raymond. *Introduction to the Philosophy of History: An Essay on the Limits of Historical Objectivity.* Translated by George J. Irwin. Boston: Beacon Press, 1961.

———. *La philosophie critique de l'histoire: Essai sur une théorie allemande de l'histoire.* 2d ed. Paris: Librairie Philosophique J. Vrin, 1950.

Baumgartner, Hans Michael. *Kontinuität und Geschichte: Zur Kritik und Metakritik der historischen Vernunft.* Frankfurt am Main: Suhrkamp, 1972.

Bischoff, Dietrich W. *Wilhelm Diltheys geschichtliche Lebensphilosophie.* Leipzig: B. G. Teubner, 1935.

Bloch, Marc. *The Historian's Craft.* Translated by Peter Putnam. New York: Knopf, 1953.

Bollnow, Otto Friedrich. *Dilthey: Eine Einführung in seine Philosophie.* 2d ed. Stuttgart: Kohlhammer, 1955.

Braudel, Fernand. "La longue durée." In *Ecrits sur l'histoire,* pp. 41–83. Paris: Flammarion, 1969.

——. *The Mediterranean and the Mediterranean World in the Age of Philip II.* 2 vols. Translated by Sian Reynolds. New York: Harper and Row, 1972–74.

——. "The Situation of History in 1950." Translated by S. Matthews. In *On History.* Chicago: University of Chicago Press, 1980.

Bulhof, Ilse. *Wilhelm Dilthey: A Hermeneutic Approach to the Study of History and Culture.* The Hague: Martinus Nijhoff, 1980.

Caputo, John D. *Radical Hermeneutics: Repetition, Deconstruction, and the Hermeneutic Project.* Bloomington: Indiana University Press, 1987.

Carr, David. "The Future Perfect: Temporality and Priority in Husserl, Heidegger, and Dilthey." In *Dilthey and Phenomenology,* edited by Rudolf A. Makkreel and John Scanlon, pp. 125–137. Washington, D.C.: Center for Advanced Research in Phenomenology and University Press of America, 1987.

——. *Phenomenology and the Problem of History: A Study of Husserl's Transcendental Philosophy.* Evanston: Northwestern University Press, 1974.

——. *Time, Narrative, and History.* Bloomington: Indiana University Press, 1986.

Comte, Auguste. *The Positive Philosophy of Auguste Comte.* Edited and translated by Harriet Martineau. New York: Calvin Blanchard, 1856.

Corngold, Stanley. "Dilthey's Essay *The Poetic Imagination:* A Poetics of Force." *Interpretation* 9 (1980–81): 301–337.

Culler, Johnathan. *On Deconstruction: Theory and Criticism after Structuralism.* Ithaca: Cornell University Press, 1982.

Danto, Arthur C. *Analytical Philosophy of History.* Cambridge: Cambridge University Press, 1965.

Derrida, Jacques. "Declarations of Independence." Translated by Tom Keenan and Tom Pepper. *New Political Science* 15 (1986): 7–15.

——. *Margins of Philosophy.* Translated by Alan Bass. Chicago: University of Chicago Press, 1982.

——. "Otobiographies: The Teaching of Nietzsche and the Politics of the Proper Name." Translated by Avital Ronell. In *The Ear of the Other: Otobiography, Transference, Translation,* edited by Christie V. McDonald. New York: Schocken, 1985.

——. *Positions.* Translated by Alan Bass. Chicago: University of Chicago Press, 1981.

——. *Speech and Phenomena.* Translated by David B. Allison. Evanston: Northwestern University Press, 1973.

——. *Spurs: Nietzsche's Styles.* Translated by Barbara Harlow. Chicago: University of Chicago Press, 1979.

——. *Writing and Difference.* Translated by Alan Bass. Chicago: University of Chicago Press, 1978.

Diwald, Hellmut. *Wilhelm Dilthey: Erkenntnistheorie und Philosophie der Geschichte.* Göttingen: Musterschmidt, 1963.

Dray, William. *Laws and Explanations in History.* London: Oxford University Press, 1957.

Ermarth, Michael. "The Transformation of Hermeneutics: Nineteenth-Century Ancients and Twentieth-Century Moderns." *Monist* 64 (April 1984).

——. *Wilhelm Dilthey: The Critique of Historical Reason.* Chicago: University of Chicago Press, 1978.

Febvre, Lucien. *Combats pour l'histoire.* Paris: A. Colin, 1953.

Gadamer, Hans-Georg. *Philosophical Hermeneutics.* Translated by David Linge. Berkeley: University of California Press, 1976.

——. *Truth and Method.* Translation edited by Garrett Barden and John Cumming. New York: Continuum Publishing, 1975. Translated from *Wahrheit und Methode.* 2d ed. Tübingen: J. C. B. Mohr, 1965.

Gallie, W. B. *Philosophy and the Historical Understanding.* 2d ed. New York: Schocken Books, 1968.

Gasché, Rodolphe. *The Tain of the Mirror.* Cambridge: Harvard University Press, 1986.

Gethmann, Carl Friedrich. "Philosophie als Vollzug und als Begriff: Heideggers Identitätsphilosophie des Lebens in der Vorlesung vom Wintersemester 1921/22 und ihr Verhältnis zu *Sein und Zeit.*" *Dilthey-Jahrbuch* 4 (1986–87): 27–53.

Hegel, G. W. F. *The Philosophy of History.* With prefaces by Charles Hegel and the translator, J. Sibree. New York: Colonial Press, 1899.

Heidegger, Martin. *Being and Time.* Translated by John Macquarrie and Edward Robinson. New York: Harper and Row, 1962. Translation of *Sein und Zeit.* Tübingen: Max Niemeyer Verlag, 1979.

——. *Gesamtausgabe,* vol. 20. Edited by Petra Jaeger, Vol. 61 edited by Walter Bröker and Käte Bröker-Oltmanns. Frankfurt am Main: Vittorio Klostermann, 1979, 1985.

——. *History of the Concept of Time: Prolegomena.* Translated by Theodore Kisiel. Bloomington: Indiana University Press, 1985.

Hirsch, E. D. *Validity in Interpretation.* New Haven: Yale University Press, 1967.

Hodges, H. A. *The Philosophy of Wilhelm Dilthey.* London: Routledge and Kegan Paul, 1952.

Hoy, David Couzens. "History, Historicity, and Historiography in *Being and Time.*"

In *Heidegger and Modern Philosophy*, edited by Michael Murray, pp. 329–353. New Haven: Yale University Press, 1978.

Husserl, Edmund. *Cartesian Meditations: An Introduction to Phenomenology*. Translated by Dorion Cairns. The Hague: Martinus Nijhoff, 1977.

——. *The Crisis of European Sciences and Transcendental Phenomenology: An Introduction to Phenomenological Philosophy*. Translated, with an introduction, by David Carr. Evanston: Northwestern University Press, 1970.

——. *Husserliana*. Vol. 10: *Zur Phänomenologie des inneren Zeitbewusstseins*, edited by R. Boehm. The Hague: Martinus Nijhoff, 1966. Translated by James S. Churchill as *The Phenomenology of Internal Time-Consciousness*. Bloomington: Indiana University Press, 1964.

——. *Ideas: General Introduction to Pure Phenomenology*. Translated by W. R. Boyce Gibson. New York: Collier Books, 1962.

——. *Ideen zu einer reinen Phänomenologie und phänomenologischen Philosophie*. Bk. 2. Edited by Marly Biemel. The Hague: Martinus Nijhoff, 1952.

——. *Logische Untersuchungen*. 2 vols. 2d ed. Halle: Max Niemeyer, 1913. Translated by J. N. Findlay as *Logical Investigations*, 2 vols., N.J.: Humanities Press; London: Routledge and Kegan Paul, 1970.

——. "Philosophy as a Rigorous Science." Translated by Quentin Lauer. In *Husserl: Shorter Works*, edited by Peter McCormick and Frederick Elliston. Notre Dame: University of Notre Dame Press, 1981. Also in *Phenomenology and the Crisis of Philosophy*, edited by Quintin Lauer. New York: Harper and Row, 1965.

Ineichen, Hans. *Erkenntnistheorie und geschichtlich-gesellschaftliche Welt: Diltheys Logik der Geisteswissenschaften*. Studien zur Philosophie und Literatur des neunzehnten Jahrhunderts, 28. Frankfurt am Main: Vittorio Klostermann, 1975.

Johach, Helmut. "Diltheys Philosophie des Subjekts und die Grundlegung der Geistes- und Sozialwissenschaften: Zur Aktualität der 'Einleitung in die Geisteswissenschaften.'" *Dilthey-Jahrbuch* 2 (1984): 92–127.

——. *Handelnder Mensch und objektiver Geist: Zur Theorie der Geistes- und Sozialwissenschaften bei Wilhelm Dilthey*. Studien zur Wissenschaftstheorie, vol. 8. Meisenheim am Glan: Verlag Anton Hain, 1974.

Kant, Immanuel. *Critique of Judgment*. Translated by J. H. Bernard. New York: Hafner, 1951.

——. *Critique of Pure Reason*. Translated by Norman Kemp Smith. New York: St. Martins, 1961.

Kermode, Frank. *The Sense of an Ending*. New York: Oxford University Press, 1967.

Kolb, Daniel C. "Thought and Intuition in Kant's Critical System." *Journal of the History of Philosophy* 24 (April 1986): 223–241.

Krausser, Peter. *Kritik der endlichen Vernunft: Diltheys Revolution der allgemeinen Wissenschafts- und Handlungstheorie*. Frankfurt am Main: Suhrkamp, 1968.

186

Bibliography

Landgrebe, Ludwig. "Wilhelm Diltheys Theorie der Geisteswissenschaften (Analyse ihrer Grundbegriffe)." In *Jahrbuch für Philosophie und phänomenologische Forschung*, 9:237–367. Edited by Edmund Husserl. Halle: Max Niemeyer, 1928.

Lessing, Hans-Ulrich. *Die Idee einer Kritik der historischen Vernunft: Wilhelm Diltheys erkenntnistheoretisch-logisch-methodologische Grundlegung der Geisteswissenschaften.* Munich: Verlag Karl Alber, 1984.

Lévi-Strauss, Claude. *Structural Anthropology.* Translated by Claire Jacobson and Brooke G. Schoepf. New York: Basic Books, 1963.

Linge, David E. "Dilthey and Gadamer: Two Theories of Historical Understanding." *Journal of the American Academy of Religion* 4 (1973): 536–553.

MacIntyre, Alasdair. *After Virtue.* Notre Dame: University of Notre Dame Press, 1981.

Makkreel, Rudolf A. *Dilthey, Philosopher of the Human Studies.* Princeton: Princeton University Press, 1975.

——. "The Feeling of Life: Some Kantian Sources of Life-Philosophy." *Dilthey-Jahrbuch* 3 (1985): 83–104.

——. "The Overcoming of Linear Time in Kant, Dilthey, and Heidegger." In *Dilthey and Phenomenology,* edited by Rudolf P. Makkreel and John Scanlon, pp. 141–158. Washington, D.C.: Center for Advanced Research in Phenomenology and University Press of America, 1987.

Makkreel, Rudolf A., and John Scanlon, eds. *Dilthey and Phenomenology.* Washington, D.C.: Center for Advanced Research in Phenomenology and University Press of America, 1987.

Merleau-Ponty, Maurice. "Eye and Mind." In *The Primacy of Perception,* edited by James M. Edie. Evanston: Northwestern University Press, 1964.

——. *Phenomenology of Perception.* Translated by Colin Smith. New York: Humanities Press, 1972.

Mink, Louis O. "Everyman His or Her Own Annalist." In *On Narrative,* edited by W. J. T. Mitchell, pp. 233–239. Chicago: University of Chicago Press, 1981.

——. "History and Fiction as Modes of Comprehension." *New Literary History* 1 (1970): 541–558.

——. "Narrative Form as a Cognitive Instrument." In *The Writing of History: Literary Form and Historical Understanding,* edited by Robert H. Canary and Henry Kozicki, pp. 129–149. Madison: University of Wisconsin Press, 1978.

Misch, Georg. *Lebensphilosophie und Phänomenologie.* Stuttgart: B. G. Teubner, 1967.

Müller-Vollmer, Kurt. *Towards a Phenomenological Theory of Literature: A Study of Wilhelm Dilthey's "Poetik."* Stanford Studies in Germanics and Slavics, 1. The Hague: Mouton, 1963.

Nenon, Tom. "Dilthey's Inductive Method and the Nature of Philosophy." *Southwest Philosophy Review* 5, no. 1 (January 1989): 121–134.

187

Bibliography

Nietzsche, Friedrich. *Untimely Meditations.* Translated by R. J. Hollingdale. Cambridge: Cambridge University Press, 1983.
——. *The Will to Power.* Translated by Walter Kaufmann and R. J. Hollingdale. New York: Vintage Books, 1967.
Novick, Peter. *That Noble Dream: The "Objectivity Question" and the American Historical Profession.* Cambridge: Cambridge University Press, 1988.
Orth, Ernst Wolfgang, ed. *Dilthey und die Philosophie der Gegenwart.* Freiburg / Munich: Verlag Karl Alber, 1985.
Owensby, Jacob. "Dilthey and Husserl on the Role of the Subject in History." *Philosophy Today* 32, no. 3 (Fall 1988): 221–231.
Paczkowska-Lagowska, Elzbieta. "The Humanities in Search of Philosophy: Dilthey and the Historical School." *Reports on Philosophy* 6 (1982): 3–16.
Plantinga, Theodore. *Historical Understanding in the Thought of Wilhelm Dilthey.* Toronto: University of Toronto Press, 1980.
Redding, Paul. "Action, Language, and Text: Dilthey's Conception of Understanding." *Philosophy and Social Criticism* 9 (1982): 229–244.
Rickman, H. P. *Dilthey Today: A Critical Appraisal of the Contemporary Relevance of His Work.* New York: Greenwood Press, 1988.
——. *Wilhelm Dilthey: Pioneer of the Human Studies.* Berkeley: University of California Press, 1979.
Ricoeur, Paul. *Interpretation Theory.* Fort Worth: Texas Christian University Press, 1976.
——. *Time and Narrative.* Vol. 1. Translated by Kathleen McLaughlin and David Pellauer. Chicago: University of Chicago Press, 1984.
Riedel, Manfred. "Dilthey und das Problem der Metaphysik." *Philosophisches Jahrbuch* 76 (1968–69): 332–348.
Rodi, Frithjof. "Die Bedeutung Diltheys für die Konzeption von *Sein und Zeit.*" *Dilthey-Jahrbuch* 4 (1986–87): 161–177.
——. "Dilthey's Concept of 'Structure' within the Context of Nineteenth-Century Science and Philosophy." In *Dilthey and Phenomenology,* edited by Rudolf A. Makkreel and John Scanlon, pp. 107–121. Washington, D.C.: Center for Advanced Research in Phenomenology and University Press of America, 1987.
——. "Hermeneutics and the Meaning of Life: A Critique of Gadamer's Interpretation of Dilthey." In *Hermeneutics and Deconstruction,* edited by Hugh J. Silverman and Don Ihde. Albany: State University of New York Press, 1985.
——. *Morphologie und Hermeneutik: Zur Methode von Diltheys Aesthetik.* Stuttgart: W. Kohlhammer Verlag, 1969.
Rorty, Richard. *Philosophy and the Mirror of Nature.* Princeton: Princeton University Press, 1979.
Sartre, Jean-Paul. *Critique of Dialectical Reason.* Translated by Alan Sheridan-Smith. London: NLB, 1976.

188
Bibliography

Sauerland, Karol. *Diltheys Erlebnisbegriff: Entstehung, Glanzzeit, und Verkümmerung eines literaturhistorischen Begriffs.* Berlin: Walter de Gruyter, 1972.

Scharff, Robert C. "Non-Analytical, Unspeculative Philosophy of History: The Legacy of Wilhelm Dilthey." *Cultural Hermeneutics* 3 (March 1976): 295–331.

Schnädelbach, Herbert. *Geschichtsphilosophie nach Hegel: Die Probleme des Historismus.* Munich: Verlag Karl Alber, 1974.

Schrag, Calvin O. *Communicative Praxis and the Space of Subjectivity.* Bloomington: Indiana University Press, 1986.

Seebohm, Thomas M. "Boeckh and Dilthey: The Development of Methodical Hermeneutics." *Man and World* 17 (1984): 325–346.

Stein, Arthur. *Begriff des Verstehens bei Dilthey.* Tübingen: J. C. B. Mohr, 1926.

Tuttle, Howard Nelson. *Wilhelm Dilthey's Philosophy of Historical Understanding: A Critical Analysis.* Leiden: E. J. Brill, 1969.

White, Hayden. "The Historical Text as Literary Artifact." In *The Writing of History: Literary Form and Historical Understanding,* edited by Robert H. Canary and Henry Kozicki, pp. 41–62. Madison: University of Wisconsin Press, 1978.

——. *Metahistory: The Historical Imagination in Nineteenth-Century Europe.* Baltimore: Johns Hopkins University Press, 1973.

——. "The Value of Narrativity in the Representation of Reality." In *On Narrative,* edited by W. J. T. Mitchell, pp. 1–23. Chicago: University of Chicago Press, 1981.

Young, Thomas J. "The Hermeneutic Significance of Dilthey's Theory of World-Views." *International Philosophical Quarterly* 23 (1983): 125–140.

Index

Acquired psychic nexus (*erworbener seelischer Zusammenhang*), 94–95; role in historical understanding, 140–143

Acting and suffering (*Wirken und Leiden*), 56

Acts, and contents of consciousness, 32, 34, 65–66

Age, 132–133

Annales school, 74–75n

Aron, Raymond, 142n

"Aufbau der geschichtlichen Welt in den Geisteswissenschaften, Der" (The formation of the historical world in the human sciences), 14–15

Ausdruck. See Expression

Authenticity, 102–104, 177

Autobiography. *See* Biography

Baumgartner, Hans Michael, 124

Bedeutung. See Meaning

Being-in-the-world, 42

Besserverstehen (understanding the author better), 145–146, 175. *See also* Hermeneutics; Understanding

Biography, 101–102; and autobiography, 74, 79–80, 98–99; and time, 98–104

Biology, 54. *See also* Life; Life-nexus

Bischoff, Dietrich W., 9n

Bollnow, Otto Friedrich, 168n

Bulhof, Ilse, 158n, 170–171

Caputo, John D., 8, 171n

Carr, David, 6–7, 102n, 112

Categories of life, 41–44, 55–56; and existentialia, 42–44; and the formation of narratives, 99–101; meaning as, 55, 56, 99, 100–101; purpose as, 56, 99, 100; value as, 56, 99, 100

Causal relations, 30, 118, 122

Completion, 141

Comte, Auguste, 118

Concept formation, Dilthey's theory of, 167–171

Consciousness, non-representational model of, 32; as a function of life, 58

Context, 120–136. *See also* Objective Spirit; Structure; Systems of Influences

Cultural systems (*Kultursysteme*), 110–113; and the external organization of society, 115–116; individuals as crossing-points of, 111–112; as purposive systems, 110–111; and systems of influences, 122

Danto, Arthur, 3–4

Das Man, and the role of sociohistorical contexts in narrative, 102–104

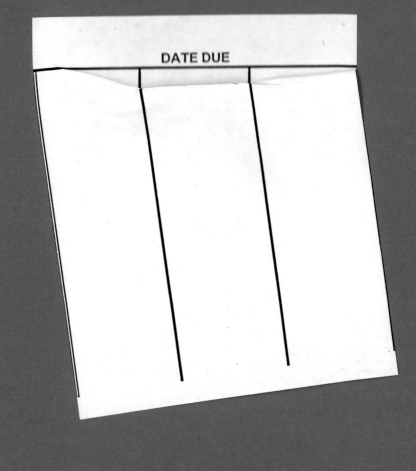

DATE DUE